HONORING THE CIRCLE:
ONGOING LEARNING FROM AMERICAN INDIANS ON POLITICS AND SOCIETY, VOLUME I

D1453011

Honoring the Circle:

Ongoing Learning from American Indians on Politics and Society,

Volume I

The Impact of American Indians on Western Politics and Society to 1800

Stephen M. Sachs, Bruce E. Johansen, Ain Haas, Betty Booth Donohue, Donald A. Grinde Jr., and Jonathon York

Waterside Productions

Printed in the United States of America

First Printing, 2020

ISBN-13: 978-1-949001-83-9   print edition
ISBN-13: 978-1-949001-84-6   ebook edition

Honoring the Circle, Volume I
ISBN-13: 978-1-949001-83-9

Honoring the Circle, Volume II
ISBN-13: 978-1-949001-85-3

Honoring the Circle, Volume III
ISBN-13: 978-1-949001-87-7

Honoring the Circle, Volume IV
ISBN-13: 978-1-949001-89-1

Note that in this volume some terms are handled per contributor preference and may appear capitalized in one section but lowercased elsewhere.

Waterside Productions

2055 Oxford Ave.
Cardiff, CA 92007
www.waterside.com

OVERVIEW OF *HONORING THE CIRCLE*

Four Volumes on What the West Has Learned and Still Might Learn from American Indians on Politics and Society

Volume I begins with a prelude, which includes an introduction to *Honoring the Circle* and chapter 1, "Traditional American Indian Politics and Society," a look at how inclusive participatory American Indian societies functioned well. Part I "The Impact of American Indian Tradition on Western Politics and Society," spans over two volumes. It begins in this volume with an introduction and chapters 2 and 3. Chapter 2, "The Impact of American Indians on Politics and Society in the American Colonies and the United States from Contact to 1800," covers the mixture of Indian and European influences on early American settlers, and the Indian influences on major leaders and on the development of American political institutions. Chapter 3, "The Considerable Effect of Contact on Europe," examines the impact of reports of Indians in Europe on all political philosophies.

Volume II continues part I. Chapter 4, "The Continuing Impact of American Indian Ways in North America and the World in the Nineteenth Century and Beyond," covers Native impacts on the development of the American philosophy of pragmatism, the women's movement, the 1960s youth movement, and the environmental movement. The volume closes with a conclusion to part I.

Volume III begins part II, "The Continuing Relevance of American Indian Ways and Values," which discusses learning from

Indians on living well together and with the Earth. It includes an introduction on changes in Western society toward Indigenous ways of seeing and other factors that make Indigenous thinking increasingly relevant for solving major contemporary problems. Chapter 5, "Applying American Indian Principles of Harmony and Balance to Renew the Politics of the Twenty-First Century," and chapter 6, "Returning to Reciprocity: Reconceptualizing Economics and Development," cover politics and economics, including how Indigenous values of inclusive participation and mutual support can provide for well-working societies today, empowering an informed active citizenry with essentially equal political and economic power to participate on an equal basis, with participatory public and private organizations.

Volume IV continues part II. Chapter 7, "Indigenizing the Greening of the World: Applying an Indigenous Approach to Environmental Issues," discusses how holistic Indigenous thinking is necessary for dealing with environmental issues. Chapter 8, "Facilitating the Unfolding of the Circle: Indigenizing Education for the Twenty-First Century," suggests how education at every level can be improved with the Indigenous approach of empowering unique people to learn experientially, as whole people, living in community. The conclusion to *Honoring the Circle* discusses how continuing to integrate Indigenous ideas into our thinking provides a path for living well together and with the planet. It shows how this approach is increasingly at the forefront of political and social discussion.

TABLE OF CONTENTS

PRELUDE

PREFACE
WEAVING THE STRANDS OF THOUGHT AND IDEAS THROUGH TIME

Stephen M. Sachs

"The universe begins to look more like a great thought than a great machine," said James Jeans.[1]

Ideas spread like organic chains over time,
Weaving and interacting with one another,
Exchanging DNA.

A chain of thought once sprouted continues on
Into the indefinite future.
Some times, in the course of exchange
With other strands,
The line of thinking diminishes,
Becomes recessive,
Only to burst forth vigorously again,
In another interaction.

Some times,
When conditions are right,
Thoughts spread rapidly

And imperceptibly
Like bursts of pollen
In an intellectual spring.

Often, new thoughts arise,
Akin to those of existing strands.
Only if the climate and season are right
Will they survive and grow,
Supported by their related strands.

Each person is unique,
A creative being thinking for themselves.
But all are related,
Receiving current and past thinking
From all they are in contact with,
By whatever means,
Reacting to what they receive
As is their nature and current state.

Some thoughts, are simply rejected,
Others may sneak in,
Even if rejected.
Some ideas cause a different,
Perhaps opposite reaction.
Others are accepted,
Yet to varying degrees transformed
By the receiver's experience.
Still others catalyze the person's thinking,
Perhaps recreating lost elements,
Other times creating,
Expanding ideas into new dimensions.
Thus, proceeds the unending weaving of minds.

---

1 Quote from "James Jeans Quotes," BrainyQuote, www.brainyquote.
com/quotes/quotes/j/jamesjeans177088.html, accessed April 28, 2016.

INTRODUCTION TO *HONORING THE CIRCLE* AND ACKNOWLEDGMENTS

Stephen M. Sachs

As yet few Americans and fewer Europeans realize that America is not just a pale reflection of Europe—that what is distinctive about America is the Indian, through and through.[1]

Contact between Native people and Europeans coming to America has had a profound and continuing effect on Western political thought and practice, and upon American life more generally. This is rarely recognized today in mainstream historical work. The emphasis in Western political life on the fundamental importance of freedom, and the idea that rights are inalienable, arose from close interaction between Europeans and the Native people of the Americas. Because of early European observers noting how well American Indian communities functioned, it can be said unequivocally that it is because of Indians that there is as much democracy as there is in the United States and across the Western world.

The Indigenous people in North America, in their different forms, and to differing degrees, practiced inclusive participatory democracy in collaborative societies in which every individual needed to be respected because all contained spirit—indeed, the Great Mystery was in all things, all beings. Moreover, the multiplicity of spirits existing within the Great Mystery were a unity in diversity that as a basic principle enhanced the functioning of inclusive participatory democracy. Human beings were seen as essentially good, but in need of appropriate experiential education to develop their character and abilities.

As is well documented by Grinde, Johansen, Weatherford, Donohue, Pratt, and others, the first three hundred years of Europeans coming to the "New World" and having close contact with Indians had a profound impact on many of the settlers and led to major contributions to the development of an American identity, different in many aspects from the dominant ways in Europe. In addition, contact with Indians brought about a significant shift in Western political and social thought that continues to shape governmental structure, function, and policy, with ongoing broader effects on social and other aspects of life across the Western world and beyond. Direct, new, Indian influence on the West has been ongoing. Good examples include the women's movement and the environmental movement.

Part I, Volumes I and II: The Impact of American Indian Tradition on Western Politics and Society

The first two volumes of *Honoring the Circle*, consisting of the prelude and part I of this project, are devoted to setting out the huge impact that American Indians have had on US and European political, social, and economic thought and practice. This is important for several reasons. First, it yields a better understanding of some of the major influences in the development of Western political thought since the end of the fifteenth century. This also shines some light upon how lines of thought move and interact over time. Second, it is important to honor the role that Native Americans have played in the development of American and European political thought and institutions. For centuries, Westerners, and particularly European Americans, have belittled Native people as being backward and ignorant. This occurred in the course of a physical and cultural genocide that has left a great many Indigenous people suffering with unresolved historical trauma.[2] Honoring the huge American Indian contribution to the United States and the world is an essential step in the healing process to return to harmonious relations between and within the two populations. Third, learning from Indians has never ceased, and for over a century Indian values have been increasingly relevant in dealing with contemporary issues.

The Problem of Determining Influences on People's Thinking

Tracing the historical influence of ideas is complex and uncertain. It raises interesting issues such as whether ideas were transferred to a person, or whether they were developed independently. If a transmission took place, what was the transmission process? Was it obvious or subtle? If an idea arose independently, did a wave of expression or trend in which that independent thought occurred provide a space in which that thought might receive notice and have a significant impact? For example, Robert Owen's guild socialism and education ideas, discussed in chapter 3, fit very well with American Indian–influenced French thinking of his era.[3] Owen said his ideas arose from his own development, and were not the result of his exposure to the ideas of others. This is arguable. But if they were, it would seem that Owen's ideas spread because they were relevant to events in a milieu in which similar thinking was already present.

Sometimes, in some way, ideas are just "in the air" and seemingly emerge within the context of the moment without any obvious direct line of transmission. *The Ever Present Origin* by Jean Gebser demonstrates that important new ideas and ways of seeing often arise independently in clusters over a relatively short period.[4]

It is always difficult to know exactly what influenced a person's thinking. Indeed, few, if any of us, can state precisely all of the influences that have shaped the development of our own thoughts, although we may have a clear memory of certain impacts on our views or way of seeing. But even then, if there was not already something in our thinking, feeling, or experience to open us to be influenced in a certain way, in most cases we likely would not have been receptive.

The problem of considering influences is made more difficult by the fact that people are creative thinkers who develop from their unique interaction with their environment. People's responses to that interaction are both conscious and subconscious. The direct experience creates and modifies ideas. The interaction also includes the transmission of ideas that may be received quite clearly, or very subtly. How one reacts to ideas received, or internally generated, varies according to many factors.

There are many cases, however, where there are very clear indications concerning the transmission of ideas, even if some aspects of that interchange are uncertain. That is the case with much of what is discussed in part I about Indian influences on Europeans and European Americans. In other instances that we consider, there are strong indications of direct or indirect Indian influence, though whether that is the case is less clear. In making our analyses of probable influence in this volume, we have attempted to make our best educated estimate of what likely occurred. We have tried to be careful in distinguishing among what seems fairly certain, what appears quite likely, and what may be fairly probable.

Part II, Volumes III and IV: The Continuing Relevance of American Indian Ways and Values

How contemporary societies might function in their politics, economics, environmental policy, and education is laid out in the last two volumes. The process of learning from Indians has been continual, and the authors of this work believe that it needs to continue.

In the midst of the turmoil of the early twenty-first century, Indigenous values and ways appeared to have increasing relevance in the West. For more than a century many of the problems that society has faced have been becoming more like those that Native peoples had already been facing. This is perhaps most obvious with environmental difficulties. Today the narrowness of Western thinking has created serious global warming and a host of other pollution problems. Returning to Indigenous ways of seeing that everything is interrelated would appear to be imperative in relating to our physical environment. On this issue and others, what we believe is needed is not to return to the details of Native ways, but to apply Indigenous values appropriately for our time and with an eye to the future.

A return to Indigenous ways of seeing and acting would not be a huge leap. As laid out in the introduction to part II, and continued in the chapters that follow, Western culture has been moving in that direction for well over a century. This is especially true in science, which lies at the center of Western culture. The change is particularly noticeable in physics, which has greatly transformed from a fixed mechanical view of the universe in the nineteenth century to a more dynamic, relativistic view today, and that increasingly has been converging with American Indian and other ancient non-Western approaches. This cultural shift has also brought a more positive understanding of Indians by the mainstream, which in turn has opened space for increasing Indian contributions in many areas.

The four volumes of *Honoring the Circle* are a continuation of the recognition of the process of the Indianization of Europeans set out by Felix Cohen in his 1952 essay "Americanizing the White Man."[5] The essay opens with:

"WHAT CAN we do to Americanize the Indian?" The question was earnestly put by a man who was about to assume control over our country's Indian affairs. He was appalled by the fact that over a hundred native tribes within the United States still speak their own languages and make their own laws on the little fragments of land that Indians reserved for their own use when they sold the rest of the country to the white man. The Commissioner-elect was a kind and generous soul, but his Anglo-Saxon pride was ruffled by the fact that so many Indians preferred their own way of life, poor as it was, to the benefits of civilization that Congress longed to confer on them. Perhaps, if Indians did not realize that they needed more Indian Bureau supervisors and bigger and better appropriations to make real Americans out of them, it might be necessary to use a little force.

A bronze-skinned figure in the audience arose. "You will forgive me," said a voice of quiet dignity, "if I tell you that my people were Americans for thousands of years before your people were. The question is not how you can Americanize us but how we can Americanize you. We have been working at that for a long time. Sometimes we are discouraged at the results. But we will keep trying. And the first thing we want to teach you is that, in the American way of life, each man has respect for his brother's vision. Because each of us respected his brother's dream, we enjoyed freedom here in America while your people were busy killing and enslaving each other across the water. The relatives you left behind are still trying to kill each other and enslave each other because they have not learned there that freedom is built on my respect for my brother's vision and his respect for mine. We have a hard trail ahead of us in trying to Americanize you and your white brothers. But we are not afraid of hard trails." (pp. 315–16)

After summarizing many of the myriad ways that Indians have contributed to the West in many fields, Cohen continues:

The real epic of America is the yet unfinished story of the Americanization of the White Man, the transformation of the hungry, fear-ridden, intolerant men that came to these shores with Columbus and John Smith. (p. 318)

There is still much that we can take from the Indian to enrich ourselves without impoverishing the Indian. We have not by any means exhausted the great harvest of Indian inventions and discoveries in agriculture, government, medicine, sport, education, and craftsmanship. (p. 326)

He concludes:

When we have gathered the last golden grain of knowledge from the harvest of the Indian summer, then we can talk about Americanizing the Indian. Until then, we might do better to concentrate our attention on the real job of the New World, the job of Americanizing the white man. (p. 327)

The Writing of Honoring the Circle

Honoring the Circle is a woven work, bringing numerous voices together in a unified whole. Included in the project are some of the leading experts in reviving the knowledge of the contributions that American Indians have made to the Unites States, the West, and the world.

Stephen Sachs acted as coordinating editor of the book, weaving its parts together. He was involved in drafting all the chapters, having previously undertaken research and publication in the fields touched on in these volumes. Sachs, an applied philosopher, is Professor Emeritus of Political Science at IUPUI (Indiana University–Purdue University at Indianapolis). He briefly taught cultural anthropology at Kirkwood Community College, Cedar Rapids, Iowa, in 1988. His Indianization began indirectly in the final three years of high school at the Putney School, in Putney, Vermont, which is in the Native-rooted tradition of John Dewey, discussed in chapter 8. Sachs has researched in and written extensively about Indian affairs, and in some of the Indian-influenced fields discussed in these volumes. He served as coordinating editor and lead drafter, with LaDonna Harris as elder, of *Re-Creating the Circle: The Renewal of American Indian Self-Determination*. The secondary theme of that volume is the relevance for the wider world of the American Indian approaches to living well in society. Sachs has served as Coordinating Editor, and is currently Senior Editor of the journal *Indigenous Policy.*

Bruce E. Johansen is one of the leading writers on the impact of American Indians upon United States institutions and culture. He also has expertise in environmental policy. He drafted much of the discussion in chapter 2 on the Indianization of the "Founding Fathers," the widespread use of Indian motifs and cultural adaptations by Europeans and European Americans in the colonial and early United States epochs, and the great Native American influence in the structuring and functioning of colonial and US political institutions. He also drafted section II of chapter 7, on applying Indigenous thinking to environmental issues, and contributed to the writing of other parts of this work. Johansen is Frederick W. Kayser Chair of Communication and Native American Studies at the University of Nebraska at Omaha, where he has been teaching and writing since 1982. Among his forty-seven published books are several on the influence of Native American political systems on United States political and legal institutions. These include *Forgotten Founders* (1982) and *Exemplar of Liberty* (with Donald A. Grinde Jr.), published in 1991. Johansen has described the present-day debate over this issue in *Debating Democracy* (1998) and *Native American Political Systems and the Evolution of Democracy: An Annotated Bibliography* (Greenwood, 1996; volume 2, 1999). Johansen writes frequently about environmental subjects, including in *The Encyclopedia of Global Warming Science and Technology* (2 vols., 2009), *Global Warming in the 21st Century* (3 vols., 2006), *The Global Warming Desk Reference* (2001), *The Dirty Dozen: Toxic Chemicals and the Earth's Future* (2003), and *Indigenous Peoples and Environmental Issues* (2004), a 200,000-word encyclopedia of Indigenous peoples' struggles with corporations with a worldwide scope. His most recent books are *Up from the Ashes: Nation-Building at Muckleshoot* (2014) and *Eco-Hustle! Global Warming, Greenwashing, and Sustainability* (2015).

Betty Booth Donohue (Cherokee) wrote the opening part of chapter 2 on the cultural impact of contact with Indians on early New England colonists. She shows how Indian influence catalyzed the rise of American literature, distinct from European letters. Donohue is an independent scholar. Among her publications are *Bradford's Indian Book: Being the True Roote and Rise of American Letters as Revealed by the Native Text Embedded in Of Plimoth Plantation* (2011). Her chapter "Remembering Muskrat: Native Poetics and the American Indian Oral Tradition" appears in the *Cambridge History of American Poetry* (2015).

Ain Haas contributed to the drafting and editing of several portions of this volume. He was a co-drafter of chapter 1 on American Indian tradition and drafted the portion of chapter 4 on the impact of Indians on the youth movement of the 1960s, and its influence on United States culture as a whole. He also made contributions to other parts of the book, including providing some research for chapter 3 and was involved in editing much of the work. Haas is Professor Emeritus of Sociology at Indiana University in Indianapolis (IUPUI). His publications include articles on Indigenous peoples of North America and North Europe, comparative social systems, juvenile delinquency, and workplace democracy. His longtime interest in Native American lore and history was reinforced while pursuing a Ph.D. minor in anthropology (focusing on North American Indian cultures) at the University of Wisconsin at Madison and visiting nearby Native American reservations, followed by a decade-long research project involving examination of ethnographic sources, described in chapter 1.

Donna K. Dial provided resources in economic history and theory, and contributed to writing and editing chapter 6 on economics. She undertook general editing of the entire volume. Dial is Associate Professor Emerita of Economics at Indiana University–Purdue University at Indianapolis, and President and Program Director of Economic Education for Clergy, and served as associate editor of *Honoring the Circle*. She is a scholar on comparative economic history and theory.

Donald A. Grinde Jr. (Yamasee) is a leading scholar on the influence of American Indians on Western political thought and institutions. He contributed to the drafting of chapter 3, on the

Indian impact in Europe, and his research was used in developing portions of chapters 2 and 4. Grinde is Professor of Transnational/ American Studies, State University of New York (SUNY) at Buffalo. His publications include *Exemplar of Liberty: Native America and the Evolution of Democracy*, coauthored with Bruce Johansen (1991); *Debating Democracy: Native American Legacy of Freedom*, coauthored with Bruce Johansen and Barbara Mann, with a foreword by Vine Deloria Jr. (1998); *A Political History of Native Americans* (2002), for which he served as author and editor, and which was awarded "Outstanding Academic Title, 2003" by *Choice Magazine*; *Encyclopedia of Native American Biography* (1997), for which he served as coeditor and author; *Apocalypse de Chiokoyhikoy, Chéf des Iroquois...*, published in French and English with Robert Griffin as translator (1997), for which Grinde served as author and editor; *Ecocide of Native America*, coauthored with Bruce Johansen, introduction by Howard Zinn (1995); *Native America: Portrait of the Peoples*, coauthored with Duane Champagne, foreword by Dennis Banks (1994); *The Unheard Voices: American Indian Responses to the Columbian Quincentenary*, coauthored and coedited with Carole Gentry (1994); *Exiles in the Land of the Free: Democracy, Indian Nations, and the U.S. Constitution*, coauthored with Oren Lyons, John Mohawk, et al. (1992); and *The Iroquois and the Founding of the American Nation* (1977).

Jonathon York drafted the section in chapter 3 on the Indian impact on the political writing of the French philosopher Montesquieu. Montesquieu has been an influential political theorist, particularly for the many of the writers of the US Constitution. York is a scholar on the Indian impact on the political thinking of the French philosopher Montesquieu. York is Instructor of Government at Mountain View College in Dallas, Texas. He is descended from the Choctaw Nation of Oklahoma, Kiowa, Kanawha River Lenape, and Cape Girardeau refugees. He has long had an interest in how those whom Montesquieu calls the Americans influenced his political thinking.

Sally Roesch Wagner, PhD, wrote the section of chapter 4 on the Indian roots of the women's movement. She is a longtime contributor of knowledge about Native American influences upon Western society, particular on women's issues. Wagner is Founding Director of the Matilda Joslyn Gage Foundation, and Adjunct Faculty in the Renée Crown University Honors Program at Syracuse University. Her publications include *Sisters in Spirit: Haudenosaunee (Iroquois) Influence on Early American Feminists* (2001); *Matilda Joslyn Gage: She Who Holds the Sky* (1999); and *A Time of Protest: Suffragists Challenge the Republic, 1870–1887* (1992).

Walter Robinson (Cherokee) drafted the section in chapter 4 on the direct and indirect contributions of Indigenous Americans to the environmental movement. He is a lecturer in the Philosophy Department and the Native American Studies Program at IUPUI. His current interests include cross-cultural philosophies, philosophical psychology of religion, Asian and American Indian philosophies and religions, and environmental ethics based on Deep Ecology. Among his publications is *Primal Way and the Pathology of Civilization* (2012).

Amy Fatzinger drafted the section on American Indian literature, film, and television and its influence on American culture in the introduction to part II, and contributed some additions and revisions to other parts of that introduction. She is a scholar with a specialty in American Indian literature and film. She is Associate Professor of American Indian Studies at the University of Arizona. Her writings include *Indians in the House: Revisiting American Indians in Laura Ingalls Wilder's Little House Books* (2008) and "Beseeching the Breath: Rediscovering the Connections in Land, Language, and Spirituality" (2000).

Christina A. Clamp drafted the section on the Mondragon cooperatives in chapter 6, on economics, and contributed to finalizing the rest of that chapter. She is a professor with the School of Arts and Sciences and is the director of Co-operatives and Community Economic Development at Southern New Hampshire University. Clamp has researched the Mondragon cooperatives for many years. Among her publications is "Social Entrepreneurship in the Mondragon Cooperative Corporation and the Challenges of

Successful Replication," coauthored with Innocentus Alhamis, *Journal of Entrepreneurship*, September 2010. She is on the board of directors of the Industrial Cooperatives Association (ICA) Group (Boston), the Food Cooperative Initiative (MN), and the Allston/Brighton Community Development Corporation (Boston). She also serves on the Steering Committee of the Mel King Institute of the Massachusetts Association of Community Development Corporations. Formerly, she was a member of the board of directors of Childspace Development and Training Institute (Philadelphia), and the National Cooperative Business Association (Washington, DC).

Phyllis M. Gagnier (Algonquin) drafted the section in chapter 5 on *Ho'oponopono*, a form of restorative justice. She has worked with numerous Indian nations on educational development, conflict resolution, and cultural projects, including the development of the Telly Award–winning substance-abuse-intervention parenting video *From the Heart of a Child*, and *Awee Sha No Tsa* (My Child Will Return to Me). She was a coauthor of *Re-Creating the Circle: The Renewal of American Indian Self-Determination*, drafting part of the education chapter, and making contributions to other portions of the book.

We are indebted to Joy Chaudhuri, Professor Emeritus of Political Science at Arizona State University; Christian L. Kraatz, Instructor in Philosophy and American Indian Studies at IUPUI; Scott L. Pratt, Professor of Philosophy and Dean of the Graduate School at the University of Oregon; and Barbara A. Mann, Professor of Humanities at the University of Toledo. Chaudhuri's research was an important source for chapter 1 on American Indian tradition, on which he commented. He made an important suggestion for considering Roger Williams in chapter 2, on the impact of American Indians in what is now the United States up to 1800. Kraatz read and commented on Walter Robinson's draft of the chapter 4 section on Native American contributions to the environmental movement. Pratt provided most of the research for the section in chapter 4 on the influence of American Indians on the development of the American philosophy of pragmatism since 1800, and made some helpful comments on Sachs's draft of that section. He also contributed some related research on Indian influence on some of the founders in chapter 2. Mann read chapters 3 and 4, and made some useful comments on them leading to revisions. The cover designs for the four volumes were produced by Kyle Malone with assistance from Reginah WaterSpirit. Joel Chamberlain compiled the bibliography, edited the endnotes for style. Copyediting was carried out by Kenneth Kales, Editorial Director and Managing Editor of Waterside Productions. Proofreading was undertaken by Emily Jerman Schuster. Indexing of each volume was accomplished by Kerin Tate, who also made final formatting adjustments of the four books. Josh Freel at Waterside facilitated final preparations for publication.

Notes to Introduction

1. Felix Cohen, "Americanizing the White Man," *American Scholar* 21, no. 2 (1952), 181, republished in "The Bibliography of Felix S. Cohen," compiled by Cohen with his own titles in June 1953; annotated and amplified by Ida K. Johnson (of the Department of the Interior Library); and Lucy Kramer Cohen, "The Indian's Quest for Justice," part II, quoted by Erin McKenna and Scott L. Pratt, *American Philosophy: From Wounded Knee to the Present* (New York: Bloomsbury, 2015), 286. See also Felix S. Cohen, *Americanizing the White Man: The Contribution of Indian Culture to the Non-Indian World* (Washington, DC: US Department of the Interior, US Indian Service, 1948).

2. On the genocide of American Indians and their struggle for renewal, see LaDonna Harris, Stephen M. Sachs, and Barbara Morris, *Re-Creating the Circle: The Renewal of American Indian Self-Determination* (Albuquerque: University of New Mexico Press, 2011).

3. For example, see the biography of Owen: "Robert Owen," Wikipedia, https://en.wikipedia.org/wiki/Robert_Owen, in addition to the discussion in chap. 3 and the references cited there.

4. Jean Gebser, *The Ever-Present Origin* (Athens, OH: Ohio University Press, 1953).

5. Cohen, "Americanizing the White Man." The page numbers are those from the republishing of Cohen's Indian writings in "The Indian's Quest for Justice."

Felix Cohen was a major figure in the reform of US Indian policy during the New Deal. Because he was a brilliant attorney involved in Indian issues, Cohen was asked by the Department of the Interior, in 1933, to serve as assistant to associate solicitor. His initial task was to help draft basic legislation that would provide Indian tribes and individual Indians greater authority over their political affairs. Cohen continued to deal with a large variety of Indian legal and administrative issues at Interior for fourteen years. In time, he became chairman of the Interior's Board of Appeals. Cohen became a special assistant to the attorney general on loan for one year in 1939, to head the Indian Law Survey of the Department of Justice. This led to his heading the compiling of a forty-six-volume collection of federal laws and treaties. Cohen summarized this work in *Handbook of Federal Indian Law* (Washington, DC: US Government Printing Office, 1945; reprint, Albuquerque: University of New Mexico Press, 1971), http://thorpe.ou.edu/cohen.html. This has been a standard sourcebook in Indian law. Cohen wrote a number of articles and papers on Indian issues, compiled in "The Indian's Quest for Justice."

CHAPTER 1

TRADITIONAL AMERICAN INDIAN POLITICS AND SOCIETY

Stephen M. Sachs and Ain Haas

Europeans coming to the Americas in general, and North America in particular, interacted with tribal and band societies that were extremely harmonious and democratic, providing mutually supportive relationships and a high quality of life for virtually all of their members. The more than five hundred Indian nations in what now makes up the United States were each unique in the details of their quite varied cultures, though they shared a common set of core values.[1] These basic values, applied in different ways by each nation, and further varied in changing circumstances, provided the basis for good lives in well-functioning societies.

Traditional Native American societies enjoyed a generally high quality of life, with virtually no poverty or crime, and with mechanisms to provide for those who were not well off. They furnished a great deal of emotional and physical support for extended family members and a sufficient variety of choices of social roles so that almost everyone could find acceptance and develop self-esteem. The virtues of these societies are attested to in numerous ethnographies and commentaries.[2]

STEPHEN M. SACHS

Traditional Indian Governance

In terms of governance, Indian nations, in different ways and to different degrees, reached decisions democratically through a variety of consensual processes,[3] the basis of which was the principle of respect for all people, and indeed for all that is. In ceremonies and in making decisions, often, all sat in a circle. Each place in the circle had a different quality and way of seeing to contribute to the whole so that each person or group could be heard. There was no circle without each of the individual places, but the places had no meaning without the context of the circle as a whole, which framed the interconnections that constituted the proper flowing of the relationships.[4] The Comanche (of the Southern Plains) state the fundamental principles as: relationships, responsibility, reciprocity, and redistribution.[5]

Thus, out of the nature of relationships, and out of the relationships everyone was in, flowed a set of mutual responsibilities that involved a reciprocity—not just of things, but of actions and concerns—which brings the redistribution necessary to continually recreate balance and harmony. In terms of decision-making, everyone affected by a decision had a right to be heard, and no decision could be made until everyone agreed, or at least acquiesced. In the rare situations when a person or a group fundamentally disagreed with the rest of the community, they had the right to leave. For example, in 1792, when the Shawnee in Ohio were unable to agree on whether to remain and continue the fight to try to protect their land in the face of US aggression or to move west across the Mississippi in hopes of living in peace, the nation divided, with one group remaining and the other moving west.[6] Similarly, in 1906, by agreement, a split in the Hopi community at Oraibi was settled with a pushing contest, with the losing group of more traditionally minded individuals leaving the village and moving to Hotevilla.[7]

Leaders, who were chosen for their good character and fine qualities appropriate to their function, acted primarily as facilitators helping the group or community to reach consensus.[8] As highly respected people, they had influence, but could not make decisions. They could only act administratively with the support of the community.

Thus, with their emphasis on finding consensus, Native American tribes and bands functioned with a politics somewhat different in character than what has been accepted by the mainstream of Western political theory as seen in Machiavelli and Hobbes. Power was an important resource for doing this, but it was not the central element for determining "the authoritative allocation of values"[9] or for determining "who gets what, when, where, how."[10] Moreover, power in traditional American Indian tribal and band societies was only partly a vehicle for control. It was also a source of empowerment. Tribal and band politics have very important cooperative elements along with competitive aspects. At the heart of this dynamic is a set of communal relationships based upon mutual respect emphasizing both the community and the individual so that in a very important sense, the whole is equal to the part.

The participatory democratic nature of Native American society places a strong emphasis on both individual freedom or rights and the good of the whole, as realized through inclusive participation; Benjamin Barber refers to this as strong democracy.[11] This can be seen in the traditional functioning of some of the Indian nations that would have been known to European political thinkers of the sixteenth to eighteenth centuries, such as Locke and Rousseau. Information about Native ways came from many detailed observations from traders, missionaries, and captives who had lived among Indigenous people for extended periods. One example is an account from James Smith, who was captured by the Lenni Lenape (Delaware Indians) in 1755:

> The chief…is neither a supreme ruler, monarch or potentate—he can neither make war or peace, leagues or treaties—He cannot impress soldiers, or dispose of magazines—He cannot adjourn, prorogue or dissolve a general assembly, nor can he refuse his assent to their conclusions,

or in any manner control them.... The chief of a nation has to hunt for his living, as any other citizen.[12]

A report dating back to 1660 on the Pennacook tribe (Massachusetts and New Hampshire) points to the typical basis of a chief's power in Native American societies:

> [T]he old sagamore, at a public feast, made his farewell speech [and gave] advice ... to his people.... [B]y his wisdom, his natural powers of eloquence, and his supposed knowledge of the mysteries of nature, [he] possesses an unbounded influence over the Indians.[13]

It proved to be difficult for Europeans to understand just how extensive the participatory democracy of Native Americans was, in part because the observers might apply terms like "king" or "emperor" to Native leaders, which carried inappropriate connotations that were more fitting for autocratic rule. As noted in Clinton Alfred Weslager's book on the Nanticoke Indians of the eastern shore of Chesapeake Bay (Maryland and Delaware):

> The so-called Emperor of the Nanticokes owned no personal real estate, received no taxes, had no court or throne, and, in the English meaning of the word, had no subjects. The Nanticokes ... were governed by tribal custom rather than by a potentate. The Emperor issued no edicts or proclamations that the members of the tribe were obliged to observe. He provided food for his own family, as other members of the tribe did for theirs, and his wife and daughters planted and cultivated the fields like the other Indian women, just as his sons hunted or trapped game.... [T]ribal decisions were arrived at jointly in consultation with great men or councillors.[14]

The risk of confusion about the true nature of Native societies' leadership roles can be seen in this excerpt from John DeForest's work on the Indians living near the Massachusetts Bay Colony; DeForest draws on the writings of the Puritan minister Cotton Mather and others:

> If [the sachem or chief] was brave, eloquent, and cunning, he might exercise a sway approaching to the despotic; but if he was deficient... his orders [were] indifferently obeyed. Yet, however great his influence might be, he was usually careful not to violate the known wishes of the people; and seldom transacted anything of importance without the advice and concurrence of his councillors. In conjunctures of great moment, general assemblies of the tribe were often called... and the different leaders sometimes enforced their views by long and animated harangues.
>
> Beneath the principal sachem was a class of inferior chieftains.... Each of these... would collect round him a band of followers. He had no positive claim to their services, however, and was obliged to... keep them in good humor, or they would forsake him and attach themselves to some rival.[15]

The situation of modern constitutional monarchs is somewhat similar, in that they are nominally the sovereign rulers of their lands but in practice must follow the wishes of their parliaments. In the time of colonization, however, European settlers knew only of monarchs who had little or no accountability to others, so they tended to use terminology they were already familiar with to characterize Native American leadership positions and authority, unaware of the terms' inappropriateness or inaccuracies.

The Example of the Wendat (Huron)

Trigger describes the traditional ways of the Wendat,[16] more widely known as the Huron,[17] living around Lakes Huron and Erie. The Wendat were a confederation of several tribes, numbering thirty thousand to forty thousand people in 1634. They lived partially intermingled with each other in settlements of up to two thousand individuals consisting of a central town and surrounding villages. Their social organization included a clan structure. In each community each clan segment had two formal chiefs, known as a Yarihawa—which literally translates as "he is a great voice"—who were chosen from among the men of the clan lineage that held the right to serve in that office.

Chiefs' primary functions were to announce decisions arrived at by a process of consensus formation involving discussion by all the adult men and women of their group, and to facilitate the discussion process. Chiefs could advise and persuade, but they could not decide. No action could be taken until it had been acceded to by every person affected.[16] In practice, that meant decision-making tended to be inclusive of the concerns of everyone involved. To reach consensus on a proposal, the group would continue to modify it to take into account each person's concerns until almost everyone reached agreement, and the few who did not agree, having been heard and seeing nothing to gain by further discussion, accepted the view of the group.

The chief's first duty was to assist his own group to come to a consensus and then to represent his people in negotiating with the chiefs of other groups. Trigger (1990) explains:

> Huron Chiefs had no constitutional authority to coerce their followers or force their will on anyone. Moreover, individual Huron were sensitive about their honor and intolerant of external constraints, and friends and relatives would rally to the support of someone who believed himself insulted by a chief. Overbearing behavior by a chief might, therefore, encourage a violent reaction and lead to conflicts within or between lineages. In the long run, chiefs who behaved arrogantly or foolishly tended to alienate support and would be deposed by their own lineages. The ideal Huron chief was a wise and brave man who understood his followers and won

their support by means of his generosity, persuasiveness, and balanced judgment.[18]

The two chiefs of each clan segment at the local level were the civil chief and the war chief. The civil or peace chiefs, who were primary, were concerned with matters of everyday life—from settling disputes and arranging feasts, dances, and games to negotiating foreign treaties. The separation of peace and war chiefs, with the primacy of the civil chiefs, is typical of many tribes.[19] This primacy of civilian over military leadership is similar to the emphasis in the US Constitution on the president, a civilian, being commander in chief over the military. It may well be that the older tribal practice is the basis, or at least a contributing factor, for the US practice.

The national government of each Wendat tribe consisted of a council made up of chiefs of the clan segments in each community, with one exception—the Tahontaenrat tribe, which lived in a single settlement so that their community and national governments were coterminous. The Confederacy Council appears to have been composed of the civil chiefs of the various national councils. However, the national and confederacy councils had no power to compel the groups whom their members represented. Their function was to develop consensus through dialog and mutual exchange among all the parties involved in the matters they considered. In order for the decisions of these councils to be effective, they had to be accepted by the constituents of the chiefs. This meant that national and confederacy affairs were discussed by citizens at the local level to a great extent, with the result being that chiefs were usually far more representative of their constituents than today's elected federal representatives are.

Underlying Wendat politics was a culture that balanced strong concern for individual, family, and clan autonomy with a strong egalitarian moral sense of working toward the good of all with respect for all views. Thus, there was an abhorrence of compelling anyone's actions. But, at the same time, both by upbringing and ongoing experience, Huron people were very sensitive to others and to the pressures of public opinion. If one acted improperly, one would lose honor, and if one went too far, then it meant eventually risking economic and other support, too. In the Huron case, as in the case of many native North American peoples, this meant that by honoring generosity, both giving and receiving, no one was allowed to be either rich or poor.

Similarly, certain political and social positions of authority might belong to certain clans or clan segments. The positions were filled on the basis of perceived merit. Thus, authority, and hence power, was widely dispersed so that individual offices carried limited authority. This worked to keep effective the primary limitation on power: public opinion. This widespread arrangement in traditional North America is somewhat similar in effect, though it is less formal and more extensive than the later use of the combination of separation of powers, checks and balances, and direct and indirect elections by the framers of the US Constitution who were directly influenced by this Indian practice. They were also indirectly influenced by English thinkers such as John Locke, who had clearly incorporated Indian ideas and practice into their own theories as presented below.

The Six Nations of the Haudenosaunee

The Wendat tribe's relatives and neighbors to the south, the Haudenosaunee, Six Nations, or Iroquois, also had a particularly strong impact upon European-American thinking. Their governance from the longhouse—a multiple-hearth residence of kinfolk—to the clan, village, nation, and confederacy was almost identical to that of the Wendat, except for a difference in the procedure by which the Six Nation Confederacy reached consensus.

The procedure for debating policies of the Confederacy began with the Mohawks and Senecas (the Mohawks, Senecas, and Onondagas are called the elder brothers).[20] After being debated by the Keepers of the Eastern Door—the Mohawks—and the Keepers of the Western Door—the Senecas—the question was then thrown across the fire to the Oneida and Cayuga statesmen (the younger brothers) for discussion in much the same manner. Once consensus was achieved among the Oneidas and the Cayugas, the discussion was then given back to the Senecas and Mohawks for confirmation. Next, the question was laid before the Onondagas for their decision.

At that stage, the Onondagas had a power similar to judicial review: they could raise objections to the proposed measure if it was believed to be inconsistent with the Great Law. Essentially, the legislature could rewrite the proposed law on the spot so that it could be in accord with the Constitution of the Iroquois. When the Onondagas reached consensus, Tadodaho, an Onondaga chief who acted as head of the Grand Council, gave the decision to Honowireton, an Onondaga chief who presided over debates between the delegations, to confirm that the decision was unanimously agreed upon by all of the Onondaga sachems. Finally, either Honowireton or Tadodaho gave the decision of the Onondagas to the Mohawks and the Senecas so that the policy could be announced to the Grand Council.

The Tuscaroras joined the Confederacy after it had been first formed. On becoming a member, they were given a direct voice within the Grand Council only when their speaking would help the nations. But when they had an issue of their own to be discussed, it was voiced through the Cayugas. Thus, they were added to the complex process without disturbing its balance.

This process reflected the emphasis of the league of six nations on checks and balances, public debate, and consensus. The overall intent of such a parliamentary procedure was to encourage unity at each step. This legislative process was similar to the mechanisms of the Albany Plan of Union, the Articles of Confederation, and the US Constitution.

Lewis Henry Morgan describes Six Nation government as extremely democratic:[21]

[S]uch was the spirit of the Iroquois system of government, that the influence of the inferior chiefs, the warriors and even the women would make itself felt, whenever the subject itself aroused a general public interest.[22]

Morgan adds there was considerable interest in public affairs by an active citizenry:

In council, public transactions of every name and character were planned, scrutinized and adopted.... It may be said that the life of the Iroquois was spent either in the chase, on the war path, or at the council fire.[23]

Furthermore, Morgan noted that no event of any importance ever transpired without passing under the cognizance of one of these councils:

Sachems [primary chiefs: "Counselors of the People"], chiefs and warriors, women and even children, deserted their hunting grounds and woodland seclusions, and taking the trail, literally flocked to the place of council. When the day arrived, a multitude had gathered together, from the most remote and toilsome distance, but yet animated by an unyielding spirit of hardihood and endurance.[24]

Morgan concludes that all of these traits combined to forge a strong bond of community with the utmost respect for the rights of the individual:

The spirit which prevailed in the nation and in the confederacy was that of freedom. The people appear to have secured to themselves all the liberty which the hunter state rendered desirable. They fully appreciated its value, as evidenced by the liberality of their institutions. The red man was always free from political bondage, and, more worthy still of remembrance, his "free limbs never wore a shackle." His spirit could never be bowed in servitude. In the language of Charlevoix, the Iroquois were "entirely convinced that man was born free, that no power on earth had any right to make any attempts against his liberty, and that nothing could make him amends for its loss." It would be difficult to describe any political society, in which there was less oppression and discontent, more of individual independence and boundless freedom.[25]

Muscogee (Creek) Confederacy

This spirit of freedom in inclusive, participatory societies was the general pattern in Indigenous North America. The Muscogee, or Creek, Confederacy that extended over much of what is now the US Southeast, though exhibiting some difference in the details of government and social organization, functioned fundamentally in the same manner.[26] Like the leagues to the north, the Muscogee Confederacy was primarily organized for peaceful interaction among highly autonomous communities. Not all of the people of the confederacy were Muscogee. Instead, membership was based on respecting all people, maintaining harmony and balance with nature and the community, and following the basic Muscogee ways. From a Muscogee perspective, there were about thirty-three major regional subdivisions of the confederacy. However, since some of these had entered the confederacy as sizable tribes with their own subdivisions, it would be more accurate to say there were more than one hundred major regions in the confederacy, which operated on the basis of consensual decision-making after full discussion among numerous interlinked councils.

Beginning at the local level, authority was widely dispersed with each of the clans having specialized functions. Elder women and men had their own highly respected bodies. In addition, through an assessment of psychological and personality traits, men were divided into white sticks and red sticks to carry out civil and military/police leadership functions, following the consensus of their communities. As was typically the case in pre-Columbian North

America, local communities were generally autonomous. Matters of general Muscogee interest were decided by councils at the confederacy level, which rotated its meetings around the Muscogee country to maintain a broad inclusiveness and balance of input over time.

Band Societies

In their own unique ways, the smaller tribes functioned on the same general basis of participatory democracy, but without the need for confederacy-level decision-making. This was the general pattern all over the Americas at the time of European contact, except in the instances of national decision-making south of what is now the United States by a few of the very large nations that were beginning to become states, as Locke recognized in differentiating between "the two great empires of Peru and Mexico" and the fully participatory tribes.[27] Yet, even these empires, such as the Aztec, Maya, and Inca societies, tended to act cooperatively and inclusively with respect for the opinions of individuals and groups, especially at the local level.[28]

An example of the smaller Indian nations, the Chiricahua Apache of the Southwest, for example, who were well-known to the Spanish, lived in small bands, each with their own consensus-based governance.[29] They lived by hunting, gathering, raiding, and agriculture. Each band, and within it each local group, was guided by one or more recognized leaders assisted by a number of subordinates. In essence, the way in which leadership functioned among the Apaches was typical for the pre-contact Americas generally, although there were differences in the details among Indian nations, such as whether eligibility for a position was limited to members of certain clans, societies, or other groups, and just how leaders were to be chosen and removed.

For the Chiricahua, important decisions were made at band or local group meetings at which all adults were present and male heads of household usually spoke to represent their families, though wives and unmarried sons and daughters might also contribute to the discussion. Typical of band and tribal societies, a man would become a leader if enough people respected him sufficiently to give him their loyalty, and he would maintain that leadership role only so long as he maintained that respect and loyalty. People dissatisfied with a local or band leader could simply move away to another community. As in many bands and tribes, being of good family was an advantage in gaining the respect necessary to become a leader, and a leader was almost always the head of an extended family. But the primary basis for leadership was being respected for one's ability and good qualities as demonstrated by the chief's achievements. He must be wise, respectful of others, able in war, capable in managing his own and his family's affairs, and generous. Thus, wealth was an aspect of qualification for leadership: as a sign of ability and as a source of the generosity that leaders were expected to exhibit in hosting prominent visitors, putting on feasts, and providing for those less well off.

For the Chiricahua Apache, as with tribes and bands in the Americas generally, the functions of a leader included being an advisor on community affairs, a facilitator in collective decision-making, and a peacemaker in disputes and the settlement of wrongs. In addition, as the Apache and some other tribal societies did not divide civil and military functions among distinct leaders, a Chiricahua leader served in war as well as in peace. While leaders could command in combat, they had no power of control in civil governance beyond what was supported by public opinion. To the extent that they were respected, and persuasive—a quality contributing to respect—leaders exercised influence in the forming of community views. Even as peacemakers, when deviant acts or major disputes occurred, they only served as mediators. Since the Chiricahuas needed each other's help in a variety of economic and social activities, as is normally the case in band and tribal societies, the main pressure for following social norms was the pressure of public opinion, which women played an important role in shaping. This was almost universally true in all traditional Indian societies.[30]

Reaching settlement in trouble cases involving a dispute or harm, which today are roughly the equivalent of torts or crimes, similarly was required by pressure public opinion, often with a respected elder or leader acting as mediator.

Hence, leaders were under continuing scrutiny to act well and to be concerned for the interests and views of the members of the community. In particular, the band leader needed to listen carefully and take into account the advice of the local group leaders. They, in turn, had to be especially responsive to leading heads of families who were obligated to be responsive to the adult members of their families. Consequently, power and influence were widely disbursed in Chiricahua society, as was generally the case in Indian societies. Respected elders had the most political influence, but their influence and respect also rested on the opinions of the community members at large in a culture that emphasized respect for all community members, and indeed all beings. This arrangement was typical in tribal societies, including among the more dispersed Ojibwa, living largely as single families engaged in hunting and gathering in the woodland and lake country of what is now the Northern Midwest and adjacent Canada,[31] the hunting and gathering Utes of the Rocky Mountains,[32] and the Yakima of the Pacific Northwest coast.[33]

The Lenni Lenape (Delaware) Bands

Among the Indigenous societies the British, Dutch, and French contacted in coming to North America were the many bands of the Lenni Lenape, or Delaware, who lived south of the Raritan River in New Jersey, Pennsylvania, and the drainage south of the Blue Mountain in Delaware. These bands were related to Algonquian-language peoples who lived from Labrador to the Rocky Mountains and from Hudson Bay to North Carolina.[34] In response to European colonization, some of the Algonquian bands farther north, including in New York, joined the tightened, but still relatively loosely tethered, Lenape Confederacy.[35] At European contact, each Lenape band dwelled in one or two villages, often of around two hundred people, where they farmed. In the late fall and winter months, the men, often accompanied by their wives, moved to cabins (wigwams) in their nearby hunting grounds. Following the general American Indian pattern, their social relations and economy were very egalitarian, with generosity and hospitality serving as central values.

As there was no overall confederacy governance, bands collaborated on occasions for mutual benefit, but the band government was paramount. The Lenape overall, and generally in each village, were members of one of three lineages or clans, in which descent was matrilineal. Marriage was exogamous, meaning individuals always married outside their own clan. The lineages were closely related, with everyone relating as members of extended families. Most matters of individual behavior were handled within the lineages of the community. Band decision-making was participatory with the facilitation of highly respected leaders chosen by its members from among the leading clan in the band. A *sachema*, whom the English for lack of an equivalent term often called "king," would convene community meetings as needed. As a respected elder he had considerable influence, but no direct power to make decisions. He announced the decisions of meetings, represented the band in negotiations, and presided at ceremonies. William Penn noted:

> Every King hath his Council, and that consists of all the old and Wise men of his Nation, which perhaps is two hundred People: Nothing of Moment is undertaken, be it War, Peace, Selling of Land, or Traffic, without advising with them; and which is more, with the Young Men too. 'Tis admirable to consider, how Powerful the Kings are, and yet how they move by the Breath of their People. I have had occasion to be in Council with them upon Treaties for Land, and to adjust the terms of Trade; their Order is thus: the King sits in the middle of an half moon, and hath his Council, the Old and Wise on each hand; behind them, or at a little distance, sit the younger Fry, in the same figure.[36]

Later, if not already in Penn's time, the council also included one or more leading warriors, whom the English often called "captains." Col. James Smith, who was captured by Indians in 1755, said of the "kings":

> I have often heard of Indian Kings, but never saw any.—How any term used by the Indians in their own tongue, for the chief man of a nation, could be rendered King, I know not. The chief of a nation is neither a supreme ruler, monarch or potentate—He can neither make war or peace, leagues or treaties—He cannot impress soldiers, or dispose of magazines—He cannot adjourn, prorogue or dissolve a general assembly, nor can he refuse his assent to their conclusions, nor in any manner control them....
>
> The chief of a nation has to hunt for his living, as any other citizen.[37]

Thus, overall, American Indian nations were almost always extremely democratic and egalitarian, with leaders acting as facilitators and advisors, and a wide dispersion of power in very participatory societies. The large empires of Mexico and Peru, which were moving toward becoming states, were partial exceptions to the otherwise almost always democratic and egalitarian pattern of American Indian nations. Even the Mayans and Aztecs largely adhered to the general pattern of inclusive participatory democracy.[38]

An example of how hard it could be to assert and centralize power in this context comes from Cherokee lore. It is reported that not too long before the arrival of Europeans on the East Coast of what is now the United States, the Ani'-Kutan'i, or priests, whose function was to ensure the proper timing and carrying out of the Cherokee nation's annual cycle of ceremonies, began to gain more power and authority.[39] As they did, they also became increasingly arrogant, violating the democratic and egalitarian sensibilities of the people. Thus, a popular resistance developed, and when one of the Ani'-Kutan'i abducted the wife of one of the younger leaders of the opposition, the people rose up and massacred most of the priests, restoring their traditional participatory culture.

Unity Though Diversity

It is important to note that the egalitarian nature of Native American societies was based upon a respect for differences, which some call the principle of "place,"[40] and a unity through diversity that provided for a high level of equality, while also allowing for differences in role and prestige. Whereas in hierarchical social systems differences of function tend to be marked by significant differences in status, participatory systems tend to minimize status differences. This was notably the case in the relations of men and women in many tribes and bands who carried out their largely separate functions with a high degree of autonomy. While their lives were different in many respects, the relations between the genders were usually those of balanced reciprocity.[41] Among the Haudenosaunee, for example, only men served as chiefs or sachems on the intertribal council, but women held considerable power, too. In certain tribes, the women of a clan, speaking through the Clan Mother, nominated the chiefs and had the power to remove them for misconduct.[42] In some tribes women could serve as chiefs, but regardless of their formal roles, women in traditional Native American societies held sway over their own lives and wielded great influence in public affairs, where they often served as the conscience of the community.[43] Similarly, tribal societies had respected roles for people who today would be considered gay, lesbian, or transgender.

"All My Relations"

The underlying principle, applied in varying ways by different peoples, was in creating and maintaining balanced and harmonious relations in a society and a larger world in which everyone and everything was seen as related. Everything was understood as being within the multiplicity of the Great Mystery, which in turn was seen as thriving in all beings. All was considered alive. Even the rocks, seen as the eldest, were living, and shared their wisdom in such ceremonies as the sweat lodge.[44] Hence, all were related in a great family, whose relations needed to be kept in balance. The Lakota, for example, when completing a prayer or passing a sacred object, said, "*Mitakue Oyasun*" (All my relations. Amen!). These words, which like the Hindu *om* representing the prime sound in the universe in which everything is vibration, when fully stated contained all the vowels in their Siouan language.[45] The Muscogee, like numerous other indigenous nations, had a very similar approach to interrelatedness. When they dance the first friendship dance, recognizing and honoring the creator that is in and surrounds all things and beings, they chant "*iyabileyuppe*," which also contains all the vowel sounds in their Muskogean language.[46]

The unity of all beings combined with their diversity, and the difference in their qualities and ways of seeing, has deep social implications in indigenous understanding. Each person, family, group, nation, tradition, as well as each of the animals, plants, and all creation has a place with its unique perspective, qualities, and talents to offer the circle of all that is. Thus, all must be respected, including taking into account future implications, and everyone affected by a decision must have a say in its making, requiring the inclusive participatory processes discussed above.[47]

American Indian thinking was necessarily quite complex and holistic, in considering the full range of relationships and factors involved in a decision, including taking into account its future implications. Long experience and careful observation had taught the prudence of being mindful of relations with the physical environment, which needed to be kept in balance. Normally, nature provided enough to live decently, if too much was not taken and environmental damage was minimized, but it was expedient to plan for shortages and difficult times. Thus, Native Americans operated under well thought out pragmatic philosophies developed from experience, and raised their young people with an education

appropriate for the functioning of their societies that was democratic, problem-solving oriented, pragmatic, and supportive of the
child in creatively developing his or her own unique qualities in
ways that fit the needs of their communities.[48]

Economy and Balanced Reciprocity

The need for balanced relationships has economic implications. An
essential dimension of living collaboratively as a harmonious family, in which individual welfare was understood as encompassing the
well-being of all, was the maintenance of the economic balance of
the community. Hence, redistribution and reciprocity were central
values, so that generosity and sharing were strongly emphasized.
Indeed, in tribal and band societies a person's identity was usually
inextricably linked with their community's identity.

Indigenous American economies functioned in varying forms
in different settings according to a tribe's cultural choices within
the ecology of its homeland. For example, the early Inuit, commonly known as the Eskimo, inhabited the Arctic and near-Arctic
regions stretching from Greenland across Canada and Alaska to
Russia, and in traditional times lived in small bands in that harsh
climate much of the year. They had few capital resources such as
wood for making the items needed for survival and well-being,
including kayaks.[49] As with most indigenous peoples, the enterprise
of living was labor-intensive.

People needed each other for economic, social, psychological,
and spiritual purposes, making considerable collaboration necessary. The need for acquiring sufficient food was such that being
a good hunter and provider was highly honored, but no one was
allowed to have much more than anyone else. The honor was not in
how much food an individual had acquired, but in how much they
had supplied to the rest of the community. As in many other Native
societies, "ownership" by individuals was more limited and subject
to greater demands by others. This tended to give the impression to
many early European observers that none of the indigenous people

owned anything, and that everything was communally owned, or simply belonged to the Creator.[50] For example, an Inuit had the right to build or properly acquire a kayak, and the right to use it whenever he wished. Because an Inuit community usually had a limited number of kayaks, which were needed for hunting and fishing, other members of the community had the right to use a kayak when the owner was not using it. An illustration of a similar notion of property ownership in an agricultural tribe can be found among the Wendat (Huron) of Ontario, where an abandoned field was no longer considered the property of the previous owner but could be cultivated by anyone.[51]

In most Native American societies, taking care of less well-off community members was a duty, and honor was given to those who provided for others. For instance, when a young Lakota man went on his first buffalo hunt or undertook some honorable action, his father would often have the camp crier go around the village announcing that he was giving away a horse to a poor family in honor of his son's deed.[52] Giving to those less fortunate was considered honorable and increased the stature of the benefactor. A woman would be honored for making beautiful articles of clothing and sharing them with others. Conversely, selfishly hoarding goods was dishonorable, and indeed any improper act reduced one's standing in the community.

European colonists became aware of this aspect of the Native American societies as soon as they engaged in trade with them and saw how payments to their Native partners circulated widely in communities. For example, William Penn, the founder of the Pennsylvania colony, made this observation about the Lenni Lenape or Delaware Indians in 1683:

> [I]n Liberality they excell, nothing is too good for their friend; give them a fine Gun, Coat, or other thing, it may pass 20 hands, before it sticks.... [They are] the most merry Creatures that live, Feast and Dance perpetually; they never have much nor want much. Wealth circulateth like the

Blood, all parts partake…none shall want what another hath.[53]

A similar observation based on the reports from Cotton Mather and others in the Puritans' Massachusetts Bay Colony was made by John DeForest about the Indians in that area:

The most popular of their dances affords a striking illustration of…improvidence…[whereby] each [dancer], in turn, divested himself of his worldly goods, going away at the end with whatever he had been able to beg from others.[54]

The role of chiefs in facilitating the circulation of material wealth is clarified in another excerpt from DeForest's writings:

[T]he sachem…was entitled…to demand from his subjects a kind of revenue. They carried him the first fruits of their corn and beans; and very often made him presents out of what they had obtained in fishing and hunting. In this way the cabin of a powerful chieftain was usually supplied with abundance of food, and his beds or couches were well furnished with…skins.

To the sachem were given the spoils taken in war.

[H]e claimed every whale and wreck that was stranded on the shore, and the skin of every wolf and deer that took to the water and was then despatched by the hunters. But, in return for the support this furnished him by his people, he was bound to exercise an unlimited hospitality towards travellers and strangers.[55]

Quantitative Evidence of Native American Egalitarianism

The extent of egalitarian arrangements among the Natives of North America can be seen in the results of the study by Ain

Haas, "Social Inequality in Aboriginal North America: A Test of Lenski's Theory."[56] He used data from ethnographic accounts for 258 of the 276 North American nations from the Inuit/Eskimo of the Arctic area to indigenous populations at Mexico's southern tip (excluding the Yucatan Peninsula and the Central American isthmus) that are delineated in George Peter Murdock's *Ethnographic Bibliography of North America*. Two measures of social inequality were obtained for testing Gerhard Lenski's theory that wealth and political inequality tended to emerge when societies developed an economic surplus and people no longer had to depend on their neighbors' cooperation and support to survive recurrent famines.

Wealth inequality was measured with the following four categories:

1) None, where there were no enduring differences between households in their standards of living (amount of food, quality of housing, valued possessions, etc.).
2) Some, where some are consistently wealthier.
3) Much, where there is a range from slaves (with no inalienable rights to property) to rich people (capable of full year-round support of individuals who make no contribution in subsistence pursuits).
4) Extreme, where the range is from expendables (doomed individuals below subsistence level) to rich people (as defined in the previous category).

The distribution of the sample on this measure was as follows (percentages rounded to nearest whole number):

1) No wealth inequality: 49 percent
2) Some: 44 percent
3) Much: 7 percent
4) Extreme: 0 percent

Political inequality was measured with these four categories:

1) None, where no position had institutionalized coercive powers over unrelated adults in other households.
2) Some, where headmen had some recognized coercive powers to apply physical or economic penalties for disobedience.
3) Much, where officials had a dependent staff of enforcers, who were paid for full-time service in implementing the leaders' decisions, by force if needed.
4) Tyranny, where the ruler had unlimited authority at the apex of a chain of command.

The distribution of the North American societies on this measure was as follows (percentages rounded to nearest whole number):

1) No political inequality: 59 percent
2) Some: 36 percent
3) Much: 4 percent
4) Tyranny: 0 percent

These results reveal that a plurality of the aboriginal North American societies had not developed wealth inequality and a majority had not developed political inequality. Where some inequality had emerged, it was often to a limited degree and often connected with public service or shared benefits. For example, chiefs in Plains Indian societies often appointed groups to enforce a coordinated bison hunt, with this responsibility typically rotated between different groups of "dog soldiers." In southwestern Indian societies, "ditch bosses" often organized mandatory participation in irrigation projects for the good of the whole community. In Northwest Coast societies, clan leaders who had accumulated great wealth for years often gave it away at potlatch feasts, which enhanced their and other clan members' prestige through generosity.

The contrast between Native American and European societies was especially evident in military activities. Most Native American societies did not have professional warriors. Instead, military skills were already widespread since hunters' skills in locating prey, self-concealment, and handling weapons were also applicable to combat with human foes. Leaders of raids typically had to persuade others to join their expeditions, and they would quickly find the ranks of their voluntary followers dwindling if things went awry. These followers might have been expected to participate in expeditions sooner or later to prove their bravery and avoid a reputation for cowardice, but no one could be forced into any particular raid against their will, especially if he had a dream about it with bad portent. Leaders of raids were typically expected to share the proceeds of their expeditions, not only with their followers but also with the wider community. If captives were spared, it was typical for them to be eventually adopted with the same rights as their captors.

The societies of northeastern North America were especially egalitarian. In contrast to the expectations of Lenski, whose theory was generally upheld in Haas's analysis, the Northeast stood out as an area where economic surplus had developed, solving the problem of recurrent famines, but political and economic inequality had not. All twelve of the nations that Murdock delineates in this region had achieved economic surplus, but in Haas's study overwhelming majorities were egalitarian on the political inequality measure (67 percent) and the wealth inequality measure (75 percent). Two-thirds (67 percent) of the northeastern nations were egalitarian on both measures, compared to one-third (34 percent) of the whole sample across the continent. In the adjacent region of eastern Canada, where about half the societies still had problems with recurring food shortages, egalitarian arrangements were even more common: all nine (100 percent) of the nations that Murdock delineates in the latter region were egalitarian on the political inequality variable, and eight out of nine (89 percent) were egalitarian on the wealth inequality variable.

This may help explain why people of British and French origin, who early on became closely acquainted with Native Americans from these very areas, were especially inspired to ponder the possibility of achieving more egalitarian arrangements in their own societies, both in their original homelands and their new colonies. However, as discussed in the introduction to part I of this book, this also had to do with the background of the people involved, the conditions and events of the nations from which they came, and the economic opportunities they found in their settlements in the New World.

The southeastern region of what became the United States was another area of early European settlement—by the British at Jamestown, Virginia, and Roanoke, North Carolina; and by the French at Fort Caroline in the Jacksonville area of Florida, though the French were soon driven out of this area by the Spaniards who settled at St. Augustine. Haas's study showed that the prosperous southeastern tribes were less likely to be in the egalitarian category of None on the measures of Political Inequality (only 4 of 21, or 19 percent of tribes lacked such inequality) or Wealth Inequality (only 7 of 21, or 33 percent), but even in this region tribes tended to have noticeably more equality than in those of the European societies from which the colonists came. In particular, the nation currently known as the Cherokee, discussed more extensively below, stood out as an especially egalitarian tribe with which the British had extensive contact in this area.

Societies as Kin Groupings

By channeling competitiveness into promoting helpfulness, American Indian societies promoted collaboration.[57] This was accomplished more directly in other ways, however. One of the most important of these was through inclusiveness, by providing every person with a role in community affairs, as exemplified by the consensus decision-making processes discussed above. An essential element in the development and maintenance of cooperation was the acculturation to collaborative values that stressed the well-being of the whole before everything else,[58] while also providing continual opportunity to participate in supporting the whole through activities involving mutual support. Thus, traditional Indian societies functioned as families. All tribal members were treated as if they were relatives, regardless of whether they were biologically related. As Ella Deloria said of the Dakota, this was a system that worked.

> Kinship was the all-important matter. Its demands and dictates for all phases of social life were relentless and exact; but on the other hand, its privileges and honorings and rewarding prestige were not only tolerable but downright pleasant for all who conformed. By kinship all Dakota people were held together in a great relationship that was theoretically all-inclusive and co-extensive with the Dakota Domain. Everyone who was born a Dakota belonged in it; nobody need be left outside. [And since being Dakota, as with Indian societies generally, was more a matter of participation in the community than blood, kinship included all who effectively joined the community, whether they married in or were adopted, a common practice throughout traditional Native America]....
>
> I can safely say that the ultimate aim of Dakota life, stripped of accessories, was quite simple: One must obey kinship rules: One must be a good relative. No Dakota who has participated in that life will dispute that. In the last analysis every other consideration was secondary—property, personal ambition, glory, good times, life itself. Without that aim and the constant struggle to attain it, the people would no longer be Dakota in truth. They would no longer be even human. To be a good Dakota then was to be humanized, civilized. And to be civilized was to keep the rules imposed by kinship for achieving civility, good manners, and a sense of responsibility toward every individual dealt with. Thus only was it possible to live communally with success; that is

to say, with a minimum of friction and a maximum of good will.[59]

Deloria goes on to point out that kinship, like all the other principles we have been discussing, while not functioning perfectly, worked quite well in Indian society:

What I have given here is, of course, an ideal picture. But I can honestly say that hardly one in a hundred dared to be thought of as deviating from its rule, although there were always a few naturally heedless persons who persistently or occasionally disregarded it. But that at once classified them as with the *witko*—the naughty, irresponsible child, the out-law adult, the mentally foolish, the drunk. No adult in his right mind cared to be so classed.[60]

A similar view of family is expressed in writing about Cherokee ways, and beyond that about traditional Native Americans in general, by Michael Garrett:

Because the survival and well-being of the individual is synonymous with that of the community, family plays a prominent role in our lives.... Many native American people *are* a family in a real sense, because they identify themselves not by their own accomplishments, but by the nature of their relations and the energy they draw from those connections.[61]

Garrett goes on to point out that for the Cherokee, as for other traditional Indian peoples, the concept of "family" was part of larger metaphysical and spiritual concerns:

The traditional view of family is universal in scope. "Family" extends well beyond immediate relatives to extended family relatives through the second cousin, members of the clan, members of the community or tribe, all other living creatures in this world, the natural environment and the universe itself. The entire universe is thought of as "a family" with each and every one of its members having a useful and necessary place in the Circle of Life, just as each strand creates the beauty and strength of the Web [of life].[62]

Harmony and Balance

Traditionally, the web of interrelationships based upon the inherent value of each being, required a striving for balance, harmony, or as the Diné, commonly known as the Navajo, say, *hozo*,[63] or beauty. Among the Muscogee (Creek), for instance, this is seen in their creation story, and in all their related stories describing that everything is interrelated and must be kept in balance. Chaudhuri and Chaudhuri write of this interconnectedness as a sacred trust to be upheld:

> The beautiful astronomical legends give us a picture of the balance of male and female energies, thereby showing the patch of darkness in light and light in darkness, all circling in the search for harmony in motion. The legends provide a humanities parallel of the science of the Creeks which also sees the search for balance between the four elements and the synergy linking the cycles of dynamic energies of the earth, the water, the sun (fire), and the sky (air). This is no romantic pipe dream, but the vision of an earth-centered culture with sacred trust responsibilities. The Earth centered physics involves exchanges between and transformations of various forms of energy and the cycles of energy among soil, water, nutrients, animals, sunlight, air and rain in an environmentally balanced manner.[64]

This dynamic balancing, necessary in the physical sphere, was also necessary in the social one in which all the elements—individuals, families, clans, moieties, societies—had their unique and essential functions that must be kept in balance, and when needed, restored to balance.[65] The same is true of the individual, who if internally out of balance cannot act socially in a balanced way. "In the Muscogee Creek cosmos, all things consist of particular combinations of body, mind and spirit. When these are not in harmony, one is truly lost and healing becomes necessary for the entity to continue."[66]

A spirituality that pervaded all of life was a central factor in Indian societies in defining the relationship of the individual to family, society, the world, and all that is. This was consistent with an expression of the social values of each people, and also an important building block in the social development of individual and collective integration.[67]

In different ways, every Native American society functioned under spiritual principles of harmony, or as the Diné or Navajo say, "beauty," which involved harmonizing the individual and the whole. Some more individualized band societies like the Comanche[68] had individual and small group ceremonies and spiritual practices, but no overarching rituals, so both the religious and the sociopolitical practices put more responsibility on the individual to find his or her place in the larger whole than was the case in those societies with stronger collective rituals such as the Pueblo nations;[69] yet they still had spiritual as well as social roles for each individual.

Many societies, such as the Lakota and the Cheyenne, had both individual ceremonies, such as those for a person seeking a deeper understanding of her or his purpose in life by going on a vision quest or an individual retreat,[70] and one or more collective rituals of renewal of the Earth and the people, such as the Sun Dance. Moreover, these individual rituals and spiritual experiences had important societal aspects. For example, for Plains tribes, messages received by an individual on a vision quest, in a dream, in a Sun Dance, or at any time, often contained important information for their community as well.[71] Thus, there were dream societies to help interpret people's dreams, and when proper, to help share them in appropriate ways with the community.

For traditional American Indian societies, the ideal for individual and community life was harmony and balance; however, attaining and maintaining those was not automatic. One had to work continually to build and keep good relations. As the Chaudhuris say of the Muskogee, "Given the unpredictable elements of nature and the quirks of human nature, the search for harmony takes sustained effort in all social institutions."[72] Hence, in personal inner work and in all relationships, including with the natural environment and its nations of plants, animals, and all creation, one continually participated in processes for returning to harmony.

Each Native culture did this in a different manner, but almost all followed the same general principle—at least until they became too large or events put them sufficiently out of balance. On the spiritual and psychological level, Indian cultures had ceremonies for reestablishing balance. For the Navajo (Diné), for example, virtually all ceremonies were healing rituals to return individuals and groups to beauty. In addition to healing rituals for rebalancing, many tribes had major rituals for the "renewal of the earth and the people," such as the Sun Dance of the Lakota and other Plains, Rocky Mountain, and Great Basin tribes.[73]

On the sociopolitical-economic level, with some spiritual-psychological aspects, all Native cultures traditionally had what were often called "peace making" processes for settling conflicts and disputes, and for redressing injuries and grievances. These were almost always facilitated participatory processes for returning the parties to a harmonious relationship. Thus, tribal people more often dealt with harms in ways that modern Western legal systems would consider torts where injuries are dealt with by civil law rather than as crimes, with the emphasis on restoring the pre-existing situation and/or resetting relations rather than on attaining justice or retribution. This could have involved a gift or payment for damages. In addition, with the importance of familial relations in Native societies, injuries concerned not only the individuals involved, but also their families.

For example, when a Kiowa or Cheyenne man eloped with another man's wife, it was required that the absconder provide a suitable compensation to the injured husband, with a peace chief facilitating the resolution of the dispute between the parties.[74] In some instances of homicide, restoration went so far as to have the party causing the death, whether intentionally or accidentally, take on a role of the deceased, as with an Aleut (Eskimo)[75] or Lakota man marrying the wife of the husband he had killed in order to ensure that the deceased's family was cared for, and particularly in the latter case, to restore harmony between the families involved in the dispute.[76]

With the importance of familial relations in Native societies, an injury concerned not only the individuals involved, but the familial group of which they were members. In some instances, the process of restoration even extended to warfare. Among the Wendat (Huron), for example, a captured individual would sometimes be adopted to replace a family member killed by the enemy, with the adoptee taking on all of the lost person's roles, including leadership positions.[77]

Since the handling of disputes and troubles was aimed at restoration and maintenance of harmony in the community, working out proper solutions often involved consideration of the whole range of relations between the parties, and the whole catalogue of ill feelings between them. This contrasts with the often narrower focus on what is specifically relevant to a legal case in deciding on fault or guilt in US courts, though they do consider wider contexts in deciding upon punishment in criminal cases.

Similarly, the emphasis on restoring harmony meant that acts of improper behavior were generally handled with a focus on rehabilitation exacted by traditional Native North Americans. Thus, when some Cheyenne young men were caught hunting buffalo on their own, which might have caused the herd to stampede away, making further hunting for everyone impossible, the miscreants were beaten and had their horses killed and gear destroyed by the members of the military society policing the hunt. But once it was clear that they had accepted their punishment, the young men were resupplied and brought back into the ranks of the hunters.[78] It was generally only in extreme cases that a person was killed or exiled. Among the Aleut, for instance, a man who killed community members several times, or someone who lied repeatedly, might be executed or forced out as a danger to the community.[79]

However, even in some extreme cases, rehabilitation might have been possible. Among the Cheyenne for example, killing another tribal member was considered so serious that the whole tribe would be polluted by the act, requiring purification and renewal of the nation's most sacred objects and the expulsion of the murderer.[80] Yet, after several years, the offender, if repentant, might be permitted to return with the permission of the family of the deceased, which there was usually social pressure for them to give.

There were also attempts to create, maintain, and reestablish harmony between tribes, though some long-term enmities did occur. Generally, there would be an effort to negotiate a settlement of issues between peoples. Often, if that was unsuccessful, it would be agreed to settle the matter with a rather rough game of stickball, today called lacrosse, rather than jump ahead to the last resort of war. European colonization, essentially invasion, disrupted relationships in North America on many levels, causing increased violent conflict between Native peoples, as well as between Europeans, and later European Americans, and tribes. Before that there were wars, but less so than in the periods of European contact. Moreover, compared with European warfare, Native American combat usually was more of a rough and sometimes deadly game with relatively few killed. Alongside direct combat, warriors also demonstrated their bravery to receive honor by touching an enemy without inflicting a wound, or undertook raids to steal from their opponents.[81] In general, in an uncertain world, avoiding and reducing conflict was an important practical approach. Peace was essential as conflict was dangerously disruptive, and since no one could be sure of future events, it was best to have as few enemies and as many friends as possible.[82]

The Practical Wisdom of Restoring Harmony

The need for harmony was not merely an ideal, but very much a practical realization learned from experience. This was exemplified in the history of creation of the Great Peace of the Haudenosaunee (Iroquois) and other confederacies, and in the need for people to collaborate and get along for survival and everyday community life, as set forth in Ella Deloria, "A System that worked," in *Speaking of Indians.*

This history is quite clear among the Haudenosaunee.[83] Their current ways, including their confederation (the Great Peace), arose to overcome internal dissension. It was a time of a blood feud among clan units and fighting between tribes reminiscent in our own time of the civil wars in Syria and Somalia, and of gang wars in major cities such as Los Angeles. Thanks to the vision and work of the Peacemaker, *Deganawidah*, and his Assistant, *Hayanwatah*, or *Hiawatha*, the Great Peace was achieved and an extremely participatory government based upon principles of equality and justice was installed, with the stipulation that each decision and action by the people be beneficial to the seventh generation yet to come.

That innovative form of government and other institutions across traditional North America were able to guide Native societies in a most democratic manner. Whatever their imperfections, these societies were remarkably peaceful, prosperous, and happy places/communities for virtually all of their citizens. For the members of these societies, acting virtuously and honorably was a practical ideal and a social necessity. Thus, in the first centuries of colonization, many of the Europeans arriving in North America in particular, and in the rest of the Americas in general, were greatly impressed by the Native peoples with whom they were regularly in close contact. To varying degrees, their contact with indigenous people in this "New World" brought positive changes in thinking, worldviews, and actions to the colonists and their descendants, and through a multitude of reports, to the Old World societies of Europe, and indeed across the world as shown in the unfolding of part I, below.

Notes to Chapter 1

1. Several authors have delineated a set of "pan-Indian" values. These have included generosity, respect for elders, respect for women as life-givers, regard for children as sacred, harmony with nature, self-reliance, respect for choices of others, accountability to the collective, courage, sacrifice for the collective in humility, recognizing powers in the unseen world, and stewardship for the Earth. See A. Timas and R. Reedy, "Implementation of Cultural-Specific Intervention for a Native American Community," *Journal of Clinical Psychology* 5, no. 3 (1998): 382–93.

2. For example, E. Adamson Hoebel gives a good brief picture of many of the virtues and problems of Eskimo, Comanche, Kiowa, and Cheyenne life in *The Law of Primitive Man* (New York: Atheneum, 1976), chaps. 5, 7.

3. Sharon O'Brien, *American Indian Tribal Governments* (Norman: University of Oklahoma Press, 1989), chap. 2; Stephen M. Sachs, "Remembering the Circle: The Relevance of Traditional American Indian and Other Indigenous Governance for the Twenty-First Century" (paper, Western Social Science Association Meeting, Reno, NV, 2001).

4. LaDonna Harris, Stephen M. Sachs, and Barbara Morris, *Re-Creating the Circle: The Renewal of American Indian Self-Determination* (Albuquerque: University of New Mexico Press, 2011), 34–35.

5. Discussed with author Stephen Sachs by LaDonna Harris, Comanche, President of Americans for Indian Opportunity (AIO), for which these "four R's" are living, traditional principles applied to guide contemporary life, particularly in AIO's Ambassadors Program. This is discussed in Stephen M. Sachs, "The AIO Ambassadors Program: Nurturing Leadership, Building a Network for Indian Country and the Indigenous World," from *Proceedings of the 2009 American Indian Studies Section of Western Social Science Association Meeting* in *Indigenous Policy* 20, no, 2 (2009). For more information on its Ambassadors program, contact AIO, 1001 Marquette NW, Albuquerque, NM 87102 (505) 842–8677, aio@aio.org, www.aio.org.

6. Dark Rain Thom, *Kohkumthena's Grandchildren: The Shawnee.* (Indianapolis, IN: Guild, 1994), 248.

    John Sugden makes a similar point in his book *Tecumseh: A Life* (New York: Henry Holt and Company, 1997). He writes that the Shawnee tribe could not agree on how to meet the threat posed by the American incursion into their Ohio territory in the late 1700s, after the campaign of

General Anthony Wayne forced their allies (Delawares, Miamis, Ottawas, and Detroit River Wyandots) to accept negotiations for territorial concessions, resulting in the Treaty of Greenville (1795). One faction of the Shawnee, under the leadership of the famed war chief Blue Jacket, lost hope of British support and made peace with the Americans. Another faction decided to move to Spanish-claimed territory in Missouri, where the French trader Louis Lorimier had gotten permission from Spanish authorities a few years earlier to bring Shawnees and Delawares to the area. Some Shawnees, including the head civil chief Kekewepelethy, decided to remain in place in Ohio in their existing territory and await help from the British. A fourth group, led by Tecumseh, listened respectfully to Blue Jacket's explanation of his decision to negotiate with the Americans and declined his invitation to join the treaty talks, setting up a new settlement in western Ohio instead, where they began to contemplate the formation of a new confederacy of tribes to resist American incursions (Sugden, 1997, pp. 52, 91–93).

7. Frank Waters, *The Book of the Hopi: The First Revelation of the Hopi's Historical and Religious World-View of Life* (New York: Ballantine, 1963), chap. 7.

8. Sachs, "The AIO Ambassadors Program." Also Hoebel, *Law of Primitive Man*, chaps. 5, 7.

9. The concept of politics as the "authoritative allocation of values (when sanctions are available)" was introduced by David Easton, *The Political System* (New York: Alfred A. Knopf, 1953), 131–32.

10. Harold Laswell, *Who Gets What, When, How* (New York: McGraw-Hill, 1936).

11. Benjamin R. Barber, *Strong Democracy: Participatory Politics for a New Age* (Berkeley: University of California Press, 1984).

12. Paul A. W. Wallace, *Indians in Pennsylvania* (Harrisburg: Pennsylvania Historical Museum Commission, 1975), 51.

13. Henry R. Schoolcraft, *Information Respecting the History, Condition, and Prospects of the Indian Tribes of the United States*, Part 5 (Philadelphia: J. B. Lippincott, 1856), 234.

14. Clinton Alfred Weslager, *The Nanticoke Indians: Past and Present* (Newark, NJ: University of Delaware Press, 1983), 33–34.

15. John W. DeForest, *History of the Indians of Connecticut* [1851] (Hamden, CT: Archon, 1964), 31.

16. Bruce G. Trigger, *The Huron: Farmers of the North* (Fort Worth, TX: Holt, Rinehart, and Winston, 1990), especially chap. 6, "Government and Law."

17. Many Indian nations were referred to by Europeans with names that were not their own, and were sometimes derogatory. "Huron," for example, is derived from an archaic French word meaning "ruffian/ rustic" or "boar's head," the latter perhaps applied as an allusion to the Natives' bristly hair-style, reminiscent of hairs on a wild boar (Bruce G. Trigger, *The Children of Ataensic: The History of the Huron People to 1660*, 2nd printing [Montreal: McGill-Queen's University Press, 1987], 27). It thus could be taken as an insult by Wyandot who are descendants of the Wendat, the Natives' own original name for their confederacy (Trigger, *Farmers of the North*, 7, 69, 131).

18. Trigger, *The Huron*, 84.

19. Among the Cheyenne, for example, a chief of one of the military societies upon becoming one of the forty-four peace chiefs, would have to resign his chieftainships of the military society, and the military societies and their leaders had no authority in regular civilian affairs, but only in leading war parties, patrolling outside the village, and policing buffalo hunts. Discussions of whether to go to war or make peace were facilitated by peace chiefs. Hoebel, *Law of Primitive Man*, chap. 7; E. Adamson Hoebel, *The Cheyennes: Indians of the Great Plains* (New York: Holt Rinehart and Winston, 1960).

20. Donald A. Grinde Jr. and Bruce E. Johansen, *Exemplar of Liberty: Native America and the Evolution of Democracy* (Los Angeles: UCLA American Indian Studies Center, 1991).

21. Lewis Henry Morgan, *League of the Iroquois* (Secaucus, NJ: Carol, 1996), 70. Morgan's work, originally published in 1851, was "the first scientific account of an Indian tribe" (according to Major J. Wesley Powell, founder of the Bureau of American Ethnology) and remains the best general book on the Six Nations ("introduction" to Morgan, *League of the Iroquois*, V). See also Johansen, *Exemplar of Liberty*.

22. Morgan, *League of the Iroquois*, 108.

23. Ibid., 109.

24. Ibid., 110.

25. Ibid., 139.

26. Jean Chaudhuri and Joyotpaul Chaudhuri, *A Sacred Path: The Way of the Muscogee Creeks* (Los Angeles: UCLA American Indian Center, 2001), chaps. 3–9.

27. John Locke, *The Second Treatise on Government* [1690] (Buffalo, NY: Prometheus, 1986), section 105 (chap. VIII, "Of the Beginnings of Political Society"). He distinguishes these empires from the more participatory tribes representing an earlier form of social and political organization.

28. William Brandon, *New Worlds for Old: Reports from the New World and Their Effect on the Development of Social Thought in Europe, 1500–1800* (Athens: Ohio University Press, 1986), 56–61. Brandon does believe the "rank conscious, and wealth conscious societies of the Northwest coast" (and also the Natchez of what is now Mississippi) were exceptions to the general tribal functioning through participatory inclusiveness. However, there is good evidence that despite social stratification in these societies, at least in matters of subsistence living and other areas, the respect for individual dignity and opinion remained functioning principles, and as cornerstones in the collaboration that communities needed to thrive (Harris, Sachs, and Morris, *Re-Creating the Circle*, 16–17).

29. See Morris Edward Opler, *An Apache Way of Life: The Economic, Social, and Religious Institutions of the Chiricahua Indians* (Lincoln: University of Nebraska Press, 1996), on politics, see particularly pp. 460–71. The Chiricahuas are typical of the Apaches generally in the nature of their politics. For example, See Veronica E. Tiller, *The Jicarilla Apache Tribe: A History* (Lincoln: University of Nebraska Press, 1983).

30. Laura E. Klein and Lillian A. Ackerman, eds., *Women and Power in Native North America* (Norman: University of Oklahoma Press, 1995); Chaudhuri and Chaudhuri, *The Way of the Muscogee Creeks* (which corrects some misconceptions about the role of women among the Muscogee in Klein and Ackerman's *Women and Power in Native North America*); and Paula Gunn Allen, *The Sacred Hoop: Recovering the Feminine in American Indian Traditions* (Boston: Beacon, 1986).

31. Opler, *An Apache Way of Life*, on politics, particularly pp. 460–71; on the Ojibwa, see Ruth Landes, "The Ojibwa of Canada," in *Cooperation and Competition among Primitive Peoples*, ed. Margaret Mead (New York: McGraw-Hill, 1937), chap. 3. Landes discusses how individual families, or some of their members, come together in common endeavors for a limited time. On those occasions one of them is accepted as the informal leader. Anyone not happy with the leadership goes elsewhere. See particularly pp. 93–96.

32. Richard K. Young, *The Ute Indians of Colorado in the Twentieth Century* (Norman: University of Oklahoma Press, 1997), 73, 255, discusses the consensus-building style of traditional Ute leaders. See also Katherine M. B. Osburn, *Southern Ute Women: Autonomy and Assimilation on the Reservation, 1887–1934* (Albuquerque: University of New Mexico Press, 1998), 21–23.

33. O'Brien, *American Indian Tribal Governments*, 16–17, 29–33.

34. Paul A. W. Wallace, *Indians in Pennsylvania*, rev. ed., Anthropological Series Number 5 (Harrisburg: Pennsylvania Historical and Museum Commission, 1989), 18–87, 119.

35. Personal communication to Stephen Sachs by a Lenape elder in New York State.

36. Wallace, *Indians in Pennsylvania*, 53, the quote taken from Henry Cook Myers, ed., *Narratives from Early Pennsylvania, West New Jersey, and Delaware, 1630–1707* (New York: C. Scribner's, 1912), 234–35.

37. Wallace, *Indians in Pennsylvania*, 55; the quote taken from William Darlington, ed., *An Account of the Remarkable Travels in the Life of Col. James Smith* (Cincinnati, OH: R. Clarke, 1870), 147.

38. Brandon, *New Worlds for Old*, 49–61.

39. James Mooney, *History, Myths, and Sacred Formulas of the Cherokee* (Ashville, NC: Bright Mountain, 1992, reprinting of Mooney's *Myths of the Cherokee* [Bureau of American Ethnology, No. 108, 1900]), 392–93.

40. Scott L. Pratt, *Native Pragmatism: Rethinking the Roots of American Philosophy* (Bloomington: Indiana University Press, 2002), chap. 7.

41. Klein and Ackerman, eds., *Women and Power in Native North America*, found a balanced reciprocity in twelve of thirteen Native North American societies studied. The one exception in the study was the case of the Muscogee, and this case was a partial exception concerning both the place of women in particular and the relative lack of hierarchy in Indian societies in general. However, Joyotpaul Chaudhuri, who was married to a Muscogee woman and lived among the Muscogee and studied their tradition for forty years, communicated to author Stephen Sachs that Klein and Ackerman's conclusion about the Muscogee is accurate only for post-contact times—not for the pre-contact. For an understanding that the traditional Muscogee maintained a balance between men and women, see Chaudhuri and Chaudhuri, *A Sacred Path*. For a longer discussion of male-female relations in traditional North America, see Harris, Sachs, and Morris, *Re-Creating the Circle*, 20–24.

42. O'Brien, *American Indian Tribal Governments*, 19–20.

43. Valerie Sherer Mathes, "Native American Women in Medicine and the Military," *Journal of the West* 21 (1982): 44; and Harris, Sachs, and Morris, *Re-Creating the Circle*, 20–24. On the roles in traditional Native societies of people who in the twenty-first century are considered gay, lesbian, or transgender, see Walter L. Williams, "The Two-Spirit People of Indigenous North America," *First People*, http://www.firstpeople. us/articles/the-two-spirit-people-of-indigenous-north-americans.

html; and Harlan Pruden and Se-ah-dom Edmo, "Two-Spirit People: Sexuality in Historic and Contemporary Native America," National Congress of American Indians (NCAI), http://www.ncai.org/policy-research-center/initiatives/Pruden-Edmo_TwoSpiritPeople.pdf.

44. Raymond A. Bucko, *The Lakota Ritual of the Sweat Lodge: History and Contemporary Practice* (Lincoln: University of Nebraska Press 1998), 38–39, 77, 82, 136, 236 (note 32), provides a large number of references to other sources.

45. Gerald Mohatt and Joseph Eagle Elk, *The Price of a Gift: A Lakota Healer's Story* (Lincoln: University of Nebraska Press, 2000), 3, 35, 145–46, 298–99; Joseph Marshall III, *The Lakota Way: Stories and Lessons of Living* (New York: Viking Compass, 2001), 211, 227.

46. Chaudhuri and Chaudhuri, *A Sacred Path*, 26.

47. For more on the variety of American Indian inclusive participatory decision-making processes in their societal context, see Harris, Sachs, and Morris, *Re-Creating the Circle*, chaps. 1 and 4, part I; O'Brien, *American Indian Tribal Governments*, chap. 2; Morgan, *League of the Iroquois*; Trigger, *The Huron*, especially chap. 6, "Government and Law"; Opler, *An Apache Way of Life*, particularly 460–71; Clyde Kluckhohn and Dorethea Leighton, *The Navaho* (Cambridge, MA: Harvard University Press, 1974), 111–23; Robert W. Young, *A Political History of the Navajo Tribe* (Tsaille, Navajo Nation, AZ: Navajo Community College Press, 1978), particularly pp. 15–16, 25–27; Alfred W. Bowers, *Hidatsa Social and Ceremonial Organization* (Lincoln: University of Nebraska Press, 1992), particularly pp. 26–64; Catherine Price, *The Oglala People, 1841–1879: A Political History* (Lincoln: University of Nebraska Press, 1996) [which drew on many sources including the Walker papers], particularly pp. 7–21, 33–34, 60–62, 98–99, 156, 168, 172–73; the second of the three edited volumes of the James R. Walker papers published by the University of Nebraska Press; Raymond DeMallie, ed., *Lakota Society* (1982), Part I, particularly documents 6–16; Landes, "The Ojibwa of Canada"; Jannette Mirsky, "The Dakota," in *Cooperation and Competition among Primitive Peoples*, ed. Mead; and Chaudhuri and Chaudhuri, *A Sacred Path*, particularly chap. 9, but throughout the rest of the work, including in the creation myth discussed in chap. 3.

48. Harris, Sachs, and Morris, *Re-Creating the Circle*, chap. 5, sec. 2; Thomas Buckley, "Doing Your Thinking," in *I Become Part of It: Sacred Dimensions in Native American Life*, eds. D. M. Dooling and Paul Jordan-Smith (New York: HarperCollins, 1989); San Gill, "The Trees Stood Deeply Rooted," in *I Become Part of It*; Elaine Jahner, "The Spiritual

Landscape," in *I Become Part of It*; and Margaret Connell Szasz, *Education and the American Indian: The Road to Self-Determination Since 1928* (Albuquerque: University of New Mexico Press, 1999).

49. Hoebel, *Law of Primitive Man*, chap. 5.
50. The misunderstandings by many Europeans of indigenous views of property come from a still common failure to see that ownership is never absolute or simple, as it involves a complexity of rights and duties concerning the item or thing involved in the particular setting or circumstance. For example, several years ago one of the authors of this volume could say he owned a particular house, because his name was on the property deed. But his rights concerning the property were few: First, he had taken out a mortgage on the property, giving the bank certain rights and himself certain duties. Second, he had sold the house on a not yet paid off contract, so he had no use rights to the property and very limited right to enter the property, but did have the right to limit the buyer's use and modification of the property within certain limits, and to receive payments from the buyer plus the right to sell the contract for future payments from the buyer, which further limited his "ownership." Similarly, his "ownership" could have been further limited if he had transferred the property's air, mineral, water, and any other conceivable rights. In addition, by law (without which there would be no official property rights or ownership), there were limits on the "owner's" rights to the property, and a set of duties for the property "owner," including paying taxes, abiding by municipal statutes (including the duty to keep the property in a certain condition), etc. For more on the rights and duties that relate to property and ownership, especially concerning indigenous people, see Hoebel, *Law of Primitive Man*, 47–50.
51. Trigger, *The Huron*, 32.
52. Luther Standing Bear, *My People, the Sioux* (Lincoln: University of Nebraska Press, 1975), chap. V.
53. Wallace, *Indians in Pennsylvania*, 17.
54. DeForest, *History of the Indians of Connecticut*, 16.
55. Ibid., 31, 33.
56. Ain Haas, "Social Inequality in Aboriginal North America: A Test of Lenski's Theory," *Social Forces* 72, no. 2 (1993): 295–313.
57. For discussion of collaboration and competition in other Native North American societies, see the discussions of the Ojibwa, Kwakiutl, Iroquois, Zuni, and Dakota in Margaret Mead, ed., *Cooperation and Competition among Primitive Peoples* (New York: McGraw-Hill, 1937). As the discussion of the Kwakiutl by Irving Goldman in "The Kwakiutl

of Vancouver Island" shows, there was a considerable amount of difference in wealth and hierarchy in that Northwest Coast society. However, the hierarchy arose from the ability to make enormous give-aways of the bounty of the region, and those on the lowest social level still enjoyed enough for a decent subsistence living, while having a say in the everyday affairs that related to that living. Similarly, while there was hierarchy among the Kiowa, and a small lowest class with little honor or property of their own, the members of this class, though disdained for having to do so, could take what they needed from those more well off in the community. Hoebel, *Law of Primitive Man*, 169–78.

58. O'Brien, *American Indian Tribal Government*, chap. 2.

59. Ella Deloria, "A Scheme of Life That Worked," part 2 in *Speaking of Indians* (Lincoln: University of Nebraska Press, 1998), 24–25.

60. Ibid., 37.

61. Michael Garrett, "To Walk in Beauty: The Way of Right Relationship," in *Medicine of the Cherokee: The Way of Right Relationship*, eds. J. T. Garrett and Michael Garrett (Santa Fe, NM: Bear, 1996), 165.

62. Ibid., 16.

63. Kluckhohn and Leighton, *The Navaho*; Downes, *The Navaho*, particu-larly chaps. 2, 3, 8; Young, *A Political History of the Navajo Tribe*; Alice Reichard, *Navaho Religion* (New York: Pantheon, 1950).

64. Chaudhuri and Chaudhuri, *A Sacred Path*, 19.

65. Ibid., chap. 10.

66. Ibid., 23, the theme pervading chap. 4.

67. For instance, if you go to a Lakota (Dakota or Nakota) Sun Dance and ask the dancers why they endure four grueling days dancing beneath the hot sun without food or drink, they will not tell you that it is to gain prestige or to receive personal spiritual power, though those things may come to them. The dancers will tell you that they give themselves away so that "the people may live." Their giveaway is first to the Great Spirit, second to the people, and lastly for themselves and only so they can play their proper part in the greater whole. (Observation by author Stephen Sachs, who has supported Lakota Sun Dances in 1984, and from 1992 to the present).

68. Hoebel, *Law of Primitive Man*, chap. 7; and Ernest Wallace and E. Adamson Hoebel, *The Comanches: Lords of the Plains* (Norman: University of Oklahoma Press, 1952).

69. Frank Waters, *The Masked Gods: Navaho and Pueblo Ceremonialism* (Athens: Ohio University Press, 1984); and Elise Clews Parsons, *Pueblo Indian Religion*, vols. 1–2 (Lincoln: University of Nebraska Press, 1966).

70. Hoebel, *Law of Primitive Man*, chap. 7; and Hoebel, *The Cheyennes*.

71. Lee Irwin, *The Dream Seekers: Native American Visionary Traditions of the Great Plains* (Norman: University of Oklahoma Press, 1994), chaps. 1, 2, 8.

72. Chaudhuri and Chaudhuri, *A Sacred Path*, chap. 9, particularly where quoted, 68.

73. On the Lakota Sun Dance, see Thomas E. Mails, *Sun Dancing at Rosebud and Pine Ridge* (Sioux Falls, SD: College of Western Studies, 1978); James R. Walker, *The Sun Dance of the Oglala and Other Ceremonies of the Oglala Division of the Teton Dakota*, Anthropological Papers of the American Museum of Natural History, vol. 16, part 2 (New York: American Museum of Natural History, 1917); and Raymond DeMallie and Elaine A. Jahner, *James R. Walker, Lakota Belief and Ritual* (Lincoln: University of Nebraska Press, 1980). On the Cheyenne Sun Dance, see Hoebel, *The Cheyennes*. On the Shoshone, Ute, and one of the Crow Sun Dances, see Joseph G. Jorgensen, *The Sun Dance Religion: Power to the Powerless* (Chicago: University of Chicago Press, 1972); and Fred W. Voget, *The Shoshoni-Crow Sun Dance* (Norman: University of Oklahoma Press, 1984).

74. Hoebel, *Law of Primitive Man*, 146, 160–67, 172–76.

75. Ibid., 87.

76. Deloria, *Speaking of Indians*, 34.

77. Trigger, *The Huron*, 58–60.

78. Hoebel, *Law of Primitive Man*, 143, 150–56.

79. Ibid., 70, 88–91.

80. Ibid., 142–43, 156–60. Murder, however, was such a heinous act for the Cheyenne that the pollution never fully left the reformed killer, who was ever after perceived not to smell quite right, and thus was not permitted to share in communal ceremonies, though he might otherwise participate in the life of the community.

81. Harris, Sachs, and Morris, *Re-Creating the Circle*, chap. 1.

82. Stephen M. Sachs, "Power and Sovereignty: The Changing Realities of American Indian Nations," from *Proceedings of the 2008 American Indian Studies Section of Western Social Science Association Meeting* in *Indigenous Policy* 19, no. 2 (2008).

83. Oren Lyons, "The American Indian in the Past," in *Exiled in the Land of the Free: Democracy, Indian Nations, and the U.S. Constitution*, ed. Oren Lyons, John Mohawk, Vine Deloria Jr., Lawrence Hauptman, Howard Berman, Donald Grinde Jr., Curtis Berkey and Robert Venables (Santa Fe, NM: Clear Light, 1992); Grinde and Johansen, *Exemplar of Liberty*; and Donald A. Grinde Jr., "Iroquois Political Theory and the Roots of American Democracy," in *Exiled in the Land of the Free*, ed. Lyons et al.

Part I

The Impact of American Indian Tradition on Western Politics and Society

Introduction to Part I

The Impact of American Indians on Western Politics and Society to 1800

Stephen M. Sachs and Ain Haas

For the relatively few Europeans coming in the first century to a new world that ecologically was for them a new place in which they were in the midst of a large number of Indigenous people, who regularly interacted with and initially attempted to educate them on Native ways, living in their new location was a profound experience.[1] Their contact with Indigenous people upon coming to America had a wide range of effects in virtually every area of the immigrants' lives that would also prove to have wide impacts on Europe and the rest of the world as well, over time. This included finding a wide variety of, for them, new plants, which Native people showed them the use of, leading to a culinary and medical revolution as these plants spread from the Americas. Today a large portion of the world's vegetable food and a great deal of the medication in use around the planet sprang from those used by Native Americans.[2] In addition, the exportation of huge amounts of resources from the New World colonies to the old countries, together with the Europeanization of some Indian ideas, is widely credited with greatly assisting the rise of the non-Native American capitalism.[3]

The impact of the experience of contact was necessarily different for different people because human beings are continually engaged in a dialogue with their ongoing experiences of all kinds, through the lenses of the impacts on their changing nature and worldview of their previous experiences.[4] These experiences encompass what people perceive directly from all their own outer and inner senses (and processes), and from the input they receive from others in the way of information, attitude, ideas, worldview, and so forth over time leading to the collective ways of seeing, knowing, and understanding that constitute culture. While culture is an ever-changing and individually varying system, in most instances it tends to be long lasting and slowly evolving. The often subtle, yet profound, effects of cultural interaction on people have been personally experienced by author Stephen Sachs: "When my then wife, a fledgling anthropologist, and I were about to embark on fieldwork, we were cautioned by an experienced colleague that while we had been extensively educated to be aware and respectful of the foreign culture we were entering, we also needed to note that even our limited one-year immersion in it would change us in ways that we would not be aware of, and that we needed to be prepared for some resulting confusion and disorientation on our return—a phenomenon that, indeed, we experienced." Going further, one might say that we are all anthropologists, and that ever-changing life is the field in which we are especially impacted by intercultural interactions.

But how one is impacted by experience, and particularly by cross-cultural experience, depends on who a person is by nature, or biological inheritance, and what they have previously experienced including the cultures and subcultures they have lived in, which while ever-changing, also have varying degrees of long-term continuity. Those who came from Europe to the Americas came from different nations, with their own unique situations, cultures, and subcultures. Thus, the impact on people coming from Europe was necessarily varied. For example, Spanish and Portuguese colonies moved forward from contact with different histories and had different impacts on the thinking and life of their home countries than did those of the English, French, or Dutch, as we show below, because of developments in those nations, as well as differences in experience in the Americas.

Differences in the colonial experience of people from different European nations arose in part from their approach to colonization, how that played out in their colonial activity and interactions with Native peoples. In England, in the opening years of North American colonization, a struggle was underway that would soon break into a civil war involving issues of religion and royal authority versus freedom, followed by a dictatorship and a restoration. This created an openness and also a resistance, in the motherland as well as for some of the colonists, to democratic ideas from Native American living experienced in practice by the colonists. At the same time, the precolonial experience in resistance to royal authority by some English colonists opened them to positive views of at least certain important aspects of Indigenous American ways. A very important example of this is Roger Williams, who is discussed below.[5]

One reason for the receptivity of the English and French in particular to new ideas from Indians had to do with the economic opportunities and challenges of their settlements in northeast North America, where the winters are quite harsh, the growing season is short, and the forest is vast. The new settlers of this region had to learn quickly how to adapt to this unfamiliar environment, and the process of learning by trial and error was more hazardous than in a more temperate or tropical environment. It made sense to pay close attention to how the Indians, who in several cases assisted them, managed to survive and even prosper in this setting.

The foodstuffs provided by the Natives as gifts or trade items were crucial to the newcomers' chances of survival, until the newcomers learned to imitate their hosts and grow the same crops and apply the same methods of hunting and fishing that the Natives relied on. After the problems of sustenance and survival were solved, the settlers also needed to find goods to trade with Europe in order to pay for their passage and imported supplies: the beaver skin fur trade was the main opportunity in this regard.[6] This meant that Indians became respected economic partners, whose traditional hunting and trapping skills and knowledge of the landscape were very valuable, and they had to be left free to move about that landscape. So the kinds of displacement, enslavement of Natives, or importation of slaves that occurred with other colonies would not have paid the same dividends to the European settlers in northeast North America.

Furthermore, the seminomadic lifestyle of the Natives of this region made it harder to exploit them through forced labor and to force their conversion to a new religion and lifestyle. Moving around with the seasons to take advantage of the varied resources in their forest and coastal environment, and relocating their main villages every few years to deal with declining fertility of fields and exhaustion of firewood supplies, the Native Americans in this region had not settled into permanent towns and could easily relocate to escape oppressive invaders. In their colonies to the south, the Spanish and Portuguese had a more captive labor force of sedentary Natives or imported slaves. Drawing on their experience in colonizing the eastern Atlantic islands, Africa, and other parts of the Old World, the Spanish and Portuguese were able to base the economies of their New World colonies on mining and plantations of cash crops, especially tobacco, cotton, and sugar, and could profit from the exploitation of less mobile Native labor or imported African slaves.[7] Thus, there was less of an economic incentive to treat the Natives with respect and to try to learn their ways.

Moreover, the situation and approach to colonization of each nation was different. The Catholic Spanish, in 1492, had just won a major war against invading Middle Eastern and North African Muslims attempting to spread Islam as well as to gain political territory and power. At home the Spanish reacted against diversity by insisting that the Muslims and Jews in Spain convert to Catholicism or leave the country. This policy was enforced by a harsh Inquisition. Spanish, and Portuguese, colonialism emphasized gaining wealth and power though conquest, with the Catholic Church having a major role in Christianizing the Native populations of the conquered, "discovered" territories.[8]

While the opinion within the Spanish elite, including the church and the colonials, was not monolithic, and the King of Spain had some doubts about the correctness of the policy, the thrust of Spanish colonial policy was to dominate, and generally not to tolerate or be open to learning new philosophical, theological, or political ideas.[9] Although at least in New Mexico the Spanish lived closely with Indian communities, life was still organized in a very hierarchical way under the casta lists, with the Spanish at the pinnacle; later more accommodation had to be made by the Spanish after the Pueblo Revolt of 1680.[10]

The French, who came as traders, and related more equally with the Indigenous people they partnered with than did the Spanish, also sent priests and attempted to convert Natives to Catholicism. But unlike the Spanish and Portuguese, most of whose colonies did not border on those of the European nations they were in conflict with, the French were often in direct competition with the neighboring English, and did not want to make enemies of tribes in their claimed territories since they needed those good relations with the Native populations for the success of their trading. This may have contributed to French priests being more tolerant of the Indians. In any case, the priests regularly sent quite favorable reports of the Indians back to France. Those reports were regularly read from the pulpit, at least in part to help raise money for continuing missionary work.[11] In addition, they were read by those who were critical of the French political system, such as Voltaire and Rousseau, and whose ideas, considerably influenced by these reports, became leading intellectual currents of the French Revolution, as is discussed in the chapter on the impact of contact with American Indians in Europe.

The Protestant Dutch also came to trade, though they generally lived apart from the Indians with whom they traded, and only held the colony of New Amsterdam from 1614 to 1664.[12] But even before their own colony was founded, they had been impacted sufficiently by the reports of and debates about Indians to decide, in agreement with North American Indigenous ways, that diversity was to be tolerated.[13]

Interaction and the Process of Indianization

Most of the few Europeans who came at first to what is now the United States largely remained in their own social groups but interacted regularly with Indians, some of whom lived with them.[14] There were also traders, missionaries, and adopted captives of European origin who lived among the Indians and became particularly well-informed sources of information about Native American cultures. The Indians taught the colonists much about the practicalities of living in their new place, while also attempting to teach them their cultural ways. The largest portion of these colonists, though, only changed slowly and to limited degrees. Yet those changes eventually proved to be profound. This is exemplified by the resulting rise of a distinctly American literature beginning in early 1650 in New England with the first important piece of this kind of literature, *History of Plimoth Plantation* by William Bradford.[15] As Betty Booth Donohue in *Bradford's Indian Book* writes:

> When Massachusetts Natives met English settlers in 1620, literary events took place. The American Indian oral tradition confronted English-speaking immigrants and changed their discursive propensities. As the English-speaking immigrants wrote, they produced a new literature that would eventually be designated American, and ... American literature is different from the continental British. It is a literature that reveals an American Indian presence, a characteristic that British literature does not have. American Indian words, characters and actions entered America's written work at contact, and these words, characters and actions have become part of a continuing European American literary tradition. Remove the Indians, and the literature is no longer American.[16]

Some evidence of the cultural impact can be found in our vocabulary: some two thousand American Indian words have been adopted into the American English language. This includes the word "caucus," reflecting the democratizing effects of Indianization of Europeans and European Americans in North America.[17] A similar indicator of cultural impact is the continuing existence of a huge number of Native American place names in the United States and throughout the Americas.[18] The Native American cultural impact on Europeans, and later European Americans, was so broad that it even influenced sports and games. This encompasses the continuation in modified forms of the sacred Native American stick game we know today as lacrosse. Lacrosse, in turn, inspired the adaptation of the ancient Indigenous ball court game we now call basketball, which initially included lacrosse strategies. Ice and field hockey also have Native American origins. Moreover, Indigenous Americans introduced the rubber ball to Europeans and as a result impacted worldwide every game that uses a bouncing ball.[19]

Going beyond sports, even the way European armies fought and applied their military tactics were greatly changed by contact with Indians. There were many similarities between Native American and colonial American approaches to warfare, both contrasting markedly with the style of fighting that was predominant in Europe two or three centuries earlier. The latter emphasized coordinated volleys fired across open fields by disciplined lines of professional soldiers wearing bright-colored uniforms (e.g., British redcoats). In contrast, the colonial American militia, especially in frontier areas where cultural exchange with Native Americans took place, tended to wear camouflage or at least clothing that made it easier to avoid detection by the enemy; to use tactics of stealth, encirclement, and ambush similar to those used in communal hunting; and to fire at the enemy from behind the protection of trees, bushes, and rocks. Such military traditions are especially evident today among the special forces of the United States and other nations. It is worth noting that the US Army Rangers officially credit the colonial woodsman Robert Rogers with organizing the force of Rangers that evolved into the American special forces. Rogers, who wrote the first manual for special forces units (*Rules of Ranging*, 1757),[20] admired the tracking skills, scouting abilities, endurance, and bravery of the Indians he had recruited to secure the northern border of the American colonies against French incursions from Quebec during the French and Indian War of the mid-1700s. Even earlier, Captain Benjamin Church of Massachusetts detailed in his diary of 1716 how observation and imitation of Indian tactics influenced his style of command.[21]

The influence of Native American traditions can also be seen among American regular troops and those of many other modern nations with the emphasis on individual initiative and commanders' respect for the dignity of their subordinates—at least after the basic training stage has habituated troops to military discipline. Although Native American warriors were more free to choose and abandon their military leaders, their example helped inspire American fighters' objections to degrading corporal punishments for disobedience (e.g., the whipping post), expectations of eventual explanations for orders, and desires for freedom to improvise if circumstances made it prudent to do so. Some of the parallels between Native American and colonial American fighting styles might be attributed to independent invention and common sense, but the textbook *American Military History* used to train military officers is explicit about how "the Indian method of warfare in the forest, perforce adopted by the white man also, was the most significant influence in developing and preserving the spirit of individualism and self-reliance in the military sphere."[22]

The degree to which Native American leaders respected the individual warrior's right to think for himself and to participate in decisions about whether to go to war and how to wage it can be seen in Leonard Mason's comments on the Cree of Canada. Although his fieldwork was from the twentieth century, long after Europeans' first contacts with Native Americans on the East Coast, his comments about the Swampy Cree of Manitoba, Canada, corroborate what many other observers noted in earlier times, and are quite consistent with the discussion of North American Native ways in chapter 1:

> A head of a family was his own master, but he... respected the advice of... more experienced men.... A war chief was informally chosen on the basis of experience and valor.... [H]is commands were implicitly obeyed until the expedition was finished.... Agreement with a chief's war strategy was formally acknowledged by the warriors when they smoked from a sacred pipe in the assemblies from which no man could be absent.... [T]he prestige of a [war] captain was primarily dependent upon his success in driving a good bargain and his conduct as leader of the expedition. He had no power to enforce his own wishes when they were contrary to the will of the band.[23]

Some Europeans and Euro-Americans were so greatly moved by contact with the Indigenous people that they quite willingly became Indians, accepting the relative kind of adoption which was a regular tribal practice.[24] As Hector St. John de Crèvecoeur said in 1782, in *Letters from an American Farmer*, "There must be in their [the Indians'] social bond something singularly captivating, and far superior to anything to be boasted among us; for thousands of Europeans are [have become] Indians, and we have no example of even one of those Aborigines having from choice become Europeans."[25]

Meanwhile, a minority of European immigrants, while remaining European or rather becoming European American, took on a considerable number of Indigenous ways of seeing and acting, as is documented by Scott Pratt in *Native Pragmatism*,[26] and additionally by Roger Williams, as is discussed below along with others including Thomas Paine and Benjamin Franklin.

Moreover, a huge number of reports on American Indian ways, and especially on the freedom Native Americans enjoyed, were sent to Europe, which—along with testimony by Europeans returning from America to Europe and some discussions with Indians brought to Europe—had a great impact on European thinking, particularly on politics and society, as is discussed below. The impact in Europe of contact with American Indians necessarily varied according to what different people heard or perceived, and with how they responded. Thus, thinkers such as Locke and Rousseau, in what is often called the liberal tradition, each spawned a variety of traditions of their own which included their different receptions of thoughts from, and reflections about, Indigenous American ways. Similarly, a major impetus to the rise of socialism and anarchism in Europe (interacting with other lines of thought and tradition, as is always the case), was the accumulation of reports on Indians.

People and lines of thought are always interacting, so that once there is an impact it continues to have influences in various ways, as is discussed by Scott Pratt below concerning the ongoing development of an American philosophy of pragmatism with strong Native roots. Similarly, the Indian impact on John Locke, in turn, had a strong influence on a number of the already Indian-impacted late colonial and early US leaders, including in the writing of major documents such as the Declaration of Independence and the Constitution. Indian influence, both direct and indirect, has continued and remains an important source of numerous strands of political, economic, and social thought and action in North America, Europe, and the world, as is significantly, but because of its vastness and complexity, only partially indicated in the unfolding of part I of this volume.

Notes to Part I Introduction

1. See Betty Booth Donohue, *Bradford's Indian Book: Being the True Roote & Rise of American Letters as Revealed by the Native Text Embedded in Of Plimoth Plantation* (Gainesville: University of Florida Press, 2011) on Indianization, particularly pp. xiv–xvi, 7–9, 16, 34–44, 47–49, 89, 93–104, 114, 133–45.

2. Jack Weatherford, *Indian Givers: How American Indians Transformed the World* (New York: Fawcett Columbine, 1988), chaps. 4–6, 10, 11; Gregory Cajete, *Native Science: Natural Laws of Interdependence* (Santa Fe, NM: Clear Light, 2000), particularly chap. 4; and William Brandon, *New Worlds for Old: Reports from the New World and Their Effect on the Development of Social Thought in Europe, 1500–1800* (Athens: Ohio University Press), 128.

   Louise Côté, Louis Tardivel, and Denis Vaugeois, *L'indien généreux: Ce que le monde doit aux Amériques* (Montréal: Boréal, 1992). The French title translates as "The Generous Indian: What the World Owes to the Americas." The book is like a dictionary, with an alphabetical list of things the Indians gave to the world, and many interesting illustrations. The information is precise with regard to which tribe(s) might be behind each donation, and which Europeans received it. Many of the items have to do with food, medicine, technology, and vocabulary. There are some social, political, economic, and recreational entries, but these are largely taken from Weatherford's books *Indian Givers* and *Native Roots: How the Indians Enriched America* (New York: Crown Publishers, 1991).

3. Weatherford, *Indian Givers*, chaps. 1–3. On the transformation of some Indian ideas, see the discussion of John Locke below.

4. See Lee Nichol, ed., *The Essential David Bohm* (London: Routledge, 2003), who makes many reference to Jean Piaget, 172–73, 176–77; Jean Piaget and B. Inhelder, *The Child's Conception of Space* (London: Routledge and Kegan Paul, 1956); and Jean Piaget, *The Origin of Intelligence in the Child* (London: Routledge and Kegan Paul, 1956).

5. John M. Bary, *Roger Williams and the Creation of the American Soul* (New York: Viking, 2012), pt. I–II discuss developments in England involving Williams and the Pilgrims that were background to their coming to New England.

6. Alden T. Vaughan, *New England Frontier: Puritans and Indians, 1620–1675* (Boston: Little, Brown, 1965), 211–15.

7. Lyle N. McAlister, *Spain and Portugal in the New World, 1492–1700* (Minneapolis: University of Minnesota Press, 1984).

8. Both Spain and Portugal undertook their colonial expansion under the Doctrine of Discovery, first announced by the Pope in 1452, to authorize and encourage Portugal's African coast colonization, as part of the country's attempt to secure a major trade route to the orient. As stated by Steve Newcomb in "Five Hundred Years of Injustice:

The Legacy of Fifteenth Century Religious Prejudice," Indigenous Law Institute, http://ili.nativeweb.org/sdrm_art.html:

Under various theological and legal doctrines formulated during and after the Crusades, non-Christians were considered enemies of the Catholic faith and, as such, less than human. Accordingly, in the bull of 1452, Pope Nicholas directed King Alfonso to "capture, vanquish, and subdue the saracens, pagans, and other enemies of Christ," to "put them into perpetual slavery," and "to take all their possessions and property." (Davenport: 20–26) Acting on this papal privilege, Portugal continued to traffic in African slaves, and expanded its royal dominions by making "discoveries" along the western coast of Africa, claiming those lands as Portuguese territory.

Thus, when Columbus sailed west across the Sea of Darkness in 1492—with the express understanding that he was authorized to "take possession" of any lands he "discovered" that were "not under the dominion of any Christian rulers"—he and the Spanish sovereigns of Aragon and Castile were following an already well-established tradition of "discovery" and conquest. (Thacher: 96) Indeed, after Columbus returned to Europe, Pope Alexander VI issued a papal document, the bull Inter Cetera of May 3, 1493, "granting" to Spain—at the request of Ferdinand and Isabella—the right to conquer the lands which Columbus had already found, as well as any lands which Spain might "discover" in the future.

In the Inter Cetera document, Pope Alexander stated his desire that the "discovered" people be "subjugated and brought to the faith itself." (Davenport: 61) By this means, said the pope, the "Christian Empire" would be propagated. (Thacher: 127) When Portugal protested this concession to Spain, Pope Alexander stipulated in a subsequent bull—issued May 4, 1493—that Spain must not attempt to establish its dominion over lands which had already "come into the possession of any Christian lords." (Davenport: 68) Then, to placate the two rival monarchs, the pope drew a line of demarcation between the two poles, giving Spain rights of conquest and dominion over one side of the globe, and Portugal over the other.

9. For a discussion of Spanish colonialism in contrast to that of the Dutch, with some brief reference to the French and English, see Nan A. Rothschild, *Colonial Encounters in a Native American Landscape: The Spanish and Dutch in North America* (Washington, DC: Smithsonian Institution, 2003).

10. Ibid., chap. 4–6, and on the casta lists per se, 169–73.

11. Reuben G. Thwaites, ed., *The Jesuit Relations and Allied Documents*, 73 vols. (Cleveland, OH: Burrows, 1896–1901); J. H. Kennedy, *Jesuit and Savage in New France* (New Haven, CT: Yale University Press, 1950); William Brandon, *New Worlds for Old: Reports from the New World and their Effect on the Development of Social Thought in Europe, 1500–1800* (Athens: Ohio University Press, 1986), 67–70, 83, 91, 100, 100–108, 162.

12. Rothschield, *Colonial Encounters in a Native American Landscape*, 28–29, 30–32, 63–93, 123–40, 152–67, 192–223, 225–31.

13. Naeem Inayatullah and David L. Blaney, *International Relations and the Problem of Difference* (New York: Routledge, 2004), pt. I.

14. Donohue, *Bradford's Indian Book*, throughout, but particularly see xiv.

15. As discussed in Donohue, *Bradford's Indian Book*, that has references to various editions of *History of Plimoth Plantation* in the bibliography, 165.

16. Donohue, *Bradford's Indian Book*, xii. As Donohue makes clear, this does not deny the primary European character of literature. It indicates an essential transformational impact.

17. Bruce E. Johansen, *Debating Democracy: Native American Legacy of Freedom*, with Donald A. Grinde Jr. and Barbara Mann (Santa Fe, NM: Clear Light, 1998), 123.

18. For example, see William Bright, *Native American Place Names of the United States* (Norman: University of Oklahoma Press, 2004). "List of Place Names in the United States of Native American Origin," Wikipedia, http://en.wikipedia.org/wiki/List_of_place_names_in_the_United_States_of_Native_American_origin, provides a large, but partial, list of Native place names in the United States. A longer, but also far from complete, list of Indigenous names in the Americas is in "List of Place Names of Indigenous Origin in the Americas," Wikipedia, http://en.wikipedia.org/wiki/List_of_placenames_of_indigenous_origin_in_the_Americas.

19. Emory Dean Keoke and Kay Marie Porterfield, *American Indian Contributions to the World* (New York: Checkmark, 2003), 26–30, 129, 152–54; and Philip P. Arnold, *The Gift of Sports: Indigenous Ceremonial Dimensions of the Games We Love* (San Diego, CA: Cognella, 2012).

20. "Rogers' Rules of Ranging (1757)," Wes Clark, http://wesclark.com/jw/rogers_r.html.

21. Stephen Brumwell, *White Devil* (London: Weidenfeld and Nicolson, 2004), 16, 100, citing the historian Burt Garfield Loescher on the importance of Rogers's legacy.

22. Robert Coakley, "The Beginnings," in *American Military History*, John E. Jessup and Robert Coakley (Washington, DC: Center of Military History, US Army), 27. Additional discussion of the impact of American Indians on first European, and later world military tactics, is in Keoke and Porterfield, *American Indian Contributions to the World*, 172, with further references.

23. Leonard Mason, *The Swampy Cree: A Study in Acculturation*, Anthropology Papers (Ottawa, ON: National Museum of Canada, 1967), 39–41.

24. Donohue, *Bradford's Indian Book*, xiv. Also, Bruce G. Trigger, *The Huron: Farmers of the North* (Fort Worth, TX: Holt, Rinehart, and Winston, 1990), 6. Most Indian nations also made it their practice to adopt captives who, at least initially, were often not so willing. See Trigger, *The Huron*, 58–62; and Ernest Wallace and E. Adamson Hoebel, *The Comanches: Lords of the South Plains* (Norman: University of Oklahoma Press, 1986), 241, 259–64.

25. Sharon O'Brien, *American Indian Tribal Governments* (Norman: University of Oklahoma Press, 1989), 37; and LaDonna Harris, Stephen Sachs, and Barbara Morris, *Re-Creating the Circle: The Renewal of American Indian Self-Determination* (Albuquerque: University of New Mexico Press, 2011), 4.

26. Scott Pratt, *Native Pragmatism: Rethinking the Roots of American Philosophy* (Bloomington: Indiana University Press, 2002).

Chapter 2

The Impact of American Indians on Politics and Society in the American Colonies and the United States from Contact to 1800

Section 1: The Indianization of American Literature

Betty Booth Donohue

Indigenous influence on the Europeans who came to the New World began at Contact and was instantaneous and far-reaching. As Natives became aware that their lands were being invaded by Europeans who showed little inclination for settling in and living in socially acceptable ways, they began a process of behavior modification that was intended to turn the intruding savages into respectable neighbors. Europeans were generally unreceptive to these attempts, but regardless of their resistance, changes did occur and Europeans were quickly hybridized or Indianized. Much of their acceptance of Indian ways was occasioned by the imperative to survive, while other aspects of Indianization were acquired by more subtle means. Whether deliberately chosen or subconsciously incorporated and whether recognized or not, Native cultural mores and intellectualism touched immigrants of all stripes as they settled the length and breadth of the continent. With the passage of time, what began as temporary cultural adaptations eventually became permanent characteristics, and a new breed of people emerged: Americans. Because many of the incoming European colonists were accustomed to writing, they continued their literary proclivities in the New World. As their social environment changed, their writing also transformed so that gradually European American writers produced literature that displayed credible evidence of Native imprinting. This section will demonstrate how certain of these cultural modifications transformed colonial literary works and thus created the literature of the United States.

The process by which colonists internalized Native practices and worldviews is called "Indianization," and the Indianization of European settlers was easily accomplished because of proximity and necessity. Unfortunately, popular theories articulated in the recent past—theories such as the "Savage Other"—have created the impression that Indigenous people and Europeans were isolated from each other and did not engage in casual, social interactions, thus making influence exchange difficult if not impossible to effectuate. A review of early texts, however, reveals that Natives and colonists had countless interactions with each other. If the two groups were not engaged in actual conversations, they were always aware of the other's presence. Sometimes this presence was real and sometimes it was imagined, so that in a manner of speaking, Indians and whites were always "in each other's minds."[1] For example, in Plymouth Colony's formative years, Indians and whites intermingled daily. When the Wampanoag leader Osamequin and the people of Plymouth Colony made their nonaggression pact in 1621, it was agreed that the Wampanoags would continue to fish in their accustomed ponds. These ponds were fitted with weirs and were located within the area that Plymouth was using for home building and gardens; consequently, Wampanoags were inside Plymouth's palisades quite frequently, and some of them eventually reestablished their former residences there. Indians and Pilgrims gossiped among themselves and told tales to each other; they fought and they got along. In Bradford's history of Plymouth there are several passages that begin with the phrase "The Indeans said." When the Indians spoke, the Pilgrims invariably listened and were changed by what they heard and experienced.

Edward Winslow was a Plymouthean leader who spent a significant amount of time with the Algonquians. His writings reveal many astute characterizations of Native leaders and their customs. Winslow enjoyed a close relationship with various Algonquian people, and his writings indicate that he liked and respected them. In the 1620s at Plymouth there was close contact between English and Natives, and there was also reciprocal empathy, understanding, conversation, and help in times of need. Wampanoags taught the Plymoutheans to cultivate corn and brought food to their first harvest festival. Wampanoags attended Bradford's wedding to Alice Southworth and stayed for the reception. Conversely, Plymoutheans nursed Natives dying of smallpox, and Winslow once healed an ailing Osamequin. American Natives and Europeans were in each other's presence and in each other's heads. They were constantly psychoanalyzing each other, anticipating actions and reactions, and learning each other's ways.

There were meetings and conferences with American Indians in other colonies as well. In Boston, the Massachusetts, the Pequots, and other Eastern Algonquian tribal leaders were occasional visitors in John Winthrop's home and he frequently conferred with them. If negotiations were not favorable to him, he would then on occasion attempt to set Natives against each other. In order to manipulate American Indians, Winthrop had to have at least some knowledge of their politics and their long-held alliances and grudges. If he formulated impressions about the Algonquians and their leaders, it is only logical to conclude that the Natives formed opinions about him as well. They read each other.

The early days of colonization were characterized by intense bilateral scrutiny, casual social relations, and formal negotiations, and it is a mistake to believe that influence traveled only from

Europeans to Natives. The exigencies of Contact forced Europeans to alter their accustomed behaviors. Their subsistence in the New World depended upon their appropriation of Native resources and culture. Raw material availability as well as climactic and geographical realities forced the settlers to observe and emulate Native food procurement methods, home construction sites and methods, and road placements. European acquisitions and adaptions to American Indian life changed the ways the immigrants farmed, hunted, fished, traded, settled, and traveled. In addition to modifying the essentials of their everyday lives, Europeans eventually replicated Natives in other ways as well. American Indian concepts regarding astronomy, zoology, medicine, and physics began to enrich European science. A new American dialect was formed when Native words were incorporated into English conversations, documents, histories, deeds, letters, court records, and literary efforts.

While redacting Sigmund Freud, the anthropologist A. Irving Hallowell pointed out that the organization of human personality and the transmission of culture are formed by "the social interaction of individuals and adaptive learning."[2] It is clear that while Europeans were diligently attempting to civilize the Indigenous savages, the Natives were diligently attempting to Indianize the invading barbarians. Change in both groups was inevitable and not all of it beneficial. Europeans picked up the tobacco habit, and Indians learned to enjoy hard spirits. For a very short period of time, a good time was had by all.

Indianization occurred for reasons other than European survival and bilateral trade. American Natives, whose populations had diminished in the seventeenth century, needed to increase their numbers and revitalize their weakened social orders. When the colonization of what is now the United States first began, American Natives tended to see Europeans as potential tribal members. This view stemmed from their motives for waging war and their logically reasoned treatment of any war captives they took. As an example, in the seventeenth and eighteenth centuries American Natives often used war as a method for replacing dead tribal members in order to increase their numbers. We know that the Iroquois, for instance, transformed war captives into contented new citizens and assigned them the names of deceased tribal members as an integral part of their annual requickening ceremonies.

That many Indigenous Americans saw the wisdom in transforming the strangers who came among them into productive new tribal members could have predisposed them to integrate foreigners into their cultures.[3] Of course, most Europeans were not receptive to becoming tribal members, but for a short time the Natives seemed to believe that the Europeans could at least be taught to be considerate neighbors who knew how to comport themselves in the expected, traditional North American ways. The thinking being that if everyone respected each other and practiced reciprocity for the good of the greater community, the region would prosper. With a minimum of effort, there would be peace and trade, social stability, and improved standards of living for all.

Not only did exposure to Indigenous Americans transform the colonists' material culture, but it promoted psychological and social changes as well. For example, gendered social roles were inflected when women, particularly in Plymouth Colony, were forced to till the fields like Native females while English males were freed from agricultural duties so that they could maintain the colony by trading, fishing, and hunting. In times of military distress, Europeans chose to emulate American Indian war maneuvers. When it was time to form a government not headed by a monarch, European Americans partially replicated Native styles of government.[3] Influence is subtle and quickly transferred in ways that are not easily controlled. For example, prevailing social attitudes and practices, body language, fashion, slang or specialized terms, music, dance, and food preferences are common vehicles of influence transfer. Europeans were either observing or taking part in many of these avenues of influence and were likely unaware that they were being changed. As Michele Espagne, French historian, has pointed out, "influence is always a two-sided and creative process." He stresses that influence does not depend on power and suppression, and in reference to colonization, he theorizes that "the material and spiritual culture of the colonizers inevitably changed under the influence of the local culture."[4]

The Indianization of European life in America certainly extended to literary matters, and several of the means by which the Indianization of European American writings occurred are quite straightforward. Early historical texts often mention persons like Pocahontas, Opechancanough, Tisquantum, Papasiquineo's unfortunate daughter, and the Pequot Wequash. These "real" Indians entered our early texts and are now part of our intellectual realities and imaginations. It is a short step from Pocahontas to Minnehaha and from Papasiquineo's daughter to Ramona. As narratives about such characters develop, we begin to find within the texts a kind of Native embedded story, one which provides a tale within a tale that often gives considerable insight into Indigenous cultures. American Indian people function not only as characters in early American works, but they supply themes as well. When John Smith was captured by Powhatans, he later detailed his experiences—experiences he found hostile and menacing—in *The Generall Historie of Virginia* (1624). Smith's experiences helped create the very popular literary themes of hostile, menacing Native behavior and colonial fears of captivity. On the other hand, William Bradford's *Of Plimoth Plantation* (1639–51) frequently depicts helpful Wampanoags like Tisquantum and Hobomok, and the Plymouth history has engendered themes of cooperative, accommodating Natives who assist whites. Additionally, as each early author wrote about his dealings with American Indians, Native thinking, actions, characters, language, and customs permeated their texts and Indianized the developing American literature. Not only did Natives populate these early texts, but American Indian agricultural products such as corn, squash, and tobacco began to function as newly conceived allusions and metaphors. Corn and tobacco are not only American Indian foods, but are also sacramentals used to bless ceremonies and lift prayer words to heaven. These substances, whether the colonists knew it or not, added symbolic value to anything associated with them.

As they went about their tasks, Europeans had many occasions to hear Native poetic works. American Indian villages and Native people were all around them. Despite the fact that at Contact most American Indians did not use an alphabetic system for recording literary compositions, they did have a vibrant and powerful literary tradition operating at the time. This tradition employed most of the genres known to Europeans and utilized others unknown to them. For example, American Indians:

> produced creation accounts, histories, orations, lyric poetry, lullabies, fables, love songs, elegies, epics, and dramatic rituals. In addition to these familiar literary modes, American Indians composed songs or poems designed to effect protection or success for a designated undertaking. They [formulated] hunting, fishing, and planting songs, traveling songs, war chants, and battle narratives. Native life began and ended with poetry. Naming songs introduced infants to the Creator; vision recitations revealed a person's life-plan or obligations, while death songs prepared the singer for his spirit journey and identified him to his Maker.... The most important of all tribal compositions, however, were the oral formulae designed to effect change or bring about healing. I call these sacred chants medicine texts.[5]

The settlers could not escape American Indian languages—either the language employed in casual conversations or the language of ceremony they overheard. The languages the immigrants first heard were conveyed by words that were not only poetic or beautifully conceived, but the verbal expressions were also efficacious and full of multiple meanings. It follows then that another avenue leading to the Indianization of early American letters was Native language absorption, appropriation, and the inevitable attendant teleological acquisitions. For example, the phrase *alakwsahla padôgi-wigi* is an Abenaki way of saying lightning. Literally the term means *star approaching from the thunder home,*[6] and that one term allows science and legend; creation accounts and visual reality; man and universe; and movement and fixity to weld and be contextualized into notions of time and space. Certain of these very beautiful and powerful words, when situated in predetermined arrangements can also effect change and alter reality. What is important to American literary theory is that the colonists frequently had occasion to hear these words; furthermore, they observed and participated in countless rites that were executed with formalized language and accompanied by ritual paraphernalia, song, and dance, all components of Native literature.

The ceremonies that the colonists likely heard quite frequently would have included greeting songs, morning prayers, corn grinding songs, and mourning obsequies. The powerful verbal codifications contained in these compositions, together with those recited in sacred chants, stories, or lyric poetry, conformed to the compositional formulae or poetics employed in the American Indian oral tradition, and these carefully chosen and arranged words had great power. Native rhetorical dynamics, whether used in ceremonial rites, household tasks, hunting expeditions, or military conventions were such a part of Native literary life that Europeans could not escape them. The colonists absorbed these Native formulae and subconsciously applied them. As they began to write their travel accounts, real estate promotions, diaries, exploration narratives, histories, and letters, their works reflected their new verbal acquisitions. Whether these early writers were aware of their compositional acquisitions or not is debatable, but it is obvious that their works were Indianized, and American literature was born.

The inclusion of Native words into English texts quickly transformed the English language and created an American mutate. Not only were Native words such as "moose" and "mugwump" absorbed into English, but the power these words contained was also passed to the developing language. Many American Indians believe that there is vigor and vitality in the spoken word and especially in the names of powerful people. Thus, any American work that incorporates Native words, and particularly Native proper nouns, lends

Indigenous American potency and efficacy to that piece. When names like Canonicus and Sassacus, Miantonomi or Osamequin enter English writings, these pieces are subtly altered. Subsequently, a new entelechy is produced. Canonicus and his peers became a part of British letters as well as British historical reality and gave both new dimensions. In short, English now has an Algonquian accent.

The practice of keeping or adjusting the Native names for geographical entities like mountains or rivers modified English as well. When English speakers encounter Mount Passaconaway or Mount Waumbek or navigate the Assonet or Coonamesset rivers and describe them in their works, their writings take on additional meanings whether or not English speakers recognize the actual denotations and connotations. For example, according to Milton Travers in *The Last of the Great Wampanoag Indian Sachems*, the word Assonet means "at the place of stones" or "at the place of the stone" referring to Profile Rock, a formation thought to resemble the face of Osamequin.[7] Once a reader is aware of Assonet's meaning, the word takes on an unexpected lexical depth, one that calls up a specific historical person as well as a familiar promontory. Assonet is then revealed to be more than a savage utterance. It suggests instead the language of a people who could extract meaning from rock formations and connect that significance to their histories and to their practical lives. Here it must be emphasized that reading land formations is essential to American Indian poetics and exegesis.

Not only were Native characters and languages absorbed into European American writings, but basic tenets of Native compositional theory were subconsciously absorbed as well. Among these components of Native poetics are creation accounts that are central to nearly all American Indian sacred rites or medicine texts. American Indian creation accounts usually relate that the earth was fashioned by ancient gods or sacred animal-like beings who prepared it for human habitation. Before leaving people alone on the earth to live their lives unassisted, these creator gods left their essences and their sacred stories relating to those essences at various geographical locations. When people return to these spots they are reminded of the stories or lessons imparted by the old gods and are refreshed.

For example, the formation known irreverently as Devils Tower in the Black Hills of present-day Wyoming is the site of many tribal narratives that connect the formation to Bear and to people who are transformed into bears. These accounts reveal that young children at this sacred site were chased by Bear and later transformed into constellations which have forever guided people like the Kiowas as they travel through the night.[8] Considered holy by many Native nations, Devils Tower is a site where narrative, sacred Beings, and Native people coalesce to reveal two major premises of Native poetics: narrative resides in the earth, and the earth and people are the same thing. The first concept, that narrative resides in the earth, is articulated in *Secrets from the Center of the World* by the Mvskogee poet Joy Harjo while she was gazing at southwestern landforms:

> Don't bother the earth spirit who lives here. She is working on a story. It is the oldest story in the world and it is delicate, changing. If she sees you watching, she will invite you in[9]

In American Indian medicine texts, as well as in the Native literature that derives from such texts, the land narratives are the most important level of interpretative meaning and should be regarded as the intended "truth" of the work. Narrators cannot always be trusted; however, the earth does not dissemble. Preoccupations with landscapes, perhaps the most telling of all Native rhetorical impulses, are now evidenced in writers ranging from William Byrd II to William Bartram, and from Henry David Thoreau to Willa Cather to modern-day eco-critics.

The second premise, that the earth and people are the same thing, is illustrated by the word "Oklahoma." This Choctaw word is usually translated "land of the red man." In reality, the "okla" means people and the "homa" or "humma" means red. Thus, the concept that there is no difference between land and red people is understood. Native poetics center on a nexus of narrative, earth, and people. As Joy Harjo explains:

> Near Round Rock is a point of balance between two red stars. Here you may enter galactic memory, disguised as a whirlpool of sand, and discover you are pure event mixed with water, occurring in time and space, as sheep, a few goats, graze, keep watch nearby.[10]

The sheep and goats in this passage lead to the third major premise of Native poetics, and that is animals are as important as humans in Native literary works. In the Indigenous American scheme of things, animals inhabited the earth before humans and they served as mentors and helpers for them. For that reason animals should be respected and their narrative must always be considered if one is to fully comprehend the meaning of a Native story. For example, readers of James Welch's *Winter in the Blood* (1974) must carefully attend to the cows, horses, and ducks in order to see how the animal narratives contribute to some of the novel's possible meanings. Indicating that Native poetics has entered European American works are the numerous animal narratives that can be observed in canonical works (ranging from William Bradford's bevers and Herman Melville's whale, to Walter Farley's horse). In *Of Plimoth Plantation* (1856), *Moby-Dick* (1851), and *The Black Stallion* (1941), the animal passages operate much like those appearing in the healing chants and creation accounts of the oral tradition in that they present alternate levels of interpretative possibilities that have no connection to the work's human-sided plot lines.

In Native works, seemingly ordinary but actually extraordinary animals, and especially trickster animals—creatures like Coyote, Spider, Raven, or Rabbit—serve myriad purposes and must be carefully and thoughtfully approached. Trickster types remind us of human frailty and keep us rooted in the human dimension of reality as opposed to the spiritual or godly as symbolized by the land and its various formations of stone, water, and earth. Tricksters spread mayhem, confusion, and hermeneutical bewilderment wherever they roam. Always on the move, Tricksters quickly migrated from their Native literary homes to many European American works. Because the trickster type enjoys history and fiction equally, he assumes the likeness of an Isaac Allerton in William Bradford's history and as Samuel Gorton in *Winthrop's Journal: History of New England* (1630–49). On a lighter side, Trickster becomes the tobacco salesman in *The Sot-Weed Factor or a Voyage to Maryland, A Satyr* (1708) by Ebenezer Cook and later morphs into Mark Twain's duke and king in *The Adventures of Huckleberry Finn* (1885).

To illustrate how American Indian rhetorical devices took root in early American literature, this chapter will discuss two works: William Morrell's *New-England. Or a Briefe Enarration of the Ayre, Earth, Water, Fish, and Fowles of the Country, with A Description of the Natures, Orders, Habits, and Religion of the Natives; IN Latine and English Verse* (1625) and Edward Johnson's *Wonder-Working Providence of Sions Saviour in New England 1628–1651* (1654). I will deal with "*New-England*" in some detail, and all quotations from the Morrell poem will come from the version published in the 1792 *Proceedings of the Massachusetts Historical Society.* Given the time restraints of a short essay, the *Wonder-Working Providence* remarks will be brief, and the quotes will be taken from J. Franklin Jameson's 1910 edition of *Wonder-Working Providence.*

William Morrell was an Anglican clergyman commissioned by the Episcopalian church to superintend the building of Anglican churches in New England. He accompanied Robert Gorges to Massachusetts in 1623, and they, with their followers, settled in Wessagusset. When the colony did not succeed, Gorges returned to England the following year. Morrell and a few others, however, remained in the area for almost another twelve months. Much of the clergyman's time there was spent observing Natives and writing about them. When he returned to England in 1625 he published his poem. This poem was among the first English American poems written in New England, and although the Native rhetorical strategies in this piece are muted, they are, nevertheless, present.

Morrell's work begins in typical European fashion. The first stanza, written in Latin, is composed in elegiac couplets, a line of hexameter followed by a line of pentameter, while the remainder of it is in epic meter, or dactylic hexameter.[11] Each Latin stanza is followed by an English translation. At first glance, the poem is seemingly written in a classical style, given its meter, its traditional nod first to Apollo and Minerva, and then its apostrophe to Morrell's own muse who is "plaine and conscise" (125). Since this muse is obviously unlike her refined Greek predecessors, she could likely be of American origin. The elegiac couplets in the first eight stanzas suggest that the work will be smaller in scale than a typical epic, but unlike what one may expect from classical Greek works written in elegiac couplets, there is no one to mourn, precisely, and no war to remember. Like epics, the poem does contain several catalogues, or lists of flora and fauna, but Morrell's catalogues are shorter than those usually found in classical epics. Other than the meter, catalogues, and apostrophes to muses, there are few typical epic characteristics in place. There is no hero, no mighty deeds, no armies, and no journey. There follows only a detailed description of New England and its people.

Jonathan Post, Distinguished Professor of English at the University of California, Los Angeles, believes that "this poem belongs to a venerable history of topographical or 'Chorographical' poems popular in late Elizabethan and Jacobean England. These are largely landscape descriptions, [evolving] from works like Michael Drayton's unwieldy 'Poly-Olbion' (1612–22) ... and Guillaume Dubartas, *Les Sepmaine,* translations gathered together and published in 1605 as *Bartas: his Devine Weekes and Workes.*"[12] Post continues, "What is unusual about *New-England* is the disproportionate attention given to the Natives. Disproportionate because the title of the poem promises a focus on the four elements ... but really turns into a description of the political, cultural, and religious practices of the Natives."[13]

His observation that the poem is "unusual [with its] disproportionate attention given to the Natives" reinforces my contention that the work does have American Indian substance. Post's remarks also open the door to the possible speculation that any contact with American Natives changed European writings. For example, an examination of works such as *A Briefe and True Report of the New Found Land of Virginia* (1588) by Thomas Harriot and *The Generall Historie of Virginia* by John Smith reveal incipient Native poetics and themes just as *New-England* does.

Morrell begins his poem with a creation account and a paean to the earth. New England is born "[a] Grand-childe to earth's Paradise" and she is "[w]ell lim'd, well nerv'd, faire, riche, [and] sweete." Her "sweet ayre, rich soile, [and] blest seas [his] penne / Shall blaze and tell the natures of her men" (125). What is significant for the Native critic is that Morrell immediately gives the earth signifying powers and connects it to Native people, particularly women, given the feminine attributes of the land. Here the landscape can "tell the natures of her men." It appears that in his two-year sojourn in New England, Morrell learned the essentials of Native poetics. Narrative resides in the earth, and people, the earth, and narrative are all components of the same narrative entity. In "Poem on New-England" Morrell not only makes a connection between narrative and humans, but includes in his verse a creation account, which is central to nearly all medicine texts. Significantly too, he discovers the American Indian oral tradition:

> The knowledge of [their] God they *say* they have
> From their forefathers, wond'rous wise and grave. (emphasis added 136)

The clergyman's opening lines also delineate New England's bounty. He describes the healthful climate and then catalogues various varieties of animals, fish, and fruit giving special attention to the ground nut, a Native staple something like a potato:

> A ground-nut there runnes on a grassie threed,
> Along the shallow earth as in a bed,

Yealow without, thin filmd, sweet, lilly white,
Of strength to feede and cheare the appetite.
From these our natures may have great content,
And good subsistence when our meanes is spent.
With these the natives do their strength maintaine (128)

In addition to the abundance of foods in New England, Morrell observes there is also a good supply of fresh water, fertile soil, ports, seafood, and whales that will open possibilities for commercial expansion. Having substantiated his claim that New England is indeed a paradise, he proceeds to his larger subject, Natives and Native culture. Although Morrell's observations lack ethnological precision and sociological tact, he nevertheless manages to convey a general sense of how Algonquian life appeared to colonists. "Poem on New-England" provides interesting details about many aspects of Native life including Algonquian food storage caches, time counting practices, adolescent male puberty rites, mourning and burial customs, and beliefs about the afterlife. Although the clergyman is troubled by Native polygamy, he concedes that this practice is necessary for producing and maintaining offspring and cultivating crops. Despite his reservations about American Indian marital conventions, he is, however, favorably impressed by the Natives' love for their children. Morrell was unable to get below the surface in his understanding of Algonquian life, but his somewhat limited grasp of their more obvious cultural practices provides an account of seventeenth-century Native life that other early writers often did not. As Eurocentric and flawed as his assumptions often are, his poem is still consulted as a reliable source for data regarding seventeenth-century Algonquian culture.[14]

Once Morrell has introduced the land and its bounty to his readers, he then takes up New England's inhabitants. According to Morrell, the Algonquian men with whom he has interacted seem to be inscrutable and intractable. They conceal "all close designes ... in their deepe brests ... if you offend once ... they're wondrous, cruell, strangely base and vile." He goes on to report that their hair is heavily greased and features warlocks, a style that intensifies their ostensible martial inclinations. He informs us that the males dress in deer, beaver, and otter skins and are "of body straight, tall and strong" (131). They do not concern themselves with domestic or agricultural labor but enjoy themselves with hunting and shooting. Perhaps to reinforce his deduction that the men are lazy, he tells us that their homes are "like to sties" and they sleep on straw (132).[15] Even though Morrell believes that the men do little useful work, he does admit that they skillfully manage land by conducting controlled burns, a practice that facilitates hunting and planting.

Morrell's opinion of Algonquian women is kinder than his impression of the men. They are

> of comely formes, not blacke, nor very faire:
> Whose beautie is a beauteous blacke laid on
> Their paler cheeke, which they most doat upon.
> [...They are] inricht with graceful presence, and delight.
> (135)

He is also struck by the skill and dexterity of Algonquian women's finger-woven grass tapestries that depict:

> rare stories, princes, people, kingdomes, towers,
> in curious finger-worke, or parchment flowers (135)

Here Morrell is light-years ahead of scholars and anthropologists who have been unable to realize, both from this passage, and from the many other similar ones found in other early American texts, that the "illiterate savages" were actually writing. And women were doing it.

Morrell seems to have appreciated the company of women during his visit to New England. He sympathizes with Native women who work while the men "play," and he implies that they may be a little superior to English women who live in "content." On the other hand, the clergyman spent enough time with the local females to know that a Native woman "long [retains] deep wrath, / and [is] nere appeas'd till wrongs reveng'd shee hath" (136)

An analysis of the poet's attitude toward the Wessagusset fairer sex as evidenced by his appreciation of their facial tattoos, their "graceful presence," and their "small and right" fingers, which is offset by his nervous apprehension of Native men, suggests that Morrell may have had some emotional involvement with at least one Algonquian woman. At the very least, he found the women easier to engage than the men.

Morrell maintains that Native society is hierarchically ordered with "kings" heading the ranks. He is under the impression that kings must marry into royalty if their offspring are to inherit their fathers' titles. He believes that the "kings give laws," but does not understand that such "laws" would have been the result of tribal discussion and consensus reached in a democratic way, not by royal pronouncement. He further feels that the kings are responsible for "aged widows and orphanes all ... and strangers when they call" (132).

In Morrell's perceived hierarchy, warriors who "protect" the kings rank immediately under the monarchs. Next in importance are the shamans who are followed by the "lowest people" or servants. He notes that the healers are "well seen men in herbes, and rootes, and plants, for medicen, with which by touch, with clamors, tears, and sweat, with their curst magicke ... [their patients] they quickly ease" (133). Here Morrell hits on a key factor in American Indian literature. It is shamans who store and transmit the sacred formulae that give the words their generative capabilities, or in other words, it is "medicine" that generates literature. As for the lower classes, Morrell seems to believe that they cannot marry or use tobacco without the sovereign's permission. This latter observation may have some merit. Theoretically, tobacco was intended to be used for ceremonial or religious rites so that Morrell's sense that it was restricted may have some merit in fact. Tobacco guaranteed the truth of one's statements and for that reason it should not be used recreationally.[16]

The clergyman-poet concludes his piece by recognizing that the Algonquians have religious beliefs:

All feare some God, some God they worship all,
On whom in trouble and distresse they call. (136)

He further believes that the Natives "keep just promise, and love equitie," and admits:

Each man by some meanes is with sense possest
Of heaven's great lights, bright starres, and influence. (137)

The clergyman fears, however, that the Natives are doomed because they do not understand or accept the concept of the Christian Trinity. In his heart Morrell knows that the Natives are not heathens. Although they worship the Creator, theoretically they are not redeemed and the officially mandated rules of salvation will not accept them. A close reading of "Poem on New-England" reveals an ironic request given the Natives' heathen state. In his closing lines Morrell writes:

If these poore lines may winne this country love,
Or kinde compassion in the English move;
Perswade our mightie and renowned state,
This pore-blinde people to comiserate;
Or painefull men to this good land invite,
Whose holy workes these natives may inlight;
If heavens graunt these, to see here built I trust,
An English kingdome from this Indian dust. (139)

These lines indicate that Morrell believes there is value in Native life and he is persuaded that American Indians can enlighten British religious practices, missionary endeavors, and culture. As the conflicted clergyman brings his poem to a close, he prays that the English will be moved to compassion for the Natives, but also prays that "An English kingdome [will be built from] this Indian dust" (139). In a sense *New-England* is prophetic. For roughly one hundred fifty years, New England was a British kingdom, but that political situation eventually changed. What did not change, however, was the signifying power of "Indian dust," the residing place of American Indian discursive practices that continue to inform American letters.

Just as "Poem on New-England" demonstrates American Indian rhetorical strategies and a Native presence, Edward Johnson's *Wonder-Working Providence of Sions Saviour in New England, 1628–1651* provides a much fuller example of these compositional protocols. Begun in 1628 and published in 1654, *Wonder-Working Providence* is one of America's earliest histories because William Bradford's history of Plymouth, written at roughly the same time, was not actually published until 1856. Johnson was born in Kent, England, in about 1599 and came to Massachusetts in 1630, presumably as part of the Winthrop contingent. He returned to England shortly thereafter, but came back again in 1636 with his wife, seven children, and three servants.[17]

Johnson settled in what is now Woburn, Massachusetts, and is considered to be one of the town's most notable founders. There he helped establish the first Congregational church and was quite active in it. He also served as the town clerk or reporter, an office having both civic and ecclesiastical prerogatives since church and state were one during that period. An extremely versatile man, Johnson did military duty when circumstances warranted and held the honorific rank of captain. He also served as a surveyor, regional explorer, and mapmaker. Because his father had been a parish clerk in England, it is possible that Johnson was educated at an English grammar school, but no record certifying either his educational or military background has ever been found. His writings suggest that he must have appreciated poetry, biography, theology, and history since *Wonder-Working Providence* employs all those genres.

Johnson is an important writer for early Americanists because he left a record of the first English settlements in Massachusetts and delineated the theological and social concerns informing those settlements and their leaders. His work, however, must be read judiciously because it is a highly subjective history given to florid Calvinist verbiage that eulogizes the colonizing ministers of various towns in Massachusetts colony. His praise for these clergymen is decidedly overblown, and what he produces is indeed a wonder. It is part history and part wishful thinking. Describing Johnson, William Trent and Benjamin Wells, editors of *Colonial Prose and Poetry* (1901), write that

> Unfortunately, the author was very uncritical, and while we cannot but admire his strenuously eulogistic tone when he writes of the great Puritan leaders and their work, we are obliged to smile at the extravagant crudity of his style.... His attempts at verse are peculiarly distressing, but when all is said ... much is to be pardoned to so sturdy a patriot.[18]

Since Trent and Wells's assessment, criticism of *Wonder-Working Providence* has been kinder to Johnson, but the main vein of it keeps the captain well within the Puritan paradigm and ignores his commentary on American Indians altogether even though a sizable amount of his chronicle is dedicated to Native agency.[19]

What makes *Wonder-Working Providence* interesting to scholars searching for Native influence in early American works is that the history has embedded within it a microhistory of New England's Indigenous people from their first significant contact with Europeans in 1614 to the Pequot Dispersal and its aftermath. Symbolically the work can be read as a Native allegory covering even a longer period of time than the history does because the population reduction of New England Natives, like the one Johnson delineates, continued throughout the colonial period. Of course, the eastern nations were not completely annihilated. They either melded with other groups, or they moved to the social margins and lived unobtrusively. Because some American Indians intermarried with non-Natives, succeeding generations often became difficult to identify as Natives, and it was assumed that the Indians had disappeared.

Wonder-Working Providence contains within it unmistakable examples of basic Native literary theory. It also displays an embedded Native text complete with Algonquian characters who act, speak, and interact with colonists. In addition to American Indian historical figures contributing to the work's action, we find Native tropes and allusions working throughout the piece. Johnson anchors his embedded Native narrative to the diegetic text by a series of vignettes that depict vivid portraits of Algonquian men and women. These vignettes spell out motivations for the Natives' political activism in ways that reveal the complexity of their reasoning. As the vignettes, with their attendant Native tropes and allusions coalesce, Johnson's Native narrative forms, and this narrative gives readers a glimpse into the Native response to colonization and possibly to the truth of what actually happened when certain events transpired.

Johnson commences his history of Sions Saviour in New England with an admonition to prospective colonists about how to behave in the New World, but once his etiquette guide, coupled with high-minded reasons for settlement, is laid out, he begins the American and larger part of his chronicle. Significantly enough, the New World portion of his history opens with a vignette of American Indians acting as interpreters of miraculous events, his titular "wonder-working providences," that presaged the English settlements in New England. Johnson, who obtained this story from local Native hearsay, relates that probably in 1614, some Massachusetts people saw a ship, probably navigated by John Smith, sail into Massachusetts Bay. The astounded Natives rowed out to the vessel and shot at it, but could not penetrate it with arrows. The seemingly invincible sailors landed their vessel and came ashore. When the Natives saw that the ship's occupants were merely humans who wanted to barter, they opened talks with them. Apparently this ship sighting and the resulting trade with its sailors were the first contact this particular Native group had

had with Europeans, and Johnson believes that this occasion, once noised abroad in Great Britain, stirred up such commercial interest in England that it paved the way for subsequent English settlement (39–40).

Johnson expands this first episode with another Native report. Apparently in 1618, an unidentified band of Indians relate the sighting of a "perspicuous bright, blazing Comet," which could be seen for thirty days (39). Johnson asserts that the Natives concluded that the comet, coupled with the ship's landing, indicated that even more unsettling events for Native people would transpire. What is significant for American literary critics is that these two events, the marvelous English ship and the mystifying comet, function as signifiers in American Indian oral history as well as in English letters, thus linking, however tenuously, the two literary genres. By analyzing these passages, modern critics can see that exchanges are taking place. In both of Johnson's accounts, American Natives are serving as characters in an early colonial work and their actions are underlining several of his history's themes: Native agency in America and divine intervention in Puritan affairs. Indians may be the "Other," but they are certainly the interactive Other. Action flows from them as well as to them, and often they are depicted as agents of God's will. More important, Johnson's history demonstrates that the English have begun incorporating bits of the American Indian oral tradition into British literature. In terms of American Indian literary theory, the connection between people and narrative is clearly established, and it is closely associated with a particular geographical location: New England.

In *Wonder-Working Providence*, American Natives serve as characters. Johnson's first depiction of Native people in New England is fleshed out by his fairly detailed catalogue of Nations living in the region. He asserts that the "Abarginny" men consist of Mattachusets, Wippanaps, Tarratines, Nianticks, Narrowganssits, and Pecods, and understands their divisions of government to be "Saggamore ships." He designates their major gods as "Squantam" and "Abbamocho," whom he assumes to be good and evil deities, and describes their "Powwowes [as doctors who] work partly by Charmes, and partly by Medicine." He relates that these groups had earlier been decimated by a "sore Consumption [that swept away] whole Families, but chiefly yong Men and Children" (41). He goes on to conflate the historical figures of Samoset and Tisquantum earlier described by Edward Winslow in *Good Newes from New England* (1624), and he recasts the two as one Native superhero who was "instrumentall" in acquainting Plimoth with her Native neighbors and reconciling them to her (43).

Before the arrival of the *Mayflower* in 1620, the Algonquians living near the east coast had been visited by an epidemic of proportions so great that entire villages had been laid waste. Johnson insists that this plague is proof providential that the Almighty's plan for New England is to allow Natives to die so that English settlers can take their land, build churches, and institute Christian communities. For example, Johnson estimates that before this wasting disease hit New England, the "Mattachusets ... consist[ed] of 30,000 able men [and were] brought to lesse then 300" (48). His numbers may be exaggerated, but his point does underscore the severity of this epidemic. The resulting weakness of the Mattachusets allowed for Winthrop's easy takeover of their lands in the Boston area. Johnson continues the theme of dying-Natives-exemplifying-Divine-will throughout his work, and as contact between the two groups increases and disagreements arise, he asserts that God takes the colonists' part in any dispute and "put[s] an end to [the] quarrell ... by smiting the Indians with a sore disease" (79). In *Wonder-Working Providence*, the Natives are characters in God's epic as well as in the English's.

The vignettes anchoring Johnson's Native narrative to the diegetic text range from the miraculous to the humorous, from the military to the political, and from the mundane to the horrific. These vignettes, taken together as a layer of Native narrative embedded within a colonial text, create an insightful portrait of Native Americana. An example of a humorous Native-English episode can be found in Johnson's relation of an occurrence that transpired on a night watch. A man named Lieutenant Walker was guarding the town of Linn. During night duty he heard noises nearby and felt something hard brush against his shoulder. The lieutenant realized that he had been shot by an arrow that had not penetrated his body, but had only grazed his upper arm. He immediately discharged his weapon toward the place he assumed that Indians were hiding and then hastened to the guardhouse for safety. His compatriots inside noticed that Walker had been shot between the legs as well and that the arrow had simply lodged in his coattails. Immediately the other guards "raised a small force" and anxiously waited. Nothing happened the rest of the night. When morning came, they could find no Indians, but felt that an attack "would be sudden" (79). To send a warning to any remaining Indians lurking about, they "discharged their Great Guns [so that there was a] redoubling eccho rattling in the Rocks." Johnson reports that the Indians, who were frightened by the noise of the guns, took flight. He surmises that it was God who "put such trembling feare in the Assyrians Army, [who] struck the like in these cruell Canniballs" (79). Johnson does not report that any Indians were actually seen. Apparently the guards had been led primarily by their sense of hearing and their active imaginations.

Once the smoke clears and the racket subsides, readers can surmise two things: either the unidentified Indian bowman was an incredibly bad shot, or Walker was very lucky. It is probably safe to conclude that this incident was trifling in the great scheme of colonization, but it does underline European paranoia about both real and perceived threats. Whether this event was really an "attack," or whether it was the work of a lone prankster is never clearly established. The only proof of an assault is the lone arrow lodged in a coattail. Johnson goes on to say that the English, who were "few in number" in the 1630s, kept a "constant watch…so much that they were exceedingly weakened with continued labour, watching, and hard diet" (78–79). This passage also shores up his frequently stated argument that as the English actualized the will of God, they were morally circumspect and amazingly courageous in the face of hardship. For twenty-first century readers, however, the statement opens the consideration that the extremely vigilant, fatigued, malnourished, and arrow-phobic settlers were prone to hallucinations.

Johnson follows the Walker vignette with the notation that one of the sad facts of the colonial period was the reality that both disease and warfare destroyed American Indians. In describing what was likely the smallpox epidemic of 1633–34, Johnson writes that the English, fearing for the souls of the dying Natives, assisted some of them. Among those ill was a headman called Sagamore John, the son of Nanepashemet. Sagamore John had been reasonably accommodating to the British and had become acculturated to some of their customs. As he lay dying, he was visited by the Reverend Mr. John Wilson, and according to Johnson, he was also visited by John Winthrop. In Johnson's relation, Sagamore John requested that Wilson and Winthrop take his two sons and convert them to Christianity and "[a]ccordingly the honoured Mr. John Winthrop, and the Reverend Mr. John Wilson tooke them home, notwithstanding the infectiousnesse of the Disease their Father died of" (80).[20] Johnson does not say what happens to these boys, but apparently at least one of them died shortly after his father. In his *History of New England 1630–1649,* Winthrop does not report taking one of the boys, but he does confirm that Wilson took one.

Johnson's smallpox narrative portrays the social demoralization of Natives ravaged by this epidemic as well as their numerical losses. He reports that the severity of the disease caused great fear because none of the Natives' known remedies were effective in treating it. Since large numbers of Indigenous people were dying, there were few relatives either able or willing to act as caregivers; thus the dying were sometimes deserted. The English sometimes felt compelled to step in to assist. "Relations were little regarded among them at this time, so that many, who were smitten with the Disease, died helplesse, unlesse they were near, and known to the English" (80).

When an unnamed village was hit extremely hard by disease, the English again went to offer assistance. Upon entering one particular wigwam, an unidentified group of colonists found all the inhabitants dead except for a small infant who was attempting to nurse at the breast of its deceased mother. What the English did with the baby Johnson does not say. He must have been somehow moved by this report because he recorded it. However, the infant's appalling condition, and that of many others similar to it, did not seem to move the Puritans to compassion for Natives generally. Johnson reiterates only that this plague allayed the Natives' "quarrelsome spirits, and made roome for the following part of [the Lord's] army" (80).

In addition to Indigenous characters, Johnson's history contains many well-fleshed-out Native rhetorical devices. His text includes an animal narrative in which beavers, raccoons, and bivalves render sustenance to the colonists and Anne Hutchinson's dogs demonstrate agency by contributing to her murder. Tricksters also heavily populate Johnson's work, and they include persons such as Archbishop William Laud and Samuel Gorton as well as Papists, Familists, Seekers, Antinomians, Anabaptists, miscellaneous prelates, and prebendaries. As Johnson's string of vignettes depicting amazed, contemplative, teasing, suppliant, and moribund Native people ends, the Native portion of his history takes an interesting turn. Johnson moves from the smallpox notation and stricken Natives to a pronounced land narrative, the most important of all being the narrative levels in an American Indian medicine text and perhaps the dominant component of Native poetics. As always, the land narrative connects to the human and often reflects the human story. Here, as Natives die and diminish in number, their land, once "savage" like them, moves out of their control and in turn reflects the order and prosperity of the English.

With *Wonder-Working Providence,* Captain Johnson has produced an early history in which Natives serve as *dramatis personae* and active participants in the colonization process. His characters' human dimensions, complete with foibles as well as nobility of spirits, stand in stark relief to his unbending and humorless Calvinist colonists. Johnson, like Morrell before him, has left a work shot through with American Indian rhetorical devices that have informed his compositional practices and left tangible proof of Native influence upon early American letters.

By the time of Cotton Mather, a third-generation Puritan divine, the Indianization of European Americans was evident and extensive. In Book V of the *Magnalia Christi Americana* (1720) Mather writes that "Christians in this land have become too much like unto Indians."[21] He continues the admonition in Book VI when he declares:

> We have too far degenerated into Indian vices. The vices of the Indians are these: They are very lying wretches, and they are very lazy wretches, and they are out of measure indulgent unto their children; there is no family government among them. We have shamefully Indianized in all of those abominable things.[22]

What is interesting about Mather's comments, other than his rather biased assessment of Native Americans, is that in an undated letter, probably written in 1713 to Richard Waller, Secretary of the Royal Society in London, he actually pleads to embody the pervasive dissipation he deplores. In this letter, Mather petitions Waller to be the Englishman's "tame Indian" in an effort to become sufficiently erudite for induction into Britain's Royal Society:

> I first render my most humble & hearty Thanks unto you for doing ye Part of a Patron on my behalf... [and I will] render myself a Master of what may be found useful & proper to be transmitted from these parts of ye World, under such a Management as yours, cannot miss of being brought unto Perfection. I must further pray you to be my Instructor,

(for S^r, you must imagine that you have now a sort of a tame Indian under your Tuition,)[23]

In his conscious mind, and seeking English approval, Mather's offer to become a "tame Indian" probably means to convey a sense of humility in the face of England's prestigious Royal Society, but out of some pre-Freudian corner of his subconscious mind, Mather actually says something quite different. In his stated request, he declares that he feels he must be Indianized in order to gain recognition as a malleable and worthy American scholar, a scholar whose *Curiosa Americana* will win him acclaim abroad and entrance into the Royal Society.

In terms of American literary history and theory, what Mather literally says, not his tone or what he perhaps theoretically means, is significant to American literary exegesis in terms of the influence of American Indians on our national literature. In the Waller letter, not only does Mather ask to be a tame Indian, but also states that America possesses information that can be "useful & proper" for Europeans. His remarks imply that it is American Indians, not European American colonists, who have something unique for British scientific studies, and obliquely recognizes the existing American Indian intellectual tradition, a tradition that included science, music, arts, and letters.

Mather's *Curiosa* contains much data gleaned from American Indians including Algonquian beliefs about the constellations, the power of rattlesnake venom, and the efficacy of dreams. In other narratives, and at other stages in his life, Mather wrote several passages about American Indians, and he seems to have learned to speak Algonquian. If he did not actually learn the language, he did have some of his sermons translated into Algonquian ostensibly for the purpose of converting his Native neighbors. Thus, this Puritan divine deliberately and consciously Indianized several of his various discourses, and by that act he arranged a meeting of English and powerful Algonquian sacred words even though some of his writings indicate that he found American Indians contemptible. On more than one occasion he refers to Natives as "diabolical," and in *The Magnalia*, he describes them as "the veriest ruines of mankind which are to be found anywhere upon the face of the earth."[24]

The irony of this dichotomy is not lost on American Natives who have long recognized that denigrating Indians yet emulating them is an ingrained American habit. It is possible, however, that strong emotions about American Indians, emotions ranging from admiration to dismissiveness to dislike, actually facilitate the influence transfer. Despite suppositions regarding the "how" of cultural transmission, one fact does emerge: American Indian literary theory and cultural praxes have penetrated and transformed European American writings and produced an Indianized American literature. It is a literature in which Chingachgook is as well-known and appreciated as Huck Finn, and for what it's worth, both characters are Natives. Like the wooden Indian standing just inside the barroom of the old television comedy, *Cheers*, there is a "tame Indian" residing in the pages of many American literary works, and for that we should all raise a glass.

The impact of European Contact with American Indians that gave rise to an American literature, which is a major reflection of culture in general, had a profound and broad effect upon European, and later European American, politics and society, which since the mid-nineteenth century often has barely been recognized, if at all. For many colonists Indianization was subtle, though Indian symbols and an appreciation of certain Indian qualities and ways had become widespread well before the American Revolution and remained prevalent in US culture until the mid-nineteenth century, as is discussed below. A fair number of colonists were considerably affected in their social and political thinking, including quite a number who became important colonial, revolutionary, and early US leaders. Several of these key people are discussed in the following, beginning with Roger Williams.

Section 2: Errand in the Wilderness: Roger Williams and "Soul Liberty"

Bruce E. Johansen and Stephen M. Sachs

I've known them to leave their house and mat
To lodge a friend or stranger
When Jews and Christians oft have sent
Jesus Christ to the Manger
Oft have I heard these Indians say
These English will deliver us
Of all that's ours, our lands and lives
In the end, they'll bereave us.
—Roger Williams[25]

First rebel against the divine church-order.[26]
—Roger Williams

Morning star in the galaxy of the American great.[27]
—Roger Williams

Vernon Parrington regarded Roger Williams as "the most provocative figure thrown upon the Massachusetts shores...the one original thinker amongst a number of capable social architects,"[28] one whose philosophy predated the ideas of John Locke by almost half a century. He has also been hailed as the first flower of Enlightenment's spring: Roger Williams, the first North American revolutionary, or at least the first of European extraction.

Although his ideas were couched mainly in religious contexts, they also engaged debates regarding political liberty that would fire the American Revolution more than a century later. Like many of the United States' founders, Williams also often used his perceptions of American Indians and their societies as reference points to hone his pre-existing desires for an alternative to the European status quo. As the founder of Providence Plantations (Rhode Island),

Williams tried to implement his ideas of "soul liberty," political freedom and economic equality. His experiment presaged the later revolution of continental scope.

During his lifetime, however, Williams was excoriated as a spreader of intellectual infections. Cotton Mather, the Puritans' chief theologian, understood the threat this rebel posed to the reigning ideology. He led his *Magnalia Christi Americana* with a description of Williams as "the chief of sinners," and as "an embodiment of mischief and ruin," comparing him, metaphorically, to a windmill in Holland that spun so fast it burned an entire town to the ground.[29] Mather directly linked Williams's "sin" to his proposal that New Englanders live in peaceful coexistence with the Native peoples they met on those new shores, instead of requiring them to convert to Mather's faith and to exterminate those who refused.

Scott L. Pratt, in his reappraisal of American pragmatism's roots, writes that "Williams represented the thing most dangerous to Mather: the potential to burn down the Puritan Jerusalem in America." Pratt makes a detailed case that Williams went beyond contact with and description of Native peoples and their cultures—that he sought to use their example, in synthesis with European ideas, as gist for an alternative ordering of human relations in his Providence Plantations, which became Rhode Island. "Williams," Pratt writes, "adopted a version of a Native attitude and supported it using conceptual resources from his own Christian and European background."[31]

Educated at London's Charterhouse School and Cambridge University, Williams became a protégé of the great English jurist Edward Coke, who was very strong on liberty, ruling "the house of every man is as his castle," and was the leader of parliamentary opposition to the expansion of royal power. As Williams's mentor, Coke did much to open him to his later actions promoting diversity and religious liberty. Also important in Williams early development was his interaction with Francis Bacon, father of the scientific method, who influenced Williams on how to look for evidence with enough detachment to be an accurate observer.[32] Williams was one of the Puritans' best and brightest when he emigrated to America. Having asserted soul liberty for the Native peoples of America as well as for dissident colonists, Williams was cast out of Puritania to found Providence Plantations, a refuge for free-thinkers, at least at its inception.

Like many other Puritans, Williams originally came to America "longing after the natives' soules."[33] More than most, his errand in the wilderness helped to shape Williams's predispositions toward freedom. He engendered a passionate debate on both sides of the Atlantic that began to hone the definitions of political and religious liberty that would frame the ideology of the American Revolution.

Within a few months of his arrival in Boston in 1631, he began learning to speak the Algonquian language. He would later grow to also master the dialects of the Showatuck, Nipmuck, Narragansett, and others. Williams's oratorical flourish and compassion won him esteem with congregations at Plymouth and Salem, as well as among Native peoples of the area, all of whom sought his "love and counsel."[34]

Williams's quick mastery of Native languages did not alarm the "soul soldiers" of Puritania. What landed him in hot ecclesiastical water was what he learned from the Native peoples as he picked up their languages. Asked by William Bradford to compose a paper on the compact which established the Puritan colony in America, Williams concluded that the document was invalid. How, he asked, could the Puritans claim the land by "right of discovery" when it was already inhabited? Furthermore, Williams argued that the Puritans had no right to deny the Indians their own religions, divine or secular. Soon, as a punishment for his progressive views, the authorities began transferring Williams farther away, from pulpit to pulpit, but still fretting over how easily he won over friends, not only among colonists, but the Native peoples of the area too.

Those friendships would be used to advantage a few years later when Williams founded the Providence Plantations. Williams became friendly with Massasoit, a sachem among the Wampanoags, also called Pokanokets, a man described by Bradford in 1621 as "lustie ... in his best years, an able body grave of countenance, spare of speech, strong [and] tall."[35] Williams met Massasoit when the latter was about thirty years of age and, in Williams's words, became "great friends with the sachem."[36] Massasoit, father of Metacom—also called King Philip by the English—favored friendly relations with the English colonists when he became the Wampanoags' most influential leader in about 1632.

Williams also became close to Canonicus, the elderly leader of the Narragansetts. With him and Massasoit, Williams traveled in the forest for days at a time, learning what he could of their languages, societies, and opinions, drinking in experiences that, along with prior European experience, would provide the intellectual groundwork for the model commonwealth Williams sought to establish in Providence Plantations. Canonicus, born about 1560, regarded Williams as nearly a son. At their height, the Narragansetts, with Canonicus as their most influential leader, held sway over the area from Narragansett Bay on the east to the Pawcatuck River on the west. The Narragansetts rarely initiated war, and their large numbers of about four thousand men of warrior age in the early seventeenth century usually prevented other Native nations from attacking them.

William Wood, in *New England's Prospect,* characterized the Narragansetts as "the most numerous people in those parts, and the most rich also, and the most industrious, being a storehouse of all kinds ... of merchandise."[37] The Narragansetts fashioned wampum in bracelets and pendants for many other Indian nations. They also made smoking pipes "much desired by our English tobacconists for their rarity, strength, handsomeness, and coolness."[38]

According to Wood's account, the Narragansetts had never desired "to take part in any martial enterprise. But being incapable of a jeer, they rest secure under the conceit of their popularity, and seek rather to grow rich by industry than famous by deeds of chivalry."[39] In this fashion, the Narragansetts built a confederacy in which they supervised the affairs of Indian peoples throughout most of present-day Rhode Island and eastern Long Island, totaling about thirty thousand Native people in the early seventeenth century.[40]

Williams shows in his book *A Key into the Language of America*, written in 1643, something of how his long association with his Indigenous neighbors contributed to the development of his views on diversity, and in setting out his conversations with Narragansett leader Miantonomi at that vulnerable point in his life in 1635 when he had just been banished from the Massachusetts Bay Colony for criticizing its policies. Williams by then knew many area Indian stories, and his interchanges with Miantonomi focused on stories dealing with cannibals and those who were different and potentially dangerous, including tales and discussions emphasizing the need, in an uncertain world, to act inclusively with them, to be tolerant, and so far as possible to harmonize one's relationship with those who may be disruptive, and on the deeper level with all people and all beings. They spoke of how this harmony is not always possible, how sometimes one has to fight or exclude another, but that this is a last resort; the main object is to be inclusive, to work to create and restore harmony, so that the differences of views and talents in a community function as major assets.[41]

By 1635, Williams was arguing that the church had no right to compel membership, or contributions, by force of law, the kernel of church-state separation. With such an argument, Williams struck at the assumption that the Puritan church subsumed the state. For example, taxes were levied to pay ministers; a law passed in 1631 required church membership to hold public office. Magistrates enforced the first four of the Ten Commandments. Williams contended that the church had no such right. Furthermore, Williams believed that civil authorities could not make an oath of allegiance to the church be a part of an oath of citizenship in the colony. He defended the rights of the area's original inhabitants as well as those of Europeans who did not wish to conform to Puritan doctrine. "Natural men," as Williams called the Native peoples, should not and could not be forced "to the exercise of those holy Ordinances of Prayers, Oathes, &c."[42]

Williams conceived a more personal religion much resembling the conceptions of Benjamin Franklin, Thomas Jefferson, and others, who reacted to the state-church power alliances in Europe by seeking to separate ecclesiastical and secular authority in their designs for the United States. Williams argued for a religion that also was closer to Native conceptions of faith than the Puritanism under which he was raised. As early as 1624, Joseph Le Caron had reminded his Recollect brethren that no "savage" had ever killed a Christian for religious reasons.[43]

Native Americans held no Star Chambers, no Inquisitions to compel obedience to any particular sachem's version of the Great Spirit's wisdom. Indians fought with each other for many reasons, but none of the reasons were religious. To Williams, there was nothing more absurd than killing in the name of eternal peace and love. Williams likened society to a ship carrying many kinds of people, each of whom valued his or her own opinions enough to debate, but not to fight. In this spirit, Williams argued against coercion of the soul and for beauty in diversity.

By January 1635, the Puritans' more orthodox magistrates had decided Williams must be exiled to England, jailed if possible, and shut up. They opposed exiling Williams in the wilderness, fearing that he would begin his own settlement, from which his "infections" would leak back into Puritania. But not all Puritans wanted Williams shut up so quickly. Governor Winthrop, for one, secretly aided plans by Williams and his confederates to establish a new colony. Winthrop's reasons were many. To begin with, the colony needed accurate intelligence about, and diplomatic liaison with, the Indians; both of which Williams could provide. On a more theoretical level, Winthrop was among those Puritans who wished to find out whether a colony established on principles of soul liberty and political democracy could work, or whether it would dissolve into atheistic anarchy. Later in his life, Williams recalled that "upon the express advice of your ever-honored Mr. Winthrop, deceased, I first adventured to begin a plantation among the thickest of these barbarian."[44]

Even so, a summons was issued for Williams's arrest and sub-sequent deportation, but he stalled the authorities by contending he was too ill to withstand an ocean voyage. At the same time, Williams and his associates were rushing ahead with plans for their new colony, from which the worst fears of the orthodox magistrates would be realized. Williams already had arranged with Canonicus for a tract of land large enough to support his vision, yet Canonicus would not accept money in payment for the land. "It was not price or money that could have purchased Rhode Island," Williams wrote later. "Rhode Island was purchased by love."[45] Meanwhile, Williams was allowed to remain in Salem until the spring of 1636, provided he refrained from preaching.

But by the winter of 1636, on about January 15, the magistrates had learned that Williams was holding meetings of more than twenty people at a time in his house and so a Captain Underhill was dispatched from Boston to arrest Williams and place him on board a ship for England. Arriving at Williams's home, Underhill and his deputies found that Williams had escaped, and no one in the neighborhood would admit to having seen him leave.

Aware of his impending arrest, Williams had set out three days earlier during a blinding blizzard, walking south by west to the lodge of Massasoit, at Mount Hope. Walking eighty to ninety miles during the worst of a New England winter, Williams suffered immensely, and likely would have died without Indian aid. Nearly half a century later, nearing death, Williams wrote: "I bear to this day in my body the effects of that winter's exposure."[46] Near the end of his trek, Williams lodged with Canonicus and his family. He then scouted the land that had been set aside for the new colony.

Week by week, month by month, Williams's family and friends filtered south from Plymouth and Salem to his new settlement. By spring, houses were being erected and fields were being turned. The growing group had also begun to erect an experimental gov-ernment very novel by European or Puritan standards of the time. For the first time among English-speaking people in America, they were trying to establish a social order based on liberty of conscience and other natural rights.

Very quickly, Williams's house became a transcultural meeting place. He lodged as many as fifty Indians at a time—travelers, traders, sachems on their way to or from treaty conferences. If a Puritan needed to contact an Indian, or vice versa, he more than likely did so with Williams's aid. Among Indian nations at odds with each other, Williams became "a quencher of our fires."[47]

When citizens of Portsmouth needed an Indian agent, they approached Williams. The Dutch did the same thing after 1636. Williams also often traveled with Canonicus, Massasoit, and their warriors, lodging with them in the forests, and the Narragansetts' council sometimes used Williams's house for its meetings.

Williams seemed happiest when he was making friends of old enemies, and unhappiest when former friends fought. On a cold, rainy Monday, September 16, 1638, he set out on a hundred-mile walk from Narragansett Bay to Hartford with Massasoit, to cement an alliance with the Mohegans. A man who often lived on the run, Williams hardly ever detailed the events of his daily life, so one can only imagine what he saw, heard, and said during that hundred-mile walk, camping three nights in woods thick with scrub, burnished by the rich colors of early autumn.

For all the time Williams spent with his Native American friends, and all that he learned from them, he retained his English habits and tastes. Unlike Thomas Morton before him, or William Johnson after him, Williams never dressed the part—his adoption of Native ideas was carried on an intellectual plane, not a physical one. He never donned war paint, nor danced ceremonially. While he would lodge with Indian people and eat their food when called upon, he did not seem to forsake his English mattress for a bed of straw and blankets in what he once called "a smoky hole." Williams also did not court Indian women. To his last, this spreader of so many intellectual infections was a Puritan Englishman in his manners, even as his mind wove the examples he saw before him with his earlier European experience.

Even though he did not keep a personal journal, he did a great deal of writing: years of letters to Winthrop and others, tracts, several books ranging in subject matter from descriptions of Indian languages to debates over fine points of theology. Williams only rarely injected himself into the rushing stream of events that propelled him through history, seeming to have trouble finding time to write all that he felt he ought to commit to paper. His writing often barrels on, full of grammatical and spelling errors that stand out even in a time when English was not standardized, and with a style that seems to bespeak a man being carried along by events so quickly that he did not have time to sit, much less consciously summon the muse.

Although he was never at home in war paint, Williams often was quick to defend the Native inhabitants' rights to live, and worship, as they saw fit. Williams did his best, as well, to act as he thought everyone should, according every person equal respect no matter what they wore, or what manner of deity, if any, they believed in. Williams more than once pointed out that he personally detested professing Quakers, but nevertheless they still were free to live and work in Providence Plantations at a time when they would have at least been locked in stocks or hanged in Boston, or possibly sent into exile. Thus, Providence and nearby settlements soon became a haven for dissenters from all of New England.

When word reached Boston that the Pequots were rallying other Indian nations to drive the Massachusetts Bay settlements into the sea, the Massachusetts Council sent urgent pleas to Williams to use his "utmost and speediest Endeavors" to keep the Narragansetts out of it. Within hours after the appeal arrived in the hands an Indian runner, "scarce acquainting my wife," Williams boarded "a poor Canow &...cut through a stormie Wind and with great seas, euery [*sic*] minute in hazard of life to the Sachim's [Canonicus's] howse."[48] After traveling thirty miles in the storm, he put into port in a Narragansett town larger than most of the English settlements of his day, knowing that the success or failure of the Pequot initiative might rest on whether he could dissuade his friends from joining them in the uprising.

Canonicus listened to Williams with Mixanno at his side. The younger sachem was assuming some duties of leadership as his father aged. The three men decided to seal an alliance, and within a few days, officials from Boston were double-timing through the forest to complete the necessary paperwork. Later, Williams also won alliances with the Mohegan and Massachusetts nations, swinging the balance of power against the Pequots and their allies. The Indians welcomed the Puritan deputies with a feast of white chestnuts and cornmeal with blackberries ("hasty pudding," later a New England tradition), as Williams translated for both sides and forged the alliance.

The Puritan deputies were awed at the size of the Narragansett town, as well as the size of the hall in which they negotiated the alliance. The structure, about fifty feet wide, was likened to a statehouse by the men from Boston. Canonicus, so old that he had to lay on his side during the proceedings, surprised the Puritans with his direct questions and shrewd answers. The treaty was finally sealed much to the relief of the Puritans, who thought the Narragansetts capable of fielding thirty thousand fighting men. Although they had only a sixth that number, the Narragansetts still were capable of swinging the balance of power for or against the immigrants, who had been in America only sixteen years at the time.[49]

The outcome of the Pequot War during the summer of 1636 radically altered the demographic balance in New England. Before it, the English colonists were a tiny minority. After it, they were unquestionably dominant. The atrocities of the war stunned Williams's conscience. He had been able to prevent a rout of the English, but at a profound moral cost: He could not prevent the war itself. Nor could be prevent the cruel retribution the Puritans took on the Pequots and their allies. Williams had put himself in the position of aiding those with whom he shared a birthright, although he disagreed with the rationale of their conquest. All during the war, Williams gleaned intelligence from Narragansett runners and traders, who knew far more about Pequot movements than any European, was doubtless deeply grieved by their deaths.

In some of his letters to Winthrop, Williams seems to be trying to answer repeated charges that he was "soft" on Indians. He seems a man straddling a knife-edged conscience, an extremely painful act when one has sympathies on both sides in a war. The very talents that made his diplomacy effective produced an especially agonizing hell for him in times of war.

He was revolted by the Puritans' slaughter of the Pequots. The war reached its climax with the burning of a thatch fort, trapping as many as six hundred Indian men, women, and children in a raging inferno. The few who managed to crawl out of the roaring furnace jumped back into it when they faced a wall of Puritan swords. Puritan soldiers and their Indian allies waded through pools of Pequot blood, holding their noses against the stench of burning flesh. The wind-driven fire consumed the entire structure in half an hour. A few Pequot bowmen stood their ground amid the flames, until their bows singed and they fell backward, sizzling to death. The massacre even frightened some Puritans. Bradford recalled: "It was a fearfull sight to see them thus frying."[50] While a few Puritans remonstrated, most put the war in the category of God's necessary business, along with all sorts of other things, from smallpox epidemics to late frosts and early freezes.

Beginning in about 1640 and continuing for most of his remaining years, Williams engaged major Puritan thinkers, especially John Cotton, in a series of published theological and political sparring matches. In these debates, Williams's image of American Indians and their societies played a provocative intellectual role. To twentieth-century eyes, these arguments may seem unceasingly windy and irrelevant, full of the sort of biblical hairsplitting that today eludes all but a covey of religious scholars and a few stump preachers. But in the Puritan world of the mid-seventeenth century, what might seem to us as so many angels sliding across so many pins was a vitally important debate that defined issues of secular and religious authority and encapsulated the American Revolution a century and a half later: "All men are created equal, and endowed by their Creator with certain inalienable rights."

Williams had collected a significant amount of material about Indian grammar during much of his adult life, but the press of events left him little time to write about it until 1643, when on a solitary sea voyage to England, he composed *A Key into the Languages of America*, the first Indian grammar publication in English, as well as a small encyclopedia of his observations among Native Americans. In the *Key*, he also began to formulate a critique of European religion and politics that would continue to be a subject of intense debate on both sides of the Atlantic for decades to come.

Williams was not an anthropologist engaged in an exercise of subject-object scholarship. What he did was enjoy the company of his Native compatriots from which emerged "sparkes of true Friendship"[51] as reflected in *A Key into the Languages of America*. "Williams, in his familiarity with Narragansett culture, would have encountered not just a vision of a peaceful community, but an alternative attitude, a way of understanding and acting in the world. This alternative was one that viewed meaning as emerging from interactions emerging from pluralism," Pratt writes,[52] and goes on to argue that this fundamental orientation has informed American political and philosophical practice and theory ever since.

"God requireth not an *uniformity of religion* to be enacted and enforced in any *civill* state," Williams writes, in a belief that such requirements were the major cause of "civill Warre" and a matter of hypocrisy that tortured the conscience of Jesus Christ for having taken millions of lives throughout history.[53] Williams explicitly tied his idea of a pluralistic, tolerant "ship of commonwealth" to the Narragansetts.[54] In England, he defended the rights of the Narragansetts (at their specific request) to practice their own concepts of spirituality: "that they might not be forced from their religion, and for not changing their religion be invaded by War."[55]

In the *Key*, Williams makes it obvious that the word "barbarian" had a more positive connotation to him than the same word would wear three centuries later. Like Peter Martyr before him and Benjamin Franklin after him, among many other observers, Williams used the Indian as a counterpoint to Europe, in words very similar to those of Montaigne:

> They [Indians] were hospitable to everybody, whomsoever cometh in when they are eating, they offer them to eat of what they have, though but little enough [is] prepared for themselves. If any provision of fish or flesh comes in, they presently give … to eat of what they have…. It is a strange truth that a man can generally find more free entertainment and refreshing amongst these Barbarians than amongst the thousands that call themselves Christians.[56]

Some of Williams's American lessons are also in verse:

> I've known them to leave their house and mat
> To lodge a friend or stranger
> When Jews and Christians oft have sent
> Jesus Christ to the Manger
> Oft have I heard these Indians say
> These English will deliver us
> Of all that's ours, our lands and lives
> In the end, they'll bereave us.[57]

Williams further disputes notions that Europeans were intellectually superior to Native Americans:

> For the temper of the braine in quick apprehensions and accurate judgements … the most high and sovereign God and Creator hath not made them inferior to Europeans…. Nature knows no difference between Europeans and Americans in blood, birth, bodies, &c. God having of one blood made all mankind, *Acts 17*…. The same Sun shines on a Wilderness that doth on a garden.[58]

Thus, by implication, the Puritans had no right to take land and resources from Native Americans by "divine right." Williams's was the first expression in English on American soil of a belief that would power the American Revolution a century and a half later: "All men are created equal, and endowed by their Creator with certain inalienable rights."

In some ways, Williams found what Europeans called "Christian values" better embodied in Native American societies: "There are no beggars amongst them, nor fatherless children unprovided for."[59] The *Key* is also a lesson in humility directed at the most pompous and ethnocentric of the English:

When Indians heare the horrid filths,
Of Irish, English men
The horrid Oaths and Murthurs late
Thus say these Indians then:

We weare no Cloathes, have many Gods,
And yet our sinnes are lesse:
You are Barbarians, Pagans wild,
Your land's the wildernesse.[60]

In another verse, Williams continues:

Boast not, proud English, of thy birth and blood;
Thy brother Indian is by birth as good.[61]

The *Key* later became a standard text for English-speaking people wishing to learn the languages of New England's Native people. The small book was printed in England, and widely distributed there, but not in Puritania. Despite diplomatic aid that might have saved the Massachusetts Bay Colony, Williams still was regarded as a dangerous radical by orthodox Puritans. Addressing Christian hypocrisy, using his image of the Indian as counterpoint, Williams writes:

How often have I heard both the English and the Dutch[,] not only the civil, but the most debauched and profane say: "These Heathen Doggs, better kill a thousand of them than we Christians should be endangered or troubled with them; they have spilt our Christian blood, the best way to make riddance of them is to cut them all off and make way for Christians."[62]

To him, the Natives of America were just as godly, even if not as Christian, as Europeans:

He that questions whether God made the World, the Indians will teach him. I must acknowledge I have received in my converse with them many confirmations of these two great points, *Heb. II.6,*
viz:
1. That God is[.]
2. That hee is a rewarder of all that diligently seek him.[63]

Indians informed Williams's perspective on political matters as well. He called Indian governmental organizations "monarchies" (as did many Europeans in the earliest colonial days), but then retracted that after catching the scent of a grievous popular opinion. In *Key,* he describes the workings of Indian governments in ways similar to the structure of his new colony Providence Plantations: "The sachims ... will not conclude of ought that concerns all, either Lawes, or Subsidies, or warres, unto which people are averse, or by gentle perswasion cannot be brought."[64]

When some Puritans asked whether a society based on individual choice instead of coerced consent would degenerate into anarchy, he countered: "Although they have not so much to restraine them (both in respect of knowledge of God and lawes of Men) as the English have, yet a man shall never heare of such crimes amongst them [as] robberies, murthurs, adultries &c., as among the English."[65]

Williams's reports of Indian attitudes toward liberty in New England resembled those of French Jesuits in the Saint Lawrence Valley at about the same time. The Jesuit Bressani refuted arguments that liberty would lead to anarchy by describing the Hurons' governance as "quite as effective as our own, since very few disorders appear in the midst of extreme liberty." He described Huron leaders as "neither king nor absolute prince ... certain as if [they] were heads of a republic." Bressani wrote that Huron leaders managed villages and tribes as fathers ought to manage their families, by power of persuasion, "obtaining everything *precario* with eloquence [and] exhortation," and, would a Jesuit dare forget, with "prayer."[66]

Among the colonists of Providence Plantations, as well as among the Indians he knew, Williams envisioned a society where "all men may walk as their consciences perswade them."[67] His ideal society also shared with the Indian societies he knew a relatively egalitarian distribution of property, with political rights based on natural law: "All civil liberty is founded in the consent of the People," with "Natural and civil Right and Privilege due ... as a Man, a Subject, a Citizen."[68]

Establishing such a utopian society was easier said than done, as he observed some of his co-settlers setting up land companies similar to those in other colonies in an attempt to hoard property set aside for future settlers. The reserved parcels were intended to help prevent the growth of a landless underclass in the colony. In a 1654 letter to Providence Plantations, Williams showed how isolated he sometimes felt in his quest for a new way of life: "I have been charged with folly for that freedom and liberty which have always stood for—I say, liberty and equality in both land and government."[69]

Upon arriving in England during in 1643, Williams was doing more than taking his *Key into the Languages of America* to be printed. He also was seeking a charter for his colony, and meeting with people who shared his opinions. His observations and arguments provided raw observational material for the philosophers of Europe and, through them, to the authors of the Declaration of Independence and France's revolutionary rhetoric. Edwin Poteat writes:

The enthusiasm and much of the political idealism of John Milton and Oliver Cromwell were derived from their personal contacts with Williams ... in so far as Thomas Hobbes, John Locke, Sir Henry Vane, and others were inspired by Milton and Cromwell, they too are intellectual heirs of Williams.[70]

In addition, Williams's *The Bloudy Tenent*, published in 1644, became a virtual textbook among the Secretarians and Levellers during the English revolution of 1648.[71] Even before its publication, he had already met in 1643 with Seekers and other radical thinkers who were spreading his ideas across England, into Wales. On August 9, 1644, the House of Commons perceived Williams to be of such a threat that they even ordered the public hangman to execute a public burning of *Bloudy Tenent*. A few weeks later another unauthorized edition appeared, along with a host of other tracts by other writers who picked up Williams's refrain of secular government and popular sovereignty, while tract writers at home and in the Massachusetts colony busied presses with arguments against his "contamination."

For example, in *The Shield Single against the Sword Doubled* published in 1654 by Henry Niccols of South Wales, the author decries "that seed that sprouts in this wild and bitter fruit, and that in such a season when the spirit of error is let loose to deceive many a thousand souls in the Nation, whose hearts are become tinder or gunpowder ready to catch and kindle at every spark of false light."[72] Niccols further accuses Williams and his associates of seeking to "take away all the Gospel ... all instituted worship of God" and embraces John Cotton's description of Williams as "the Prodigious Minister of Exorbitant Novelties."[73]

The debate became an impassioned one on both sides. "Forcing of conscience is soul-rape," Williams writes, pointing out that even Jesus Christ "commands tolerance of anti-Christians." After citing Christ, Williams adds his observations of the Narragansetts, among whom the "civil commonwealth" and the "spiritual commonwealth...are independent the one of the other.... The very Indians abhor to disturb any conscience at worship."[74] Later in his life, he expanded on this theme:

> God requirth not an uniformity of religion to be enacted and enforced in any civil state; which enforced uniformity (sooner or later) is the greatest occasion of civil wars.... It is the will and command of God that...a permission of the most Paganish, Jewish, Turkish, or Anti-Christian consciences and worships be granted to all men in all nations and countries.[75]

To Williams, the only way to prevent wars based on religion was to actively sanction tolerance. He argued vehemently against assertions that one had to be Christian to have a conscience and a soul. If all people were religiously equal, Crusades made less than little sense—this, Williams took to be God's word, and like many preachers he often spoke for himself by invoking a deity. He saw that religion seemed to mean less of a professed doctrine than a possession of an innate sense of justice and morality, and he saw that capacity in all people, Christian and non-Christians alike. From observing the Indians, he learned that such morality was endowed in humankind naturally, not by membership in a church or adherence to a theology: "It is granted, that nature's light discovers a God, some sins a judgement, *as we see in the Indians*."[76] In his extensive travels with the Narragansetts, Williams sensed "the conscience of good and evil which every savage Indian in the world hath."[77]

As a peacemaker between races as well as religions, he often expressed amazement at authorities whose horizons were narrow and whose self-interests were evident. When Williams returned again to England in the early 1650s, one of the items of his agenda was a petition from the Native peoples of New England requesting the aid of the British government to preserve their religions against intrusions by the Puritans:

I humbly pray your consideration, whether or not it be only possible, but very easy, to live and die in peace with all the natives of this country.... Are not the English of this land, generally, a persecuted people from their native soil? And hath not the God of peace and father of mercies made these natives more friendly in this, than our native countrymen in our own land to us? ... Are not our families grown up in peace amongst them? Upon which I humbly ask, how can it suit with Christian ingenuity to take hold of some seeming occasions for their destruction?[78]

Where Puritans often saw heathens and devils, Williams saw people, usually friends, with intelligence, moral sense, and a workable political system based on consensus, and reasoned they had the right to judge Christianity, and decide without coercion whether they preferred its doctrines over their own traditions; to make the decision "according to their Indian and American consciences, for other consciences it is not supposed they should have."[79] He further argued that societies in Arabia, the Far East, and elsewhere had managed to sustain themselves, and even flourish, without knowledge of, nor devotion to, "a true Church of Jesus Christ."[80]

Perhaps the greatest backhanded tribute to his life was paid by his master antagonist John Cotton, who wrote that Williams's "dangerous opinions subverted the state and government of this country, and tended to unsettle the kingdoms and commonwealths of Europe."[81]

Despite Cotton and other Puritan polemicists, they knew they needed his frontier diplomacy. Williams's yeoman efforts did much to maintain a shaky peace along the frontiers of New England for nearly two generations after the Pequot War ended in 1638. In 1645, his efforts averted another Native uprising against encroaching settlements. By the 1660s, however, the aging Williams watched his lifelong pursuit of peace in the colonies begin to unravel yet again. This time, he felt more conflicted than ever: his English ancestry seemed to have driven him to protect English interests, even though wave after wave of colonists provided Native peoples with plenty of grievances by usurping their land without permission or compensation. Yet, in this matter, Williams had never changed his mind: neither the Puritans, nor any other Europeans, had any right, divine or otherwise, to take Indian land: "that we have not our land by Patent of the King, but that the Natives are the true owners of it; and that we ought to repent of such receiving it by Pattent."[82]

The final years of Williams's life were profoundly painful for a sensitive man who prized peace and harmony above all. Entering his sixties, his body weakened quickly. In 1663, he complained often of "old pains, lameness, so th't sometimes I have not been able to rise, nor goe, or stand."[83] He found himself using his pastoral staff as more than a ministerial ornament. Mixanno, Massasoit's son, had been assassinated in 1643 and his murder had never been avenged. Rumors circulated that the English had plotted the murder and were harboring the assailant. Then, when another of Massasoit's sons, Alexander, visited Boston in 1662, he fell gravely ill and died as a party of Wampanoag warriors rushed him into the relative safety of the wilderness. When he died, the warriors beached their canoes, buried his body in a knoll, and returned home with rumors that he, too, had been a victim of the English.

The mantle of leadership then fell to Metacom, called King Philip by the English. About twenty-five years of age in 1662, Metacom distrusted nearly all whites, with Williams being one of few exceptions. He also was known as a man who did not forgive insults easily. It was once said that he chased a white man named John Gibbs from Mount Hope to Nantucket Island after Gibbs had insulted his father. Throughout his childhood, Metacom had watched his people dwindle in the English advance. By 1671, about forty thousand people of European descent lived in New England. The Native population, double that of the Europeans before the Pequot War, was now about half that of the Europeans. European farms and pastures were crawling toward Mount Hope, driving away game, creating friction over land that the Indians had used without question for so many generations, but by 1675, the Wampanoags held only a small strip of land at Mount Hope, and settlers wanted even that.

Metacom grew more bitter by the day seeing his nation being destroyed before his eyes. English cattle had trampled Indian corn fields; English farming had forced game farther from Indian hunting grounds. He had been summoned to Plymouth to answer questions, while others in his nation had been subjected to more exploitation. Traders had fleeced Indians, exchanging furs for liquor. The devastation of alcohol and disease and the loss of land had destroyed Indian families and tradition. This was Metacom's world as he prepared to go to war.

When rumors of war reached Williams, he again tried to keep the Narragansetts out of it. This time, though, he failed. Nananawtunu, son of Mixanno, told his close friend that while he opposed going to war, his people could not be restrained. They had decided the time had come to die fighting, rather than to die slowly. Williams's letters of this time were pervaded with sadness, as he watched the two groups he knew so well slide toward war.

Shortly after hostilities began in June 1675, Williams met with Metacom, riding with the sachem and his family in a canoe not far from Providence Plantations. He warned that war would lead the Wampanoags people to extermination. He compared the Indigenous to a canoe on a stormy sea of English fury. "He answered me in a consenting, considering kind of way," Williams writes. "My canoe is already overturned."[84]

When Indians painted for war appeared on the heights above Providence, Williams picked up his staff, climbed the bluffs, and told the war parties that if they attacked the town, England would send thousands of armed men to crush them. "Well," one of the sachems leading the attack told Williams, "let them come. We are ready for them, but as for you, brother Williams, you are a good man. You have been kind to us for many years. Not a hair on your head shall be touched."[85]

Williams was not injured, but his house was torched as he met with the Indians on the bluffs. He watched the flames spread throughout town. "This house of mine now burning before mine eyes hath lodged kindly some thousands of you these ten years," Williams told the attacking Indians.[86] The date was March 29, 1676.

If the colony was to survive, Williams, for the first time in his life, had to become a military commander. With a grave heart, he sent his neighbors to do battle with the sons and daughters of the Native people who had sheltered him during his winter trek from Massachusetts forty years earlier. He and others watched from inside a hastily erected fort nearly all of Providence burn to the ground. Fields were laid waste. Cattle were slaughtered or driven into the woods.[87]

Colonists, seething with anger, captured an Indian, and Williams, as commander, was put in the agonizing position of ordering him to be killed rather than watching him be tortured. The war was irrefutably brutal on both sides, as the English fought with their backs literally to the sea for a year and a half before going on the offensive. At Northfield, Indians hung two Englishmen on chains, placing hooks under their jaws. At Springfield, colonists arrested an Indian woman, then threw her body to dogs, which tore her to pieces.[88]

By August 1676, King Philip's War had ended. The Mohawks and Mohegans opted out of their alliance with the Wampanoags, and left after the English had exterminated the Narragansetts. Nearly all of Metacom's warriors, their families, and friends had been killed or driven into hiding. Metacom himself fled toward Mount Hope, then hid in a swamp. When English soldiers found him they dragged him out of the mire, then had him drawn and quartered. His head was sent to Plymouth on a giblet, where it was displayed much as criminals' severed heads were on the railings of London Bridge. Metacom's hands were sent to Boston, where a local showman charged admission to have a glimpse. The remainder of his body was hung from four separate trees.[89]

In terms of deaths in proportion to total population, King Philip's War was among the deadliest in American history. About one thousand colonists died in battle; many more died of starvation and war-related diseases.[90] Every Native nation bordering the Puritan settlements was reduced to ruin—those were the same ones who in happier days had offered the earliest colonists their first Thanksgiving dinner. Many of the surviving Indians were sold into slavery in the West Indies, which served the colonists in two main ways: this removed them from the area and raised money to help pay off enormous war debt.[91] Metacom's son was auctioned off with about five hundred other slaves, following a brief, but intense, biblical debate over whether a son should be forced to atone for the sins of his father.[92]

Roger Williams died in 1683 in Providence. The pain of the world had bowed his creaking shoulders, and he likely realized just how out of step he was with the temper of that era. He was a peacemaker in time of war, a tolerant man in a world full of ideologues, a democrat in a time of ecclesiastical and secular sovereigns, a dissenter wherever self-interest masqueraded as divinity. Williams had planted seeds in American soil that would not fully flower for more than another century. He would have relished the company of Thomas Jefferson, for example, at a time when his ideas were the common currency of a revolution. He twice returned to London, where he had considerable influence particularly during the English Civil War era. There he persuaded Oliver Cromwell and other leaders to protect Rhode Island from being absorbed by Massachusetts and to stop Massachusettsans from pressuring Narragansett Indians to convert to Christianity.[93]

Williams's Indian-inspired influence in England having a return impact in North America was an early example of the regular interweaving of ideas back and forth across the Atlantic that on numerous occasions found Native American influences coming back to what is now the United States from Europe. Other instances of this are laid out below.

Williams would have enjoyed meeting two Creek sachems who visited England in 1791, "where, as usual, they attracted great attention, and many flocked around them, *as well to learn their ideas of certain things* as to behold `the savages.'" Asked their opinion of European religion, one said that the Creeks had no priests, or established religion, and that people were not expected all to agree on mere matters of opinion. "It is best that everyone should paddle his own canoe in his own way," the two Creeks told the assembled English—a simple American notion that had engaged the public hangman a century and a half earlier when he burned Williams's *The Bloudy Tenent.*[94]

Section 3: A New Chapter: Images of Native America in the Writings of Benjamin Franklin, Thomas Jefferson, and Thomas Paine

Bruce E. Johansen and Stephen M. Sachs

Introduction

During the eighteenth century, direct experience with American Indian leaders and their political systems became common for European-descended opinion leaders on both sides of the Atlantic Ocean. This period included struggle between the empires of France and England in which the Iroquois and other Native nations played crucial roles. During King George's war (1744–1748), the British colonists sought Iroquois support against the French. Ironically, many of the United States' founders received their initial exposure to Iroquois and other Native leaders and the political systems within which they operated from diplomacy and other activities at the behest of Britain, beginning two generations before the Revolutionary War.

Those who believed and still believe that the United States was molded primarily in Europe's image might think otherwise after listening to Benjamin Franklin, who so much embodied the spirit of America in Europe that he came to be called a "savage as philosopher."[95]

111

Whoever has traveled through the various parts of Europe, and observed how small is the proportion of the people in affluence or easy circumstances there, compared with those in poverty and misery; the few rich and haughty landlords, the multitude of poor, abject, rack-rented, tythe-paying tenants, and half-paid and half-starved laborers; and view here [in America] the happy mediocrity that so generally prevails throughout these States, where the cultivator works for himself, and supports his family in decent plenty, will, methinks, see the evident and great difference in our favor.[96]

The assertion of an independent identity for America and Americans sometimes became almost messianic. Thomas Paine enthused: "We see with other eyes; we hear with other ears; we think with other thoughts, than those we formerly used."[97]

Jefferson described the class structure of Europe as "hammer and anvil," "horses and riders," and "wolves over sheep."[98] As a student of government, Jefferson found little ground less fertile than that of Europe in his day. The political landscape of England was, to Jefferson, full of things to change, not to emulate. Writing to John Adams, he said that force or corruption had been "the principle of every modern government, unless the Dutch perhaps be excepted." He continued:

I am sure you join me in the detestation of the corruption of the English government that no man of earth is more incapable than yourself of seeing that copied among us, willingly. I have been among those who have feared the design to introduce it here, and that has been a strong reason with me for wishing there was an ocean of fire between that island and us.[99]

Jefferson also told the Earl of Buchan: "Bless the almighty being who, in gathering together the waters of the heavens, divided the dry land of your hemisphere from the dry land of ours."[100]

Franklin, Jefferson, and Adams's
Early Experience with Indians

An important example of the many colonists who were significantly influenced by interaction with Indians is Benjamin Franklin.[101] Franklin had considerable interaction—including diplomacy—with Indians over a long period of time, which slowly acculturated him to many Indigenous ways of thinking. By 1764, as shown in his *The Narrative of the Late Massacre in Lancaster County, of a Number of Indians, Friends of this Province,* Franklin had gained a respect for diversity, consistent with Native principles of relationship and place, that went well beyond mere tolerance including considering differences to be a good thing when harmonized with the whole. This was demonstrated again later in Franklin's participation in coauthoring the Declaration of Independence. Not only was the declaration a statement of fundamental freedoms, but also an expression of the principle of place and encompassing differences, including the propriety of a community to be sovereign and assert that sovereignty.

Similarly, beginning in his childhood Jefferson's life was rich in association with Native peoples. His father, Peter Jefferson, was an avid naturalist who introduced young Thomas to Indian sachems who lodged at the family home on their way to or from official business in Williamsburg. Late in Jefferson's life, in a series of published letters that reconciled his political differences with John Adams, both retired presidents by then, he wrote that he believed his early contacts with Native Americans were an important influence on his development.

> Concerning Indians... in the early part of my life, I was very familiar, and acquired impressions of attachment and commiseration for them which have never been obliterated. Before the Revolution, they were in the habit of coming often and in great numbers to the seat of government *where I was very much with them.* I knew much the great

Ontassete, the warrior and orator of the Cherokees; he was always the guest of my father, on his journeys to and from Williamsburg.[102]

Adams replied:

I also have felt an interest in the Indians, and a commis-eration for them with my childhood. Aaron Pomham and Moses Pomham ... of the Punkapang and Neponset tribes were frequent visitors at my father's house ... and I, in my boyish rambles, used to call at their wigwam.[103]

Franklin's Early Diplomacy

Beginning nearly two generations before the Revolutionary War, the circumstances of diplomacy arrayed themselves so that opinion leaders of the English colonies and the Iroquois Confederacy were able to meet together to discuss the politics of alliances and con-federations. Beginning in the early 1740s, Iroquois leaders strongly urged the colonists to form a federation similar to their own. The Iroquois' immediate practical objective was a unified management of the Indian trade and prevention of fraud. The Iroquois also stressed that the colonies should have to unify as a condition of alliance in the continuing "cold war" with France.

This set of circumstances brought Benjamin Franklin into the diplomatic equation. As a printer of Indian treaties, he was among the first to read of the Iroquois' urgings to unite. By the early 1750s, Franklin was more directly involved in diplomacy itself; at the same time he was already was becoming an early, forceful advocate of colonial union. He expressed ideas along this line in the late 1740s, but became more forceful in the early 1750s. All of these circumstantial strings were tied together in the summer of 1754 when colonial representatives, Franklin among them, met with Iroquois sachems at Albany to address issues of mutual concern, and to develop the Albany Plan of Union, a design that echoed both English and Iroquois precedents and which would become a rough draft for the Articles of Confederation a generation later.

In 1742, Pennsylvania officials met with Iroquois sachems in council at Lancaster to secure Iroquois alliance against the threat of French encroachment. Canassatego, an Iroquois sachem, spoke on behalf of the Six Nations to the Pennsylvania officials. He confirmed the "League of Friendship" that existed between the two parties and stated that "we are bound by the strictest leagues to watch for each other's preservation."[104]

Two years later, Canassatego would go beyond pledging friendship to the English colonists. At Lancaster, Pennsylvania, in 1744, the great Iroquois chief advised the assembled colonial governors on Iroquois concepts of unity:

> Our wise forefathers established Union and Amity between the Five Nations. This has made us formidable; this has given us great Weight and Authority with our neighboring Nations. We are a powerful Confederacy; *and by your observing the same methods, our wise forefathers have taken,* you will acquire such Strength and power. Therefore whatever befalls you, never fall out with one another.[105]

Franklin's press issued Indian treaties in small booklets that enjoyed lively sales throughout the colonies. Beginning in 1736, he published Indian treaty accounts on a regular basis until the early 1760s when his defense of Indians under assault by frontier settlers cost him his seat in the Pennsylvania Assembly. Franklin subsequently served the colonial government in England.

In October of 1753, Franklin, early in a distinguished diplomatic career that would later make him the United States' premier envoy in Europe, attended a treaty council at Carlisle, Pennsylvania. At this treaty with the Iroquois and Ohio Indians—Twightees, Delawares, Shawnees, and Wyandots—Franklin absorbed the rich imagery and ideas of the Six Nations at close range. On October

1, 1753, he watched the Oneida chief, Scarrooyady, and a Mohawk, Cayanguileguoa, console the Ohio Indians for their losses against the French by recounting the origins of the Great Law of the Iroquois.

Franklin and the Albany Plan of 1754

All diplomatic roads during the 1750s led ultimately to Albany.[106] Even before the Albany Conference, Benjamin Franklin had been musing over the words of Canassatego. Using Iroquois examples of unity, he sought to shame the reluctant colonists into some form of union in 1751 when he engaged in a hyperbolic racial slur (subsequent evidence shows that Franklin had a healthy respect for the Iroquois):

> It would be a strange thing...if Six Nations of Ignorant savages should be capable of forming such an union and be able to execute it in such a manner that it has subsisted for ages and appears indissoluble, and yet that a like union should be impractical for ten or a dozen English colonies, to whom it is more necessary and must be more advantageous, and who cannot be supposed to want an equal understanding of their interest.[107]

Franklin's knowledge of the Iroquois Confederacy appears in his letters as early as 1747 to the noted scientist, political figure, and Iroquois scholar Cadwallader Colden, when he requested and received copies of Colden's *History of the Five Nations* first published in 1727, then expanded and revised in 1747. On January 27, 1748, he wrote to Colden in a letter that he had read the *History of the Five Nations* and thought "that 'tis a well wrote, entertaining and instructive Piece," which must have been "exceedingly useful to all those Colonies" who had anything to do with Indian affairs."[108]

Colden wrote that the Iroquois' skill at oratory and statecraft had "outdone the Romans," a popular conception in the eighteenth century that helped the colonists and European philosophers integrate their observations of Native societies with what they believed had been their own history.

Characterizations of Native polities as "confederate republics" were part of intellectual discourse in the colonies as Franklin began to assemble plans for an inter-colonial federation. Lewis Evans's *Brief Account of Pennsylvania*, published in 1753 while Franklin was at Carlisle, stated:

> They are all Republicks in the Strictest sense; every Nation has a general Council, whither deputies are sent from every village; [and] by a majority of votes everything is determined there. What is most singular in American Government is that there is no such thing as coercive power in any Nation.... [Their] National Councils have Power of War and peace... [but] they can neither raise men nor appoint officers [leaving such matters to those who of] their own accord unite in a Company [and choose] their war Captain, nor has this Captain any power to compel his men, or to punish them for neglect of duty [and] yet no officer on earth is more strictly obeyed, so strongly are they influenced by the principle of doing their Duty uncompelled.[109]

On the eve of the Albany Conference, Franklin was already persuaded that Canassatego and Hendrick's words were good counsel. By the time the Mohawk leader Hendrick was invited to address the delegates at the Albany Congress, he was well known on both sides of the Atlantic, among Iroquois and Europeans alike. Hector St. John de Crèvecoeur, himself an adopted Iroquois who had sat in on sessions of the Grand Council at Onondaga, described Hendrick in late middle age, preparing for dinner at the Johnson estate, within a few years of the Albany Congress:

> [He] wished to appear at his very best.... His head was shaved, with the exception of a little tuft of hair in the back,

to which he attached a piece of silver. To the cartilage of his ears... he attached a little brass wire twisted into very tight spirals. A girondole was hung from his nose. Wearing a wide silver neckpiece, a crimson vest and a blue cloak adorned with sparkling gold, Hendrick, as was his custom, shunned European breeches for a loincloth fringed with glass beads. On his feet, Hendrick wore moccasins of tanned elk, embroidered with porcupine quills, fringed with tiny silver bells.[110]

The Albany Congress convened June 19, 1754, five days after its scheduled opening because many of the Iroquois and some of the colonial commissioners had arrived late. On June 28, 1754, the day after Hendrick arrived with the Mohawks, New York governor James DeLancey met with him. The two hundred Indians in attendance sat on ten rows of benches in front of the governor's residence, with colonial delegates facing them in a row of chairs, their backs to the building.

Hendrick was openly critical of the British at the Albany Council and hinted that the Iroquois would not ally with the English colonies unless a suitable form of unity was established among them. In talking of the proposed union of the colonies and the Six Nations on July 9, 1754, Hendrick stated, "We wish this Tree of Friendship may grow up to a great height and then we shall be a powerful people." Hendrick followed that admonition with an analysis of Iroquois and colonial unity: "We the United Nations shall rejoice of our strength [as we will] have now made so strong a Confederacy."[111]

In reply, DeLancey said: "I hope that by this present Union, we shall grow up to a great height and be as powerful and famous as you were of old." These words of Hendrick and DeLancey are significant in that they go beyond Covenant Chain rhetoric and talk of the symbol of the Great Law[112] (the Great Tree).

Franklin was commissioned to draw up the final draft of the Albany Plan that same day, two months to the day after his *Pennsylvania Gazette* had published the "Join or Die" cartoon, and the next day, July 10, 1754, he formally proposed his Plan of Union before the Congress. Franklin wrote that the debates on the Albany Plan "went on daily, hand-in-hand with the Indian business."[113]

In drawing up his final draft, he met several diplomatic demands: the Crown's for control; the colonies' for autonomy in a loose confederation; and the Iroquois' for a colonial union modeled on their own in form and function. For the Crown, the plan provided administration by a president general to be appointed by England. For the individual colonies, they were allowed to retain their own constitutions, except as the plan circumscribed in particular areas. The plan retained internal sovereignty within the individual colonies in ways that closely resembled the Iroquois system, and had no existing precedent in Europe.

Franklin chose the name "Grand Council" for the plan's deliberative body, the same name generally applied to the Iroquois central council. The number of delegates, forty-eight, was also close to the Iroquois council's fifty.[114] Each colony was allocated a different number of delegates, just as each Haudenosaunee nation had sent a different number of sachems to Onondaga, though the Albany Plan was based in rough proportion to tax revenues while the Iroquois system was based on tradition. The Indian influence was so great that Julian P. Boyd wrote in 1942 that Franklin "proposed a plan for the union of the colonies and he found his materials in the great confederacy of the Iroquois."[115]

Iroquois Observe Debates over Independence

In the midst of debate regarding independence during 1776, twenty-one Iroquois Indians came to meet with the Continental Congress. For more than a month, the Iroquois observed their operations and its president, John Hancock, as they lodged on the second floor of the Pennsylvania State House, later called Independence Hall, just above the chambers of the Continental Congress.

On June 11, 1776, while the question of independence was being debated, the visiting Iroquois chiefs were formally invited into the meeting hall of the Continental Congress. There a speech was delivered in which they were addressed as "Brothers" and told of the delegates' wish that the "friendship" between them "continue as long as the sun shall shine [and the] waters run." The speech also expressed the hope that the new Americans and the Iroquois act "as one people, and have but one heart."[116] After this speech, an Onondaga chief requested permission to give John Hancock an Indian name. The Congress graciously consented, and so the president was renamed "Karanduawn," meaning the Great Tree.

The following rules of Congress were passed on July 17, 1776, a few days after the Iroquois sachems' visit; they appear to reflect some Iroquois ideas about the conduct of government:

> Rule No. 3 No Member shall read any printed paper in the house during the sitting thereof, without the leave of Congress.

> Rule No. 4 When the house is sitting, no member shall speak to another, so as to interrupt any member who may be speaking in the debate.[117]

Certainly, no such civility was required in the British House of Commons to deal with the shouts and hoots of the "back benchers." American Indian observers of colonial assemblies had noted early on that those legislative bodies lacked decorum and respect.

Native Americans in the Intellectual Calculus of Franklin, Jefferson, and Paine

While serving as ambassador to France during the American Revolution, Franklin discussed issues with Enlightenment philosophers "with great exactness" on the ways of Indians and on the elements of the book *Politics of the Savages*.[118] The French Enlightenment philosophers observed that Franklin believed American Indian ways were more appropriate for the good life than were the manners of "civilized nations."[119] Pierre Jean George Cabanis noted that in Franklin's discussions among the *philosophes*, which included Cabanis, Turgot, Helvetius, La Rochefoucault, Condcorcet, and others, he often referred specifically to the Iroquois and made use of their rhetoric: "[He] loved to cite and to practice faithfully the proverb of his friends the American Indians, 'Keep the chain of friendship bright and shining.'"[120]

Both Franklin and Jefferson admired the egalitarian nature of Native societies, and made no secret of their preference when they journeyed to Europe. As United States ambassador to France after Franklin, Jefferson had admired that nation's neat farming fields and the beauty of its music, but he reacted with a kind of smug horror when beggars gathered around his carriage nearly every time it stopped in a town or city. "Behold me at length on the vaunted scene of Europe," Jefferson wrote Charles Bellini.

> You are perhaps curious to know how this new scene has struck a savage from the mountains of America. Not advantageously, I assure you. I find the general state of humanity here most deplorable. The truth of Voltaire's observation offers itself perpetually that every man here must be the hammer or the anvil.[121]

When Jefferson first arrived in Paris, the city was the largest in the Christian world with a population of about 600,000; a fifth of the adult population was unemployed, a number larger than the total populations of New York, Boston, and Philadelphia combined. Tens of thousands more were only marginally employed. He writes, "Of twenty millions of people supposed to be in France, I am of the opinion that there are nineteen millions more wretched, more accursed in every circumstance than the most conspicuously wretched individual of the whole United States."[122]

Thomas Paine, feeling the British government repressive, left England and came to America on the eve of the American Revolution to teach, but was quickly swept up in the events of the times. In his publication *Common Sense,* Paine called the English common-law constitution "the base remains of two ancient tyrannies, [the monarchy and the Peers] compounded with some new republican materials [the Commons]." To Paine, Britain was surely no place to look for inspiration vis a vis life, liberty, and the pursuit of happiness. Iroquois America was "the only real republic, in character and practice, that now exists."[123]

Jefferson believed too much government and law bred tyranny. When comparing the governments of France and Britain to those of the American Indians, Jefferson left no doubt as to which he favored:

> As for France, and England, with all their preeminence in science, the one is a den of robbers, and the other of pirates, as if science produces no better fruits than tyranny, murder, rapine and destitution of national morality. I would rather wish our country to be ignorant, honest and estimable as our neighboring savages.[124]

As they decried contemporary Europe, architects of the new nation such as Franklin, Jefferson, and Paine described American Indian societies in ways strikingly similar to their visions of the state they hoped to erect, modified to suit a people of Old World ancestry. In many ways, these revolutionary Americans took up where Roger Williams had left off on the argument for American freedom. All were pragmatic enough to understand that a utopian vision of a society based on natural rights could not be instantly grafted onto thirteen recent British colonies. Writing Madison on January 30, 1787, from Paris, Jefferson examined three forms of societies:

1. Without government, as among our Indians.
2. Under governments wherein the will of every one has a just influence, as is the case in England in a slight degree, and in our states in great one.
3. Under governments of force, as is the case in all other monarchies and in most of the other republics...

It is a problem, not clear in my mind, that the [first] condition [the Indian way] is not the best. But I believe it to be inconsistent with any great degree of population.125

Most "Americans"—a word that still sounded odd when also applied to people with European ancestry rather than just to American Indians—avidly sought relief not only from a raft of British taxes, but also from the entire European way of social and governmental order. This was to be Jefferson's "new chapter" in the history of humankind. He so loathed European class distinctions that as president he rather enjoyed mixing up seating assignments at state dinners so he could watch various self-conscious aristocrats stumble over each other as they sought to settle the correct hierarchies at their tables.

Not only was America distinct from Europe, but Britain, according to Franklin, had no right under natural law to even claim land in the New World. To support his position, he used an argument strikingly similar to that which Native Americans made at treaty councils when he started his diplomatic career in the 1750s. Franklin argued that the land belonged to its native inhabitants by natural right. The colonists could lay claim to portions of it by negotiating a transfer of ownership by treaty or by winnings in war. The mere claim of a European secular or religious sovereignty was not enough. His argument also was strikingly similar to that of Roger Williams's Puritans' claim a century and a half earlier. Franklin's argument was political while Williams's was religious, but both invoked the Indians' title to America by natural right, and used this right as an example by which property rights should be governed.

When still in England, Franklin had sponsored Thomas Paine's visit to America in 1774. Paine's ideas served as a good example of the transference of New World ideas to the Old. His publication *Common Sense* illustrated how imbued Americans were with the "self-evident" truths of natural rights. His examples of free government in a natural state exemplified the need for religious freedom in America. *Common Sense* captured the essence of the American spirit by saying that civil and religious liberties stemmed from governments in a natural state. In discussing the origins of American government, he felt, using the Iroquois imagery, that a "convenient tree will afford...a State House, under which [the colonists] may assemble to deliberate on public matters." He believed that in the "first parliament every man by natural right will have a seat."[127]

"Among the Indians," he writes, "there are not any of those spectacles of misery that poverty and want present to our eyes in the towns and streets of Europe."[128] To Paine, poverty was a creation "of what is called civilized life. It exists not in the natural state.... The life of an Indian is a continual holiday compared to the poor of Europe."[129] As one who sought to mold the future in the image of the natural state, Paine admired the Indians' relatively equal distribution of property, but he realized it impossible "to go from the civilized to the natural state."[130]

With knowledge of the natural state, however, Paine, with Franklin and Jefferson, could attain what Franklin called "happy mediocrity," a compromise between the nearly pure democracy of the Indian nations with their egalitarian distribution of property and the "rack-rented" hierarchies of Europe. The "natural state" of the Indian, as they became familiar with it, could be used as a cultural influence to lighten Europe's cultural baggage in America. What emerged was a republican form of government—representative, not a direct democracy—with a relatively flat but hardly absent class structure, allowing people to rise or fall by their own efforts in what Jefferson sometimes called an "aristocracy of merit."

While Franklin, Jefferson, and Paine were too pragmatic to believe they could copy this "natural state," it was woven into America's national ideological fabric early and prominently. Jefferson wrote: "The only condition on earth to be compared with ours, in my opinion, is that of the Indian, where they have still less law than we."[131] When Paine wrote that "government, like dress is the badge of lost innocence," and Jefferson again "that government is best which governs least," they were recapitulating their observations of native American societies, either directly or through the eyes of European philosophers, such as Locke and Rousseau, who were also influenced by the Indians as discussed in chapter 3.

During the few years that Paine lived in America, he spent considerable time with American Indians, especially the Iroquois. On January 21, 1777, he was appointed by Philadelphia's Council of Safety as a commissioner to negotiate a treaty with the Iroquois and allied Indian nations at Easton, Pennsylvania. The commissioners toted a thousand dollars' worth of presents with them to the Dutch Reformed Church in Easton where, by Paine's account, "after shaking hands, drinking rum, while the organ played, we proceeded to business."[132] Paine, his prominent nose, lofty forehead, ruddy complexion and eyes that Charles Lee said shined with genius, was particularly well-known among the Senecas. John Hall, who emigrated from Leicester, England, to Philadelphia in 1785, recorded in his journal for April 15, 1786:

> Mr. Paine asked me to go and see the Indian chiefs of the Sennaka Nation. I gladly assented...Mr. Paine...made himself known...as Common Sense and was introduced into the room, addressed them as "brothers," and shook hands cordially[.] Mr. Paine treated them with 2s. bowl of punch.[133]

Government and the "Natural State"

Jefferson was especially interested in native languages. For more than twenty years after he first discussed Indians' languages in 1782, in *Notes on the State of Virginia*,[134] Jefferson collected Indian vocabularies, doing work similar to that of Roger Williams. By 1800, Jefferson was preparing to publish what would have been the most extensive vocabulary of Indian languages in his time. It also was the year that he became president, so his work was delayed until he left office in 1808, at which time he packed up his research papers at the presidential residence and ordered them sent to Monticello. Contained in the cargo were Jefferson's own fifty vocabularies,

as well as several compiled by Lewis and Clark. Tragically, boat-
men piloting Jefferson's belongings across the Potomac ripped
them open and, disappointed that they could find nothing salable,
dumped the priceless papers into the river.[135]

Jefferson also occasionally promoted intermarriage with Native
peoples to create a "continental family." In January 1802, he told an
Indian delegation: "Your blood will mix with ours, and will spread,
with ours, over this great island."[136] Patrick Henry even advocated
state subsidies for Indian-white marriages. In the fall of 1784, he
introduced such a measure into the Virginia House of Delegates.
The bill directed the state to pay an unspecified sum for the marriage, and an additional sum on the birth of each child. In addition, Henry proposed that Indian-white couples live tax-free. He
pushed the bill with his usual enthusiasm and oratorical flourish as it survived two readings, but by the time it reached a third
reading, he had been elected governor of Virginia. Without him
in the House of Delegates, the intermarriage bill died.[137] However,
Franklin used his image of Indians and their societies to critique
Europe for Henry:

> The Care and Labour of providing for Artificial and fash-
> ionable Wants, the sight of so many Rich wallowing in super-
> fluous plenty, while so many are kept poor and distress'd for
> want; the Insolence of Office … [and] restraints of Custom,
> all contrive to disgust them [Indians] with what we call civil
> Society.[138]

American Indians and their societies figured into conceptions
of life, liberty, and the pursuit of happiness in the mind of Jefferson,
who authored the phrase in the Declaration of Independence, and
Franklin, who operated in many ways as Jefferson's revolutionary
mentor. A major debate at the time resulted in the phrase "happiness" being substituted for "property."[139] The two founders' descriptions of American Indian societies played a provocative role in that
both sought to create a society that operated as much as possible on

consensus and public opinion, while citing the same mechanisms in Native societies. Both described Indians' passion for liberty while making it a patriotic rallying cry. Both admired Indians' notions of happiness while seeking a definition that would suit the new nation. Franklin turned for help to all "the Indians of North America not under the dominion of the Spaniards":

> who are in that natural state, being restrained by no 'aws, having no Courts, or Ministers of Justice, no Suits, no prisons, no governors vested with any Legal Authority. The persuasion of Men distinguished by Reputation of Wisdom is the only Means by which others are govern'd, or rather led—and the State of the Indians was probably the first State of all Nations.[140]

Jefferson called up the same images in his *Notes on Virginia* in a section inserted into the 1787 edition while the Constitutional Convention was meeting. He wrote:

> [The Native Americans have never] submitted themselves to any laws, any coercive power and shadow of government. Their only controls are their manners, and the moral sense of right and wrong.... An offence against these is punished by contempt, by exclusion from society, or, where the cause is serious, as that of murder, by the individuals whom it concerns. Imperfect as this species of control may seem, crimes are very rare among them.[141]

The lesson here seemed clear to Jefferson:

> Insomuch that it were made a question, whether no law, as among the savage Americans, or too much law, as among the civilized Europeans, submits man to the greater evil, one who has seen both conditions of existence would pronounce it to be the last.[142]

Writing to Edward Carrington in 1787, Jefferson linked freedom of expression with public opinion as well as happiness, further citing American Indian societies as an example:

> The basis of our government being the opinion of the people, our very first object should be to keep that right; and were it left to me to decide whether we should have a government without newspapers or newspapers without a government, I should not hesitate for a moment to prefer the latter.... I am convinced that those societies [as the Indians] which live without government enjoy in their general mass an infinitely greater degree of happiness than those who live under European governments.[143]

"Without government" could not have meant without social order. Jefferson, Franklin, and Paine all knew Native societies too well to argue that Native Americans functioned totally without social cohesion, in the classic Noble Savage image as autonomous wild men of the woods. All three had experience with Native leaders as peers and treaty negotiators. Throughout the American Revolutionary War and into the early years of the United States, major Native nations that bordered the colonies, and later the states comprising the United States, were a primary focus of the Native's statecraft. It was clear that the Iroquois, for example, did not organize a confederacy with alliances spreading over much of eastern North America "without government," but in fact organized themselves through a non-European conception of government, one of which Jefferson, Franklin, and Paine were appreciative students and factored "natural law" and "natural rights" into their designs for the United States during the revolutionary era.

Jefferson provided the following description of Indian governance, which in some respects resembled the one the founders were erecting with a pattern of states within a state that they called federalism:

The matters which merely regard a town or family are settled by the chief and principal men of the town; those which
regard a tribe...are regulated at a meeting or a council of
the chiefs from several towns; and those which regard the
whole nation...are deliberated on and determined at a
national council.[144]

By using "men," Jefferson glossed over the reality that women
played an important role in many of the Indian nations that bordered the new America. In analyzing the nature of Native American
polities, Jefferson rather accurately described the deliberations of
Native national councils that could have been drawn from many of
the eastern North American Native nations, including the Iroquois,
Wyandots (Hurons), Cherokees, or Choctaws.

David Ramsay, physician, politician, and one of the first chroni-
clers of the American Revolution, felt that geography and the
American environment were very important in shaping American
character:

[T]he natural seat of freedom [was] among the high mountains and pathless deserts...of America.... The distance of
America from Great Britain generated ideas in the minds
of the colonists favorable to liberty.... Colonists growing up
to maturity, at such an immense distance from the seat of
government, perceived the obligation of dependence much
more feebly, than the inhabitants of the parent isle, who not
only saw but daily felt, the fangs of power.[145]

Furthermore, Ramsay also believed that principles of government were radically changed during the Revolution and the political character of the people was altered. In 1802, he stated that the:

political character of the people was also changed from
subjects to citizens.... [A] a citizen is [by definition] a
unit of a mass of free people which collectively possess

sovereignty ... [and each] ... contains within himself by nature and the constitution as much of the common sovereignty as another.[146]

One of these symbols of equality and liberty in the American environment was the American Indian. Franklin, Jefferson, and Paine were all acquainted with some of the fundamental concepts of the Iroquois and other American Indian societies. They used those concepts in their discourse to stress that the American experience was different from many of the European values that they found lacking. Their critique found a ready audience in the American people during the American Revolution. Indeed, knowledge of Indians, and the use of Indians as symbols of freedom, were widespread among European American leaders and people in general during the late colonial and revolutionary periods, as was illustrated in colonists' acts of resistance against British policies.

Mohawks, Axes, and Taxes: Symbolic Identity as a Prelude to Revolution

Few events of the revolutionary era have been engraved in America's popular memory like the Boston Tea Party. To this day, nearly everyone, regardless of sophistication in matters American and revolutionary, knows that the patriots who dumped tea in Boston Harbor were dressed as American Indians—Mohawks, specifically. However, *why* the tea dumpers chose this particular form of disguise is something we are less informed about. Judging by the dearth of commentary on the matter, one might conclude that Mohawks were chosen out of sheer convenience, as if Paul Revere and a gaggle of late eighteenth-century "party animals" had stopped by a costume shop on their way to the wharf and found the Mohawk getups the only ones available in quantity and on short notice.

But Boston's patriots were hardly so indiscriminate. The Tea Party was a form of symbolic protest, one step beyond random violence, one step short of organized, armed rebellion. The tea dumpers chose their symbols with utmost care: the imported tea symbolized British tyranny and taxation, so the image of the Indian, and the Mohawk, represented its antithesis: a "trademark" of an emerging American identity and a voice for liberty in a new land. The image of the Indian also figured into tea dumpers' disguises in cities the length of the Atlantic seaboard. The tea parties were not spur-of-the-moment pranks, but the culmination of a decade of colonial frustration with British authority. Likewise, the Mohawk symbol was not picked at random. . It was used as a revolutionary symbol, in opposition to the tea tax.

The image of the Indian, particularly the Mohawk, also appears at about the same time and in the same context in revolutionary songs, slogans, and engravings. Paul Revere, whose "midnight rides" became legendary in the hands of Longfellow, played a crucial role in forging that sense of identity.

Colonists also formed the Sons of Liberty and participated in the Stamp Act Congress that met in New York City in the fall of 1765. By the spring of 1766, the Sons of Liberty had an office in New York and kept "minutes and record them & ... [send] their correspondence ... throughout the different Provinces."[147] As the unrest grew and the British began to reinforce the troops in New York City, they observed that the New York Sons of Liberty had sent "Belts of Wampum to the 6 Nations to intercept his Majesty's troops on their march" to New York City. After corresponding with the Iroquois, the Sons of Liberty in New York erected a "pine post ... called ... the Tree of Liberty" where they conducted their daily exercises.

Revere had been one of the earliest Sons of Liberty, a clandestine society that agitated against the British. The Boston Tea Party was only one of its many acts of agitation, propaganda, and creative political mischief. The use of American Indian imagery as a counterpoint to British tyranny ran through the group's activities. Some of the Sons of Liberty's units themselves were even named after Native peoples a long while before they had dressed as Mohawks at the Tea Party. The "Mohawk River Indians" was the most notable.

Within the Sons of Liberty John Pulling was called "a bully of the Mohawk Tribe" by an unnamed British satirist.[148]

The Sons tormented Tories and their supporters, often stripping, tarring, and feathering tax collectors, then walking free at the hands of sympathetic colonial juries. They later would form the nucleus of a revolutionary armed force, but in the early years, their main business was what a later generation would call "guerilla theater." The Boston Tea Party fell squarely within this genre.

For several years before the Boston event, colonial propagandists had admonished Americans to substitute "Indian tea" for the British variety imported by the East India Company. Also called Labradore or Hyperion Tea, Indian tea was made from the red-root bush that grew profusely in swamps near many New England rivers. Boosters of it had invented stories to spur its consumption. One such fable had it that Indian tea had become so popular in France that the East India Company was lobbying to have its importation banned. Meanwhile, verse in colonial newspapers used a dash of romantic appeal to promote the patriotic brew:

> Throw aside your Bohea and Green Hyson Tea, and all
> things with a new-fashioned duty;
> Procure a good store of the choice Labradore
> For there'll soon be enough here to suit ye;
>
> These, do without fear, and to all you'll soon appear
> Fair, charming, true, lovely and clever;
> Though the times remain darkish, young men may be sparkish, and love you much stronger than ever.[149]

In the many years before the Tea Party, Bostonians had been getting up to 80 percent of their imported tea from Dutch smugglers,[150] while the East India Company's British warehouses were bursting with seven years' worth of unsold tea inventory. Through the company, the largest mercantile organization of its time, though verging on bankruptcy, and the British government looking for ways to levy taxes in the colonies, a marriage was born between flag and commerce to create a colonial monopoly that blocked out other importers and also levied tariffs. In short order, the "detested tea" became a symbol of British tyranny the length of the Atlantic seaboard.

Two months before the Boston Tea Party, on October 18, 1773, the Pennsylvania legislature condemned the tea tax, urging the East India Company's agents to resign their commissions. A patriot's committee paid less-than-cordial visits to the agents to tell them that selling tea in Pennsylvania could be hazardous to their health. Some agents in Philadelphia resigned and booked passage for England as the Philadelphia Committee for Tarring and Feathering warned pilots entering the Delaware River with British tea that they would get a gooey welcome: "What think you of a Halter around your neck, then gallons of liquid tar decanted on your pate, with the feathers of a dozen live geese laid over that to enliven your appearance?"[151]

In Charlestown and New York, as well as Philadelphia and Boston, committees of "Mohawks" mobilized to meet the incoming ships. Secret committees of correspondence coordinated their efforts using special riders on horseback, of which Paul Revere would become the best known. In New York City, a broadside appeared signed "THE MOHAWKS," warning anyone who aided in the landing of British tea to expect "an unwelcome visit, in which they shall be treated as they deserve."[152] But in New York, the patriots backed down, not wanting to risk a mauling by General Gage and two divisions of Redcoat regulars under his command, and in Charlestown both sides decided that their rhetoric had outgrown the issue. The "Mohawks" stayed inside, as did the tea, which was quietly padlocked in wharf-side warehouses by the agents who hoped to sell it when the issue cooled. It never did.

Boston's patriots though were not known for their civility in the face of British authority, and it was Boston's "Mohawks" who sparked physical confrontations over the tea tax the length of the seaboard. On November 3, 1773, about one thousand people met around

Boston's Liberty Tree to condemn the Tea Act. Afterward, protestors marched to the waterfront and presented East India Company agents with letters of resignation, complete except for their signatures. When the agents refused to resign, several other meetings were held. The last one, in and near the Old South Church, rallied roughly five thousand people, almost a quarter of Boston's population at that time and the largest public gathering in American history to date.

In early December, handbills signed "A Ranger" warned that Redcoats who tried to put down Boston's protests by force would be answered with the same tactics that the French and their Indian allies had used to defeat General Braddock twenty years earlier: "We can *bush fight* them and cut off their officers very easily, and in this way we can subdue them with very little loss."[153]

Another handbill was boldly entitled "Mohawk Tea Proclamation," and purportedly was the work of "Abrant Kanakartophqua, chief sachem of the Mohawks, King of the Six Nations and Lord of all Their Castles." The broadside asserted that tea is "an Indian plant...and of right belongs to Indians of every land and tribe." It urged "Indians [to abstain from the] ruinous Liquor Rum, which they [the British] have poured down our throats, to steal away our Brains." The "Mohawk Tea Proclamation" concluded that British tea should be "poured into the Lakes," and that any true American should be able to break addictions to European beverages in favor of pure, cold American water.[154]

On Monday, December 13, 1773, Bostonians learned that Philadelphia tea agents had resigned, and by the time five thousand Boston patriots had gathered at Old South Church the following Thursday, they were ready for action. It was said that the tea was being sold for less in the colonies than in England. Who, then, was the first to "dump" tea?

Suddenly, a war whoop went up from the gallery, then another. A line of "Mohawks" formed in the crowd outside the church, and began ambling toward Griffin's Wharf at the foot of Pearl Street. They marched single-file ("Indian fashion"), carried axes (which they called "tomahawks"), and shouted slogans: "Boston Harbor a tea-pot tonight" and "The Mohawks are come." As the first group of "Mohawks" boarded the tea ship *Dartmouth* and began to rip open 35,000 pounds of symbolic oppression, others boarded the *Beaver* and *Eleanor*. Several thousand people gathered along the waterfront in the cold, dark, drizzly air, cheering as each tea chest hit the water. During the three hours it took to lighten the three ships of 10,000 pounds sterling worth of tea, the "Mohawks" play-acted in a secret sign language using Indian hand symbols and sang:

> Rally Mohawks, and bring your axes
> And tell King George we'll pay no taxes on his foreign tea;
> His threats are vain, and vain to think
> To force our girls and wives to drink his vile Bohea!
> Then rally, boys, and hasten on
> To meet our chiefs at the Green Dragon!
> Our Warren's here, and bold Revere
> With hands to do and words to cheer, for liberty and laws;
> Our country's "braves" and firm defenders shall ne'er be
> left by true North Enders fighting freedom's cause!
> Then rally, boys, and hasten on
> To meet our chiefs at the Green Dragon.[155]

After the last of the tea had been dumped, the "Mohawks" marched off the three ships single file, passing Admiral Montague's lodgings at a friend's residence at the foot of Griffin's Wharf. The admiral shouted from a window, "Well, boys, you have had a fine, pleasant evening for your Indian caper, haven't you? But mind, you have got to pay the fiddler yet!"

"Never mind," growled Lendall Pitts, one of the "Mohawks," as he waved his tomahawk at the admiral. "Never mind, squire, just come down here, if you please, and we'll settle the bill in two minutes!" Admiral Montague then yanked the window shade shut.[156]

Within hours, Revere had stripped off his Mohawk disguise and begun the first of his "midnight rides," carrying news of the

Boston Tea Party to other cities: Springfield, Hartford, New Haven, New York City, and Philadelphia. In Philadelphia, on December 27, more than eight thousand people gathered at the State House to hear Revere, including one unwilling participant: a certain Captain Ayres, captured as he tried under the cover of darkness to guide the tea-ship *Polly* up the Delaware River. The captain seemed suitably impressed as he was guided by a group of "American Braves" through a crowd that comprised a quarter of Philadelphia's population, most of whom loudly promised another tea party on Ayres' ship if he tried to land any more British tea. The next day the captain sailed south, back to England, with 598 chests of tea still on board.

A spark had ignited into a fire throughout the colonies as patriots openly agitated against the British tea trade. Newspaper reports ascribed a galaxy of ailments to "the vile Bohea."[157] In a letter to James Warren dated December 22, 1773, John Adams asked whether any "Vineyard, Mashpee [or] Metapoiset Indians" would intercept a tea ship reportedly bound for Providence.[158] Other reports told of a peddler passing through Shrewsbury who was forced by "Indians" to toss his tea onto a hastily built bonfire. In Lyme, Connecticut, another itinerant trader lost one hundred pounds of tea the same way. In March, 1774, the brig *Fortune* arrived in Boston Harbor with twenty-eight tea chests on board. The crew expressed astonishment at their discovery of the small cargo and agreed to return it to England, but a customs collector named Harrison ordered the tea unloaded. The next evening, the "Mohawks" climbed on board and dumped all of it.[159]

In Weston, Massachusetts, an innkeeper named Isaac Jones stood accused of selling "the detested tea." He watched as thirty patriots dressed in Indian garb reduced his inn to shambles. In Annapolis, patriots not only disposed of two thousand pounds of tea aboard the brig *Peggy Stewart,* they also burned the ship to its waterline. Students at Princeton College built a tea-fueled bonfire and tossed in the flames several effigies of Massachusetts governor Thomas Hutchinson.[160]

In 1773, Britain had exported 738,083 pounds of tea to the colonies. In 1774, the figure fell to 69,830: from 206,312 pounds to 30,161 in New England; 208,385 to 1,304 pounds in New York; and 208,191 pounds to *zero* in Pennsylvania.[161]

Between the Boston Tea Party and his most famous midnight ride on April 18, 1775, Revere created a remarkable series of engravings that bore messages akin to modern political cartoons. The engravings were meant to galvanize public opinion against the British and contribute to the revolutionary cause; they portrayed an Indian woman as America's first national symbol, long before Brother Jonathan or Uncle Sam came along. However, the use of an Indian woman as a symbol of America was not invented by the rebellious English colonists; it had been used as early as 1581 in Philippe Galle's *America*. The revolutionary Americans *did* adapt it, though, as an icon of an emerging national identity. In addition, Revere also contributed the logotype of the *Royal American Magazine* showing an Indian figure, representing America, offering a calumet—an American Indian pipe—to the genius of knowledge, a figure out of European mythology: a graphic illustration of the colonists' awareness that America and its Native people had something to teach the Old World.

One of his engravings titled "The Able Doctor, or America Swallowing the Bitter Draught," portrays the Indian woman being held down by several powerful British officials and forced to drink "the vile Bohea." Lord Mansfield, in a wig and judicial robe, holds America down as Lord North, with the Port Act in his pocket, pours the tea down her throat. Lord Sandwich occupies his time peering under "America's" skirt as Lord Bute stands by with a sword inscribed "Military Law." The bystanders, Spain and France, consider aid for the colonies, while in the background Boston's skyline is labeled "cannonaded" and in the foreground a petition of grievances lies shredded, symbolic of the British government's failure to provide justice for America. This engraving, published in the *Royal American Magazine*'s June 1774 edition, had been copied from a similar work in England's *London Magazine* two months earlier.

Revere also used an English engraving as a model for *America in Distress*, published in the March 1775 edition of the *Royal American Magazine*, one month before his midnight ride. He made one enormously significant change in the British version that had been published years earlier in the *Oxford Magazine*'s February 1770 edition: for the figure of Britannia, with a shield at her side, Revere substituted America with an Indian woman flanked by a quiver of arrows, a bow, and a feather headdress.

In this engraving, Lord North stands at the left, in front, proclaiming: "She is mad and must be chained!" Behind him stands Lord Bute, saying: "Secure her now, or it is all over with Us!" Lord Mansfield, in a judicial costume, joins in: "She must lose more blood. Petitions are rebellious." Thomas Hutchinson, governor of Massachusetts, is pictured as a loyal crony of the British lords, concurring: "Right, my Lord. Penalties of that kind seem best adapted."

As he contributed these engravings to the revolutionary cause, Revere was also taking part in more direct actions as a member of the Sons of Liberty. The Redcoats were preparing for war, building fortifications that Revere, himself a veteran of the war with the French, ridiculed as "beaver dams."[162]

The Redcoats had trouble getting much of anything done. Wagonloads of straw were reported waylaid for no apparent reason. Shiploads of bricks sank at sea on clear days. Hired hands leaned on their shovels. General Gage was forced to order more workmen from Nova Scotia when it became obvious that colonial Bostonians would not work for the British military not only because of political reasons, but also because the soldiers were economic competitors.

Soon, the Sons of Liberty were going on the offensive as well: in December 1774, Revere helped plan the seizure of Fort William and Mary, surprising an undermanned British force. The patriots waded through the icy waters of Portsmouth Harbor under the stark moonlight of a clear, cold winter's night, and stole ninety-seven kegs of powder and about a hundred firearms, then hid their haul in a pit under the pulpit of a local meeting house.

About the same time Revere was contributing political engravings to *Royal American Magazine,* another artist believed to be named Henry Dawkins was using the same ideas in Philadelphia with patriots also being depicted as Indians. Instead of shouldering Britain's burdens as they had a dozen years earlier, these Indians, drawn on the eve of the Declaration of Independence, are aiming their arrows across the Atlantic Ocean straight at Lord North's heart while British officials line the English shore discussing the tea crisis and related events. On the North American side Tories do the same, dressed in European garb, unlike the newly aggressive "Indians."

In Dawkins's representation, from the English side Lord North eyes the arrow aimed at him and says: "We must manage this business with a great deal of Art: or I see we shall not succeed." Lord Bute adds: "God's curse, mon ye mun [must]." An East India Company director says: "I wish we may apply to establish our monopoly in America." The fourth British consort from the right is "The Infamous K[ ]y"—Dr. John Kearsley of Philadelphia, an outspoken loyalist—who says, "Gov. T[ ]n will cram the tea down the throats of New Yorkers!" Next to him stands Beezelbub, "The Prince of Devils," who invites Kearsley to take advantage of the situation: "Speak in favor of ye scheme. Now's the time to push your fortune." Poplicola, publicist for the tea tax, tells the tea-company director: "I have prostituted my reason and my conscience to serve you, and therefore I am entitled to some reward." At the upper left, Britannia weeps, as an angel asks her: "Why so much distress?" She replies: "The conduct of those of my degenerate sons will break my heart."

An anonymous engraving created at the beginning of the Revolutionary War in 1776 pits "The Female Combatants," an English woman in an enormous beehive hairdo, against an Indian woman symbolizing America. The English woman says: "I'll force you to Obedience, you Rebellious Slut," to which America replies: "Liberty, Liberty forever, Mother, while I exist."

The use of an Indian woman as a symbol of America was not invented by the rebellious English colonists; the symbol was used as early as 1581 in Philippe Galle's *America*.

Section 4: The Impact of Contact on the Development of American Political Institutions

Stephen M. Sachs

The development of democratic institutions in what became the United States was strongly influenced by Indigenous Americans almost from the first moment that colonists landed in North America. The Plymouth colonists, living in close contact with the Wampanoags, witnessed their first of innumerable Indian meetings and soon adopted that form of governance for themselves, with Governor Bradford acting primarily as moderator and influential elder.[163] They also adopted the Wampanoag system of land rights or ownership, which was different from the British. When Bradford sought to increase his own authority by having the community elect two assistants to the governor, a number of the older colonists moved to other towns. There they also adopted the town meeting Indigenous style of governance, which became codified in Massachusetts in the General Court in Cambridge in Ordinance of 1635/6 for the regulations of towns.

While the town meeting form of local government was primarily a New England development, the use of elected governing bodies throughout the colonies, though less participatory than representative among the various tribes and tribal federations in the British colonial areas, clearly was reflective of the tribal practices, whatever British or other European elements it embodied. Moreover, the more democratic practice of recall introduced by progressives into a number of US state governments in the late nineteenth and early twentieth centuries was precisely derived from Indigenous practices, as exemplified by the Haudenosaunee practice of the clan mothers, following consultation with the community, having the authority to remove leaders from office for cause.[164] Similarly, initiatives, referendums, and equal suffrage also have Indian origins.[165]

The Plymouth Colony also became the first European experience with an Indian federation, when a few days after the Pilgrims landed, Samoset and Squanto arranged with Massasoit for the adjacent Wampanoags to include the colony in their federation.[166] The colonists became closely familiar with numerous Native federations throughout the territory they inhabited, and many grew quite impressed with the idea of federation. For example, in the seventeenth century William Penn, who thought highly of Indian governance, proposed an outline named "A Plan for the Union of the Colonies in America" that stemmed from his observations of Native politics.[167]

Later, in 1744 Onondaga chief Canassatego and Speaker of the Haudenosaunee suggested to a colonial meeting in Lancaster, Pennsylvania, that the colonies would be stronger if they formed a federation like that of the Haudenosaunee—he said it would simplify and improve Haudenosaunee and colonial relations. Benjamin Franklin, who was also well acquainted with the Haudenosaunee and had engaged in diplomacy with numerous Indian nations, proposed the Albany Plan of Union of the colonies in 1754.[168]

The Articles of Confederation was based on the Albany Plan of Union. The Articles were developed with leaders of the Haudenosaunee taking part in the initial discussions, and several of the delegates to Continental Congress saying in the debate that they were proposing a union of the former colonies based on the Haudenosaunee federation. The resulting Articles of Confederation was established with a strong legislature representing the people through the states, a weak executive consisting of a committee, and a requirement that all decisions of the congress be unanimously agreed upon. All of this was very much along the lines of the Haudenosaunee and other Indigenous American federations.[169] The governments of most of the states in the early years of US independence similarly functioned with weak governors and strong legislatures, reflecting the governance of all the tribes in and around the former colonies and beyond.

Indeed, indicative of the Indian Nations of North America model of government having been widely adopted by the former colonies was a Navajo Nation option introduced in the mid-2000s offering the nation a return to traditional values; in 2008, the last of four options proposed by the Diné Policy Institute at the request of the Speaker of the Navajo Nation Council looked very much like the original Articles of Confederation and the state governments of the mid-1700s. Option 4 called for replacing the Navajo Nation President with an eleven-member Executive Board. The Council, though, was left nearly as-is, with the exception of adding twelve non-voting delegates specifically dedicated to certain social subgroups and nonprofit organizations, and decentralizing more authority to the 110 chapters through reorganizing agency councils. This decentralization addressed gender issues by balancing the men, predominately in leadership positions in the central government, with the women predominately in leadership positions in chapters and the growing numbers of nongovernmental organizations.[170]

The Declaration of Independence also directly reflected Indian ways in declaring that "all men are created equal and endowed by their creator with certain inalienable rights," but did so through the influence of John Locke in quoting him; declaring, in one version, that these rights are to "life, liberty and property," and modifying this in another draft to "life, liberty and the pursuit of happiness."[171] The various governments of the United States under the Articles of Confederation operated with a fair amount of democracy, but less than that of the Indian Nations. To begin with, outside of town meetings, the legislatures were less participatory than their Native equivalents as elected representatives generally functioned with more autonomy from, and in less consultation with, their constituents. Also in contrast to Indian communities, under the Articles women did not have the right to vote. And some states practiced permanent slavery with the children of slaves continuing to be slaves compared to some tribes which might temporarily make some captives slaves until they could earn citizenship—not through financial purchase, but through demonstrating their good character.[172]

The founders of the US Constitution in reaction to what they perceived as difficulties with the Articles of Confederation in drafting the new document decreased the amount of democracy. Under the Constitution, only members of the House of Representatives were directly elected, and the checks and balances, which less fully distributed power than the wide dispersion of authority in Indian nations, tended to further reduce the voice of the people.[173] At the same time, in the opening of the Preamble to the Constitution, "We the People" is a clear statement of democracy commensurate with Native traditions, and in fact there are indications the phrase may well have been taken from a Haudenosaunee document:[174] It is reported that one of the Founding Fathers brought with him a description of the Haudenosaunee constitution,[175] and Franklin alluded to the Native influence in the document with: "We have gone back to ancient history...all around Europe, but find none of their constitutions suitable to our circumstances."[176]

The Preamble itself is a good statement of the traditional purposes of governance in the Indigenous nations at the time of the first European colonists' arrival on the East Coast of the present-day United States.[177] The Constitution did continue the federalism of the Articles, but even by strict interpretation, it also greatly strengthened the powers of the national government over those of the states which more directly represented the people, by granting the Congress a set of powers in domestic as well as foreign affairs (Article I. Section 8), and by providing for a strong, hierarchical executive branch headed by a single president (Article II).

There are also several direct references to Indians in the Constitution, but these are not so much indications of Native influence as a setting out of means for relating with Native nations: in commerce (Article I, Section 8, 3); in diplomacy, which might include exercising military force, through treaties (Article II, Section 2, 1); in war powers (Article 1, Section 8, 11, and Article II,

Section 2, 2); and in providing for the entrance of new states into the Union which could include territory from the acquisition of Indian land (Article 1V, Section 3); and recognizing Indian nation sovereignty, in part by not taxing citizens of Indian tribes (Article 1, Section 3).[178]

Thus, despite some retreat from Indigenous democratic principles in the writing of the Constitution, the entire structure and functioning of government in the early years of the United States was pervaded by Native influences, which remain central to US government's operation even to this day.

Notes to Chapter 2

1. Betty Booth Donohue, *Bradford's Indian Book* (Gainesville: University Press of Florida, 2011), xiv.
2. A. Irving Hallowell, "The Rorschach Technique in the Study of Personality and Culture," *American Anthropologist* 47, no. 2 (1945), 197.
3. See Francis Jennings, *The Invasion of America: Indians, Colonialism, and the Cant of Conquest* (New York: W. W. Norton, 1975); James Axtell, "The White Indians of Colonial America," *William and Mary Quarterly* 32, no. 1 (1975): 55–88; and Daniel Richter, "War and Culture: The Iroquois Experience," *William and Mary Quarterly* 40, no. 4 (1983): 528–59, for more on the treatment and integration into Native society of noncombatants and captives.
4. "What Is Cultural Transfer?" European University at St. Petersburg, May 26, 2014, https://eu.spb.ru/en/news/14094-what-is-cultural-transfer.
5. Donohue, *Bradford's Indian Book*, xiii.
6. "The Abenaki Language: Let Us Talk About the Weather," http://freepages.genealogy.rootsweb.ancestry.com/~abenaki/Wobanaki/main13.htm 11/16/2013 (unfortunately this webpage no longer works).
7. Milton Travers, *The Last of the Great Wampanoag Indian Sachems* (Boston: Christopher, 1963), 87.
8. N. Scott Momaday, *The Way to Rainy Mountain* (Albuquerque: University of New Mexico Press, 1969), 8.
9. Joy Harjo and Stephen Strom, *Secrets from the Center of the World* (Tucson, AZ: Sun Tracks, 1989), 54.

10. Ibid., 6.

11. Thomas Benediktson, email message to author, October 31, 2013. Benediktson, who is professor of Classics and Comparative Literature at the University of Tulsa, discovered the elegiac couplets and verified my scansion of the remainder.

12. Jonathan Post, email message to author, January 17, 2014.

13. Ibid.

14. See Karen Ordahl Kupperman, *Indians and English: Facing Off in Early America* (Ithaca, NY: Cornell University Press, 2000) and Neal Salisbury, *Manitou and Providence: Indians, Europeans, and the Making of New England, 1500–1643* (New York: Oxford University Press, 1982) for ethnological data retrieved from "Poem on New-England."

15. As Kathleen Bragdon and other anthropologists have pointed out, American Indians had a division of labor that usually required women do the farming, cooking, and indoor chores while men did the hunting, fishing, and heavy land clearing. Such a division of labor did not indicate that Native men were lazy. Europeans who migrated to America came from societies in which hunting and fishing were either leisure activities or pursuits allowed primarily to the wealthy; they transferred that conception to Native life without thinking it through. Providing food for a family while using primarily a bow or a club was not easy or leisurely, yet the unfortunate notion that Indians generally are lazy has persisted through the generations.

16. Tobacco is used ritually to lift one's prayers to heaven and to guarantee the truth of one's words. Even though there are protocols for tobacco use, it is safe to suggest that the protocols may or may not be observed in all instances, human nature being what it is. Even though it is common for early American writers to record instances in which it appears that males smoked recreationally, the context is often so blurred that it is impossible to tell what is really occurring.

17. Edward F. Johnson, *Captain Edward Johnson of Woburn, Massachusetts, and Some of His Descendants* (Boston: D. Clapp, 1905), 4.

18. William Peterfield Trent and Benjamin Willis Wells, eds., *Colonial Prose and Poetry: The Beginnings of Americanism, 1650–1710* (New York: Thomas Crowell, 1901), 1–2.

19. For representative modern criticism of *Wonder-Working Providence*, see Stephen Arch, "The Edifying History of Edward Johnson's 'Wonder-Working Providence,'" *Early American Literature* 28, no. 1 (1993): 42–59; Ursula Brumm, "Edward Johnson's 'Wonder-Working Providence' and the Puritan Conception of History," *Jahrbuch für Amerikastudien* 14

(1969): 140–51; Edward Gallagher, "An Overview of Edward Johnson's 'Wonder-Working Providence,'" *Early American Literature* 5, no. 3 (1971): 30–49; and Jesper Rosenmeier, "'They Shall No Longer Grieve': The Song of Songs and Edward Johnson's 'Wonder-Working Providence,'" *Early American Literature* 26, no. 1 (1991): 1–20.

20. See Benjamin Thatcher, *Indian Biography* (New York: A. L. Fowle, 1900), 1–9, and John Winthrop, *Winthrop's Journal*, vol. 1 (New York: Barnes and Noble, 1908), 114–15, for more on this event. Accounts regarding who accompanied Wilson to Sagamore John's deathbed vary as do the number of John's children. B. B. Thatcher says the other person with Wilson was a deacon in Wilson's congregation but does not mention Winthrop specifically. There is also a discrepancy in the number of sons Sagamore John bequeathed to the Puritans. Some early writers, like Winthrop, indicate there was only one son and he was delegated to Wilson. Surely Winthrop would have reported receiving a son had he been given one. Johnson's willingness to adjust the facts in order to increase Winthrop's moral standing may explain this possible fabrication. It is important to note that Winthrop's account differs significantly from Johnson's. The governor of Massachusetts Bay writes that it was a Rev. Mr. Maverick who administered to the stricken Natives for the duration of the epidemic and this clergyman buried thirty Winnisimmet Natives in one day. Winthrop does not indicate that Wilson did much to nurse the suffering Indians, and he implies that he himself was stuck at Agawam in a snowstorm during some of this time of sickness, thus leaving Maverick to do the work that Johnson attributes to Wilson (114–15).

21. Cotton Mather, *Magnalia Christi Americana*, vol. 2 (Hartford, CT: Silas Andrus, 1853), 323.

22. Ibid., 400.

23. George L. Kittredge, "Cotton Mather's Election into the Royal Society," *Publications of the Colonial Society of Massachusetts* 14 (1913): 86.

24. Mather, *Magnalia*, vol. 1, 558–59.

25. Sidney S. Rider, *The Lands of Rhode Island as They Were Known to Caunonicus and Miantunnomu When Roger Williams Came in 1626* (Providence, RI: Author, 1904), 22.

26. Vernon L. Parrington, *Main Currents of American Thought*, vol. 1 (New York: Harcourt, Brace, 1927), 6.

27. Max Savelle, "Roger Williams: A Minority of One," in *The American Story*, ed. Earl S. Miers (Great Neck, NY: Channel, 1956), 1.

28. Parrington, *Main Currents of American Thought*, vol. 1, 63.

29. Scott L. Pratt, *Native Pragmatism: Rethinking the Roots of American Philosophy* (Bloomington: Indiana University Press, 2002), 79–80.

30. Ibid., 80.

31. Ibid., 84.

32. John M. Barry, "Roger Williams," letter to the editor, *New York Times*, January 20, 2012.

33. Henry Chupack, *Roger Williams* (New York: Twayne, 1969).

34. James Ernst, "Roger Williams and the English Revolution," Rhode Island Historical Society, *Collections* 24, no. 1 (1931).

35. Cyclone Covey, *The Gentle Radical: A Biography of Roger Williams* (New York: MacMillan, 1966), 125.

36. Samuel H. Brockunier, *The Irrepressible Democrat: Roger Williams* (New York: Ronald, 1940), 47.

37. William Wood, *New England's Prospect* (Amherst: University of Massachusetts Press, 1977), 80–81.

38. Ibid.

39. Ibid.

40. Howard H. Chapin, *Sachems of the Narragansetts* (Providence: Rhode Island Historical Society, 1931), 7.

41. Pratt, *Native Pragmatism*, chap. 5 (especially 84–97).

42. James L. Giddings, "Roger Williams and the Indians," unpublished typescript, Rhode Island Historical Society (1957), 21.

43. James Axtell, *The European and the Indian: Essays in the Ethnology of Colonial North America* (New York: Oxford University Press, 1981), 78–80.

44. Henry Crawford Dorr, "The Narragansetts," Rhode Island Historical Society, *Collections* 7 (1885): 187–88.

45. Elizabeth Ola Winslow, *Master Roger Williams* (New York: MacMillan, 1957), 133.

46. Reuben Aldridge Guild, *Footprints of Roger Williams* (Providence, RI: Tibbetts and Preston, 1886), 20.

47. Ernst, "Roger Williams and the English Revolution," 252.

48. Covey, *Gentle Radical*, 162.

49. Ibid.

50. Ibid., 200.

51. Glenn W. LaFantasie, *The Correspondence of Roger Williams*, vol. 1 (Providence, RI: Brown University Press/University Press of New England, 1988), 107.

52. Pratt, *Native Pragmatism*, 106.

53. Roger Williams, *Publications of the Narragansett Club*, vol. 3 (Providence, RI: Providence Press, 1866–1874), 3–4.

54. Pratt, *Native Pragmatism*, 116.

55. LaFantasie, *Correspondence of Roger Willliams*, vol. 2, 409.

56. Sidney S. Rider, *Lands of Rhode Island as They Were Known to Caunonicus and Miantunnomu When Roger Williams Came in 1626* (Providence, RI: Author, 1904), 22.

57. Ibid., 44.

58. Ibid., 49, 53, 78.

59. Ibid., 29.

60. Ibid., 9.

61. Samuel H. Brockunier, *The Irrepressible Democrat: Roger Williams* (New York: Ronald, 1940), 141.

62. Ernst, "Roger Williams and the English Revolution," 251.

63. Roger Williams, *A Key into the Languages of America* [1643] (Providence, RI: Tercentenary Committee, 1936), 123.

64. Roger Williams, *The Complete Writings of Roger Williams*, vol. 1 (New York: Russell and Russell, 1963), 225.

65. Ibid., vol. 1, 225.

66. J. H. Kennedy, *Jesuit and Savage in New France* (New Haven, CT: Yale University Press, 1950), 161.

67. Ibid., 42–43.

68. Ernst, "Roger Williams and the English Revolution," 276–77.

69. Perry Miller, *Roger Williams: His Contribution to the American Tradition* (Indianapolis, IN: Bobbs-Merrill, 1953), 221–22.

70. Edwin M. Poteat, "Roger Williams Redivivus," unpublished manuscript of speech to Northern Baptist Convention, Atlantic City, NJ, May, 1940, Archives of the Rhode Island Historical Society.

71. Ernst, "Roger Williams and the English Revolution," 2.

72. Ibid., 8, for both quotes.

73. Ibid., 9.

74. Oscar S. Straus, *Roger Williams: The Pioneer of Religious Liberty* (New York: Century, 1894), 139.

75. Jack L. Davis, "Roger Williams among the Narragansett Indians," *New England Quarterly* 43, no. 4 (1970): 603.

76. Williams, *Complete Writings*, vol. 4, 441. Emphasis added.

77. Ibid., 443.

78. Ibid.

79. Ibid., vol. 3, 250.

80. Ibid., vol. 3, 331.

81. Ernst, "Roger Williams and the English Revolution," 445.

82. Williams, *Complete Writings*, vol. 2, 4.

83. Winslow, *Master Roger Williams,* 267.

84. James L. Giddings, "Roger Williams and the Indians," 33.

85. Straus, *Roger Williams,* 220.

86. Bradford Swan, "New Light on Roger Williams and the Indians," *Providence Sunday Journal Magazine,* November 23, 1969, 14.

87. Ernst, "Roger Williams and the English Revolution," 500.

88. George Howe, *Mount Hope: A New England Chronicle* (New York: Viking, 1959), 40.

89. Straus, *Roger Williams,* 222, says the head of Metacom was sent to Boston and the hands to Plymouth. The version used in the text is adapted from Ernst, *Roger Williams,* 501.

90. Richard Slotkin and James K. Folsom, eds., *So Dreadful a Judgment: Puritan Responses to King Philip's War 1676–1677* (Middleton, CT: Wesleyan University Press, 1978), 3–4.

91. Benjamin L. Labaree, *America's Nation-Time: 1607–1789* (Boston: Allyn and Bacon, 1972), 53.

92. Straus, *Roger Williams,* 222.

93. Barry, "Roger Williams."

94. Samuel G. Drake, *Biography and History of the Indians of North America* (Boston: Sanborn, Carter, and Bazin, 1857), 37–38. Emphasis added.

95. Peter Gay, "Enlightenment Thought and the American Revolution," in *The Role of Ideology in the American Revolution,* ed. John R. Howe (New York: Holt, Rinehart, and Winston, 1970), 48.

96. Benjamin Franklin, "The Internal State of North America" [1786], in *The Revolution in America, 1754–1788,* ed. J. R. Pole (London: MacMillan, 1970), 573.

97. Moncure Daniel Conway, ed., *The Writings of Thomas Paine,* vol. 2 (New York: Putnam's, 1894–1896), 105.

98. Andrew A. Lipscomb and Albert Ellery Bergh, eds., *The Writings of Thomas Jefferson,* vol. 1 (Washington, DC: Thomas Jefferson Memorial Association of the United States, 1903–1904), 444.

99. Dumas Malone, *Jefferson and His Time,* vol. 3, *Jefferson and the Ordeal of Liberty* (Boston: Little, Brown, 1962), 265–66.

100. Henry Steele Commager, *Jefferson, Nationalism, and the Enlightenment* (New York: George Brazille, 1975), 119.

101. Pratt, *Native Pragmatism,* chaps. 8, 9.

102. Lipscomb and Bergh, *Writings of Thomas Jefferson,* vol. 11, 160. Emphasis added.

103. Ibid., 288.

104. Cadwallader Colden, *History of the Five Nations*, vol. 2 (New York: New Amsterdam, 1902), 18–24.

105. Carl Van Doren and Julian P. Boyd, eds., *Indian Treaties Printed by Benjamin Franklin 1736–1762* (Philadelphia: Historical Society of Pennsylvania, 1938), 75. Emphasis added.

106. Donald A. Grinde Jr., *The Iroquois and the Founding of the American Nation* (San Francisco: Indian Historian, 1977), 34–36; and Bruce E. Johansen, *The Forgotten Founders: Benjamin Franklin, the Iroquois, and the Rationale for the American Revolution* (Ipswich, MA: Gambit, 1982), 9–13.

107. Albert H. Smyth, ed., *The Writings of Benjamin Franklin*, vol. 3 (New York: Macmillan, 1905–1907), 42.

108. Leonard W. Laberee, ed., *The Papers of Benjamin Franklin*, vol. 5 (New Haven, CT: Yale University Press, 1959), 272.

109. Lewis Evans, "Brief Account of Pennsylvania," in *Lewis Evans*, ed. Lawrence H. Gipson (Philadelphia: Historical Society of Pennsylvania, 1939), 92.

110. St. John de Crèvecoeur, *Letters from an American Farmer* [1782] (New York: E. P. Dutton, 1926), 176.

111. Samuel Hazard, ed., *Colonial Records of Pennsylvania*, vol. 6 (Harrisburg, PA: Theo. Fenn, 1851), 98.

112. Ibid.

113. John Bigelow, ed., *Autobiography of Benjamin Franklin* (Philadelphia: Lippincott, 1868), 295.

114. E. O. O'Callaghan, ed., *The Documentary History of the State of New York*, vol. 6 (Albany, NY: Weed, Parsons, 1849), 889.

115. Julian Boyd, "Dr. Franklin: Friend of the Indian" [1942], in *Meet Dr. Franklin*, ed. Roy N. Lokken (Philadelphia, PA: Franklin Institute, 1981), 244–45. The quote is on pages 244–45, and the chapter begins on page 239.

116. Charles Thomson, "History of the Articles of Confederation," in *Papers of the Continental Congress, 1774–1789*, National Archives M247, Roll 22, Item No. 9.

117. Worthington Chauncey Ford, Gaillard Hunt, John Clement Fitzpatrick, Roscoe R. Hill, Kenneth E. Harris, and Steven D. Tilley, eds., *Journals of the Continental Congress, 1774–1789* (Washington, DC: Government Printing Office, 1904), 532.

118. Pierre Jean George Cabanis, *Oevres Posthumes de Cabanis*, vol. 5 (Paris: Firmin Didot, Pere et fils, 1825), 246.

119. Ibid.

120. Ibid.

121. Julian Boyd, ed., *Papers of Thomas Jefferson*, vol. 8 (Princeton, NJ: Princeton University Press, 1950–), 568.

122. Carl Binger, *Thomas Jefferson: A Well-Tempered Mind* (New York: W. W. Norton, 1970), 309.

123. Philip S. Foner, *The Complete Writings of Thomas Paine*, vol. 1 (New York: Citadel, 1945), 370.

124. Lester J. Cappon, ed., *The Adams-Jefferson Letters*, vol. 2 (Chapel Hill: University of North Carolina Press, 1959), 291.

125. Boyd, *Papers of Thomas Jefferson*, vol. 11, 92–93.

126. Foner, *Complete Writings of Thomas Paine*, vol. 1, 610.

127. Conway, *Writings of Thomas Paine*, vol. 1, 70.

128. Foner, *Complete Writings of Thomas Paine*, vol. 1, 610.

129. Ibid.

130. Conway, *Writings of Thomas Paine*, vol. 1, 70.

131. Commager, *Jefferson, Nationalism, and the Enlightenment*, 119.

132. Moncure Daniel Conway, *The Life of Thomas Paine*, vol. 1 (New York: Putnam's, 1908), 88.

133. Ibid., vol. 2, 462.

134. Thomas Jefferson, *Notes on the State of Virginia* [1784], in *White on Red*, eds. Nancy B. Black and Bette S. Weidman (Port Washington, NY: Kennikat, 1976), 109–10.

135. Boyd, *Papers of Thomas Jefferson*, vol. 20, 451–52.

136. Saul K. Padover, *The Complete Jefferson* (New York: Duell, Sloan, and Pearce, 1943), 503–5.

137. William Wirt, *The Life of Patrick Henry* (Philadelphia: Desilver, Thomas, 1836), 258–59.

138. Laberee, *Papers of Benjamin Franklin*, vol. 17, 381.

139. The statement that the legitimate ends of government are the preservation of "life, liberty and property" came from John Locke, *Second Treatise on Government*. As is shown in the discussion of Locke in this text, he was greatly influenced on this point, as well as others, by American Indians, whom he knew through numerous reports by Europeans from the "New World," and by discussions with Indigenous Americans who came to England.

140. Marginal Notes in Allan Ramsay, *Thoughts on the Origin and Nature of Government*, cited in Staughton Lynd, *Intellectual Origins of American Radicalism* (New York: Pantheon, 1968), 85.

141. Thomas, Jefferson, *Notes on the State of Virginia* [1784] (Chapel Hill: University of North Carolina Press, 1955), 93.

142. Paul Leicester Ford, ed., *The Works of Thomas Jefferson*, vol. 3 (New York: G. P. Putnam, 1904–1905), 195n.

143. Boyd, *Papers of Thomas Jefferson*, vol. 2, 49.

144. Ford, *Works of Thomas Jefferson*, vol. 3, 198–99.

145. David Ramsey, *History of the American Revolution*, vol. 1 (London: J. Stockdale, 1793), 29.

146. David Ramsey, "Dissertation on the Manner of Acquiring the Character and Privileges of a Citizen of the United States," Manuscript 34-297, South Carolina Historical Society, Charleston, 1802.

147. "Journals of Captain John Montresor 1757–1778" [April 4, 1766], in *Collections of the New York Historical Society* 14 (1868–1949), 357, 367–68.

148. Esther Forbes, *Paul Revere and the World He Lived In* (Boston: Houghton-Mifflin, 1969), 126.

149. Benjanun W. Labaree, *The Boston Tea Party* (New York: Oxford University Press, 1954), 27–28.

150. Ian R. Christie and Benjamin W. Labaree, *Empire or Independence: A British-American Dialogue on the Coming of the American Revolution* (New York: W. W. Norton, 1976), 168–72.

151. *Providence Gazette*, June 12, 1773.

152. Ibid.

153. Benjamin W. Labaree, *The Boston Tea Party* (New York: Oxford University Press, 1964), 133.

154. Eldridge Henry Goss, *The Life of Colonel Paul Revere* (Boston: Gregg, 1972).

155. Ibid., 123–24, 164.

156. Forbes, *Paul Revere and the World He Lived In*, 198–99.

157. Christie and Labaree, *Empire or Independence*, 198.

158. Robert J. Taylor, ed., *The Papers of John Adams*, vol. 2 (Cambridge, MA: Harvard University Press, 1977), 3.

159. Christie and Labaree, *Empire or Independence*, 198.

160. Ibid.

161. Labaree, *Boston Tea Party*, 331.

162. Forbes, *Paul Revere and the World He Lived In*, 227–28.

163. John Mohawk, "The Indian Way Is a Thinking Tradition," in *Indian Roots of American Democracy*, ed. José Barreiro (Ithaca, NY: Akwe:kon, 1992), 26, on the town meeting developing from Indian influence at Plymouth; Bruce A. Burton, "Squanto's Legacy: The Origin of the Town Meeting," in *Indian Roots of American Democracy*, 107–14, on both the development of the New England town meeting from experience with Indians and the adoption of the Indian system of land rights

or ownership. It is important to note that the word "ownership" simply indicates the existence of one or more rights of whatever extent relating to the thing in question. Ownership is virtually never total, as there are always limits on the rights involved (and/or rights that others have related to the thing), and that certainly was the case in Indian societies (for example, see Hoebel, *The Law of Primitive Man*, chap. 4, with the principles developed there applied in chaps. 5, 7).

164. Oren Lyons, "Land of the Free, Home of the Brave," in *Indian Roots of American Democracy*.

165. Johansen, *Debating Democracy*, 25, quoting Felix Cohen, *Handbook of American Indian Law* (Albuquerque: University of New Mexico Press, 1942), 128.

166. Burton, "Squanto's Legacy," in *Indian Roots of American Democracy*.

167. Donald A. Grinde, "Iroquois Political Concept and the Genesis of American Government," in *Indian Roots of American Democracy*, 50–51.

168. Bruce E. Johansen, *Debating Democracy* (Santa Fe, NM: Clear Light, 1998).

169. Grinde, "Iroquois Political Concept and the Genesis of American Government," in *Indian Roots of American Democracy*.

170. Stephen M. Sachs, "Returning Tribal Government to the Traditional Wisdom of the People: Applying Traditional Principles Appropriately for the Twenty-First Century," *Indigenous Policy* 22, no. 2 (2010). In more detail, the fourth proposal is a decentralization model stressing national and community issues with greater empowerment to social subgroups and agencies. It outlines a government that reflects more fully traditional and customary laws and norms. The authors of the proposal stated:

Our reasoning for this transition is based on Navajo history and current social behavior. The Navajo Nation historically resembled a parliamentary system and had decentralized political units. We believe that our proposed model would move us back in this direction.... Therefore, we have established four major steps to move our current system of governance from a presidential model to something more like the historic *naachid*. These steps are: 1) moderate the concentration of power in the executive branch; 2) restructure agency councils to balance power between legislative and chapter house members; 3) increase the power of the agency councils; and 4) create new mechanisms through which nongovernmental organizations can influence formal governmental processes. (63)

We would replace the Office of President and Vice President with an 11 person Executive Board, comprised of five female members, five male members, and the Navajo Nation Speaker who is the rotating chair. The members are elected, two from each of the five agencies, whereas the Speaker is a member of the Navajo Nation Council and therefore represents the interests of both the legislative branch and his or her particular community. Though the Speaker is a member of the 11 person Executive Board, he or she does not have ultimate authority over the rest of the council and therefore is a minor and not controlling member of it.... Secondly, the Agencies would gain more autonomy than what they have now. Each Agency addresses different concerns due to the surrounding topography. Therefore, the chapters would address their concerns at Agency Council, and the Agencies would have more autonomy and more representation since they have elected representatives on the Executive Board.

Thirdly, the 88 Delegates would be elected in the same fashion as they are elected today.... However, the major difference of the Legislative Branch would be the 12 Non-Voting Members of the Council. So, in total the Council would consist of 100 members. The Non-Voting Members would represent the non-profit sector on the Navajo Nation and the youth of the Nation. Since the youth population is growing at an astonishing rate and the role of women is needed, the implementation of the Non-Voting Members of Council will help eliminate some of the gender and age discrepancies. Lastly, with the removal of the entire Executive Branch, the Committees, Commissions and Divisions would have to be restructured. Therefore, we put into place four Committees: the Social Committee, the Economic Committee, the Families Committee and the Environmental Committee. Under each Committee, we placed the appropriate Program or Division. For example, under the Environmental Committee, we place the Division of Natural Resources, the Navajo Environmental

Protection Agency and the Navajo-Hopi Land Commission. Each Committee would consist of 12 members, which would include ten Delegates, and 2 Non-Voting Members of the Council. The Executive Board would appoint the Committee Members.

171. Robert W. Venables, "The Founding Fathers: Choosing to Be Roman," in *Exiled in the Land of the Free*, Oren R. Lyons, John C. Mohawk, Vine Deloria Jr., Laurence M. Hauptman, Howard R. Berman, Donald A. Grinde Jr., Curtis G. Berkey, and Robert W. Venables (Santa Fe, NM: Clear Light, 1992), 95. Compare Locke, *The Second Treatise*, chap. 9, #124, with Jefferson's writing either "life, liberty and property," or "life, liberty and the pursuit of happiness" in the alternate versions of the Declaration of Independence. See also a brief history of the Declaration of Independence on the US National Archives web site: http://www.archives.gov/exhibits/charters/declaration_history.html.

172. Laurence Armond French, *Legislating Indian Country: Significant Milestones in Transforming Tribalism* (New York: Peter Lang, 2007), 1–2; and LaDonna Harris, Stephen M. Sachs, and Barbara Morris, *Re-Creating the Circle: The Renewal of American Indian Self-Determination* (Albuquerque: University of New Mexico Press, 2011), chap. 1, sect. 1.

173. See Madison's discussion of faction in *Federalist Papers* #10.

174. Johansen, *Debating Democracy*, 61.

175. Ibid.

176. Ibid., 116.

177. Ibid.

178. The text of the Constitution of the United States is available in many places, including: http://www.archives.gov/exhibits/charters/constitution.html.

Chapter 3

The Considerable Effect of Contact on Europe

Stephen M. Sachs, Donald A. Grinde
Jr., and Jonathon York

Section 1: The Early Reports and the Discovery of Freedom

Stephen M. Sachs and Donald A. Grinde Jr.

During the first two centuries of European contact with Indians in the Americas, numerous reports from Europeans coming to the Americas were quickly and widely disseminated, and discussed in the Old World. This created a profound impact on European thought, particularly in the realm of politics and society,[1] at a time of openness to and actual change. Contact took place just as the Renaissance was spreading from Italy to France and the rest of Europe. Political change was already in progress with power centralizing to kings in nation-building. In response to this situation, an openness for democratic thinking was created. Meanwhile, corruption in the Catholic Church and other institutions brought forward movements for reform within the church, as well as the development of the Reformation.

During the same period great economic change was occurring, partly fueled by resources coming from the New World under the policy of mercantilism, together with the rise of Western science and the beginnings of the Industrial Revolution. These developments, in time, drove the rise of capitalism and the growth of the middle class, creating pressures for political change, including openings for democracy as well as shifts in the thrust of public policy. The movement for change centered first in England, and later in France, each of which went through their own revolutionary periods in a major long-term process of transformation. There, as elsewhere on the continent, a few European Indigenous vestiges of local arrangements/traditions, important in the Middle Ages, still remained as elements in the democratizing movements.[2] While many of the reports on the peoples of the Americas, and the interpretations of them in Europe, were overly positive, overly negative, or otherwise to greater or lesser degrees inaccurate, the resulting variety of stereotypes of Native peoples had a most significant effect in Europe, especially on promoting the idea of freedom. This was the most dominant result of these reports.[3]

The positive reports began with Christopher Columbus's first impression in his diary of Native people:

> They are loving people, without covertness.... They love their neighbors as themselves, and their speech is the sweetest and gentlest in the world.[4]

But the Old World view of conquest was also set into his first contact entry:

> I could conquer the whole of them with fifty men, and govern them as I pleased ... [and] I determined to pass none of these islands without taking possession, because being once taken, it would answer for all times.[5]

A leading theme in many of the reports about Indians in the Americas that spread rapidly and widely in Western Europe was that of liberty. Brandon's survey of these reports presents numerous examples, such as Lery's account from his own observation, "They have neither kings or princes, and consequently each is more or less as much of a great lord as the other." Macer, on the basis of what he had heard and read, declared, "They do not recognize a King or any superior, and will not subject themselves to the orders of anyone. Each there is King, master and Lord." Going further, Acosta, one of the best-informed Americanists of his day, stated: "A number of peoples and nations of the Indies have never suffered Kings nor Lords of an absolute and sovereign sort. They live in common and create and ordain certain Captains and Princes for certain occasions only, during which time they obey their rule. Afterward, these leaders return to their ordinary status. The greatest part of the New World governs itself in this fashion."[6]

Thomas More and Early Writings
Reflecting Indians in Europe

From very early on, important western European thinkers began reflecting ideas from the New World in their writing. In 1519, Sir Thomas More wrote *Utopia*, the work of fiction intended as a critique of early sixteenth-century English society. The book, which is largely responsible for his being well-known to this day,[7] tells of a fictitious society in South America, taking many of the ideas for the book from Amerigo Vespucci's two accounts of his voyages to the Americas between 1497 and 1502, which were published in the first five years of the sixteenth century.[8] Indeed, More tells the story as a conversation he had with one of the "24 Christians" Vespucci had left to maintain a base on the Brazilian coast and who had traveled to the isle of Utopia. In describing the society of Utopia, More, though clearly not describing an actual Indian society, is quite consistent with Vespucci's accounts, which More says were "common reading everywhere."[9]

In these accounts, Vespucci states of the aboriginal Americans, "Each is a master of himself.... These have neither king nor master, nor do they obey anybody; For they live in their individual liberty... [and] [t]heir dwellings are in common. They live communally. Neither do they have goods of their own, but all things are held in common."[10] Thus More's traveler to Utopia, Raphael Hythloday, says, with reference to European society:

> as long as there is any property, and while money is the standard of all other things, I cannot think that a nation can be governed either justly or happily: not justly because the best things will fall to the share of the worst men; nor happily because all things will be divided among a few (and even these are not in all respects happy), the rest being left to be absolutely miserable. Therefore when I reflect on the wise and good constitution of the Utopians—among whom all things are so well governed, and with so few laws; where virtue has its due reward, and yet there is such an equality, that every man lives in plenty—when I compare them with so many other nations that are still making new laws, and can never bring their constitution to a right regulation, where not withstanding everyone has his property;[11]

In setting out the governance of Utopia, More applies American Indian inclusive participatory democratic principles along the lines of Haudenosaunee and Wendat (called Huron by the French) traditional societies, discussed above. The thirty families in a municipality annually elect representatives initially called "Syphogrant," later "philarch"—numbering two hundred in total—and above these representatives, though not stated by which means of election or appointment, are senators initially called "Tranibor," later "archphilarch." The representatives then choose the prince, who serves for life, unless removed for cause, from among four individuals nominated by the people of the four divisions of the city. The senators meet in council every third day, or more often, with the prince and a different pair of representatives at each session, to discuss the business of the community. To promote thoughtfulness on the issues, a matter introduced at one session will have to wait until the next meeting to begin being discussed, and it must be considered in three separate meetings before finally being decided. Important issues are sent by the council to the representatives, who discuss it with the families they represent, and some matters are taken up by the people as a whole at a general assembly.[12]

Similarly, reflecting the communitas and reciprocity that was the general practice of New World Native communities, in Utopia everyone worked—but because all worked, only a short, six-hour workday was needed, leaving time for public discussion, education, and recreation; while everyone was provided with what they needed, beginning with the sick and infirm.[13] Thus, More's *Utopia* contributed directly to the rise of socialism as seen in those Marx later called utopian socialists, most notably Robert Owen, who launched the cooperative movement, or in guild socialism, which initiated the movement of worker and consumer cooperatives. The cooperative movement was a major element in the rise of contemporary employee participation and ownership, and later in the scientific socialism of Marx and others, as well as in the anarchist tradition. Karl Kautsky, much later, commented of More, "His socialism makes him immortal.... [And] as a socialist he was ahead of them all [his contemporaries]."[14] Thus Peter Kropotkin in *Mutual Aid* and Engels in *The Origin of the Family, Private Property and the State* include early chapters on Native Americans' relevant traditional practice.

More was not alone in assisting the rise of socialism and anarchism. The positive view of American Indians living "without thine and mine" was widespread. The term "anarchy," meaning without government, was coined by Louis-Armand de Lom d'Arce, Baron de Lahontan, who wrote several short books on the Algonkin and Huron based on his journeys to Canada from 1683 to 1694. These works made him a celebrity in Europe[15] and served as a source for other writers and playwrights.[16] This whole thrust by More and others was also a root of the political and social ideas that constituted Franklin Roosevelt's New Deal liberalism, at least partially via such Indian-impacted thinkers as Jean-Jacques Rousseau (discussed in detail below).

The Many European Writers Reflecting on Indian Ways

Numerous other writers in the first three centuries of contact also reflected upon aboriginal American ways, especially on liberty, including Rabelais, Ronsard, and even Shakespeare briefly in *The Tempest*, among many others. In Michel de Montaigne's *Essays* published in 1580, the essay "On Cannibals"[17] appears to show some influence from More. Montaigne begins his discussion of Native Americans, as did More, by saying he had met someone who had been to Brazil, and, in Montaigne's case, later, Indians themselves, though he was hindered by a poor translator. Like his predecessor, Montaigne applies Indigenous principles to criticize contemporary European society, which he finds corrupt and misguided, as indicated by its terrible religious wars, but his tone and approach are different than More's. Montaigne, Rousseau tells us, praised "the savages of America, whose simple and natural mode of government Montaigne preferred, without hesitation, not only to the laws of Plato, but to the most perfect vision of government philosophy can suggest."[18] Montaigne comments in the preface of his *Essays*, "If I might have been among those nations that are said to live still under the sweet liberty of the first laws of nature, I assure you that I would very willingly paint myself all over and go naked."[19] He considered the Indigenous peoples to be the "Antarctic [opposite] of France,"[20] still in a naturally virtuous state, without the corruption into which he believed European societies had fallen:

> I do not believe from what I have been told about this people, that there is anything barbarous or savage about them, except that we call barbarous anything that is contrary to our own habits.... These people are wild in the same way we say that fruits are wild, when nature has produced them by herself and in her ordinary way; whereas, in fact, it is those we have artificially modified, and removed from the common order, that we ought to call wild.[21]

How easy it would have been to turn to good account minds so innocent and so eager to learn, which had, for the most part, made such good natural beginnings! On the contrary, we have taken advantage of their innocence and inexperience to bend them more easily to treachery, lust,? covetousness, and to every kind of inhumanity and cruelty, on the model and after the example of our own manners.[22]

Further, Montaigne finds the Indigenous Americans to live harmoniously, finding their freedom in collaborative relations:

If of the same age they generally call each other brothers; those who are younger are called children, and the old men are fathers to all the rest. They leave to their heirs the undivided possession of their property, to be held in common, with no other title than the plain one which nature bestows on her creatures when she brings them into the world. [23]

.   .   .   .

The inhabitants of the kingdom of Mexico were rather more civilized and more advanced than the other nations of those parts.[24]

.   .   .   .

As for pomp and magnificence, which were the cause of my entering on this discourse, neither Greece, nor Rome, nor Egypt has any work to compare, either for utility, or difficulty, or grandeur, with that road, to be seen in Peru, which was constructed by the kings of that country and led from the city of Quito [in modern-day Ecuador] to el Quisco [in Chile]—a distance of 900 miles.[25]

.   .   .   .

The astonishing magnificence of the cities of Cuzco and Mexico, and among many similar things, that the king's garden in which all the trees and fruit, and all the plants were fashioned out of gold to the same size and in the same order as they would have in any ordinary garden; also animals in his private apartments, which were modeled after every kind that lived in his land or his seas; and, in addition, the beauty of their workmanship in precious stones, feathers, cotton and painting; all these things show they were no way inferior to us in industry either. But as to religious conduct, obedience to the law, goodness, liberality, loyalty, and honest dealing, it was greatly to our advantage that we had not so much as they. By excelling us in these virtues, they ruined, sold and betrayed themselves.[26]

. . . .

They are still governed by natural laws and very little corrupted by ours. They are in such a state of purity that it sometimes saddens me to think we did not learn of them earlier, at a time when there were men who were better able to appreciate them then we. I am sorry that Lycurgis did not know them, for I think what we have seen of these people with our own eyes surpasses not only the pictures with which poets have illustrated the golden age, and all their attempts to draw mankind in the state of happiness, but the ideas and the very aspirations of philosophers as well. They could not imagine an innocence as pure and simple as we have actually seen; nor could they believe that our society might be maintained with so little artificiality and human organization.

This is a nation, I should say to Plato.... How far from perfection would he find the Republic that he imagined: "men fresh from the hands of the gods."[27]

Some critics of Montaigne say that he often overstated the virtues of Indians. But this is questionable, as Montaigne spoke with Indians, and from what is known from ethnographies and some early reports, he appeared to be quite accurate on many points. To what degree he may have magnified the virtues of these societies, or overstated his view of the extent of their superiority over those of Europe, as a literary device to strengthen his argument, is tangential to the current discussion. In any case, he was influential in furthering a strong general positive perception of Indians in Europe, particularly in France, both in his own time and later.

There were numerous writings in Europe, especially in France, in which the Natives of America, often referred to as "noble savages," were used as vehicles to critique European institutions and societies. These literary efforts reached their climax in Voltaire's *L'ingenu; or, the Sincere Huron: A True History*. While Voltaire ridiculed the idea of the "noble savage," as he did most everything, seeing the absurdities in life, he still presented a quite virtuous, if not perfect, Huron Indian—who by blood was also half French—to illuminate problems in French society. Voltaire's Huron hero, Ingenu, arrives in France without the learning of long-developed civilizations, and says of Europe in comparison to North America, "The human species of this continent appear to me superior to that of the other. They have extended their being for many ages by arts and knowledge" (85–86).[28] Yet his elder scholarly companion, Gordon, says of young Ingenu, "Have I consumed fifty years of instruction, and I fear I have not attained to the degree of good sense of this child, who is almost a savage!" (89–90). Ingenu is clearly shown by Voltaire to be honest and perceptive, brave and able, so that eventually, at the end of the book, "Mons. de Louvois at length succeeded in making an excellent officer of the Huron, who has appeared under another name in Paris and in the Army. He was applauded by all honest men, being at once a warrior and an intrepid philosopher" (167–68).

Meanwhile, as Voltaire's story unfolds, both Ingenu's observations and experiences illuminate shortcomings in French society. An example is his discovery of the actions of the French crown under Louis XIV forcing fifty thousand Huguenot (Protestant) families to flee, some of whose members joined the enemy English army, while fifty thousand more were forced to convert to Catholicism under military duress. "Whence arises," said he, "that so great a king whose renown expands itself even to the Hurons, should deprive himself of so many hearts that would have loved him, and so many arms that would have served him?" (60–61). More telling is the experience of, first, the Huron, and then of his fiancée. After heroically leading a repulsion of an English attack on the French coast, Ingenu is sent to Paris to be rewarded by the King. But on arriving at the palace, he is thrown in prison without any clear cause, investigation, or opportunity to defend himself. The only way his fiancée can obtain his release is to sleep with the king's minister, which is so troubling to her that with the ineptitude of two incompetent physicians, it leads to her death. Thus, Voltaire's influential volume uses a virtuous and able Indian to expose his country's typical corruption.

Important sources, particularly in France, of ideas about Indians were the regular reports, books, and letters of Jesuits, written for an avidly interested public, sent back to France from Quebec from 1610 to 1810.[29] Many of the Jesuit accounts, which were very detailed and quite accurate, requested money to support their efforts to convert Indians to Christianity. The letters also are interesting in that they report that the Natives have no kings, everyone is equal, and so forth. These letters were read in the French pulpits for more than two hundred years and promoted great interest among the French people. One would guess that the popular message to send money for missionary work was not as interesting for French peasants as the revelation that "these people have no Kings."[30]

Section 2: Hobbes and the Beginning of Two Major Shifts in European Political Thought

Stephen M. Sachs

While the main thrust of discussion in Europe in the first centuries after contact was in favor of the new idea of liberty, not all commentators were positive, and those in the establishment, threatened by the idea, were resistant.[31] Among those with a negative view of Indians was Thomas Hobbes, who was most fearful of disorder. He had said that when the Puritan Revolution of the 1640s began in

England, he was among the first to flee. Thus for Hobbes, his misimpression was that traditional life in America was a terrible anarchy, the remedy for which was the authority of the sovereign—whatever the form of a regime—so long as the sovereign was able to protect the citizen. On this issue, however, Hobbes reflects one of two major points of change from contact first seen in his writings. He is sometimes called the first liberal for asserting that since the first law of nature is self-preservation, every person has a corresponding set of rights to protection from being killed. Thus, normally, one must look to the sovereign for protection of that set of rights to life. But if the ability of the sovereign to continue to provide that protection comes into question, then each person has the right to continue to follow their sovereign, or choose another.[32]

Hobbes was not the only political thinker of his era who emphasized the need for order. One of his contemporaries, Hugo Grotius, had a similar concern, but had a much more positive view of Indians. Foreshadowing the religious tolerance of Roger Williams's Rhode Island colony, Grotius was impressed with the Indigenous view of the value of diversity. In a Calvinist debate over whether difference was an aid or a danger to society, in a discussion that also concerned theories of the origins of Indians, Johannes de Laet argued that to be orderly, societies needed to be uniform in their religious belief.

Grotius countered, citing the smooth functioning of Indian societies as evidence that when properly handled, diversity was consistent with order and could be helpful to society.[33] Later, Grotius put this view into practice as a member of the Dutch Committee of Counsellors. From 1613 to 1614 he drafted an edict on religious tolerance, holding that only the basic tenets necessary for social order, a belief in God and his providence, should be required, with further views on theological matters left to private individual conscience.[34] It also seems likely that Grotius's view of international relations was Indigenously influenced. His view that there was a natural law under which nations were required to interrelate peacefully (except under certain circumstances) and on the basis of mutual agreement is quite similar to the American Indian practice of deciding by consensus on the basis of mutual respect.[35] It also fits with what was known in Europe of the history and functioning of the then Five (later Six) Nations confederacy.

The second shift in European thought resulting from contact was first voiced by Hobbes in *Leviathan*. Until the time of contact the classical view going back to Plato and Aristotle was that nature is in the telos, the ideally most developed form of something (e.g., the nature of the acorn is in the perfect oak tree). Beginning with Hobbes, nature was to be found not in ends, but in origins: in an original state of nature. For Hobbes, human beings needed to overcome the state of nature through forming societies through irrevocable social compacts. These social contracts are only dissolved if the sovereign collapses or is destroyed. From this perspective, whether one, as Hobbes saw human beings in their original state as bad, or as Rousseau saw people as naturally good but subject to being degraded or corrupted by negative experience, Indians were seen either as being in (Hobbes) or close to (Rousseau) the state of nature. A reflection of this, even today, is that one of the main kinds of places for the study and provision of information about Indigenous peoples are museums of natural history. As with most of the shifts in European thought from 1500 to 1800, contact with Native Americans was only one source, though an extremely important one, behind the shift. In the case of the transformation of the idea of nature, another factor is the development of Western science, which was a very important part of Hobbes's thinking.[36]

The Native Roots of the Idea of Inalienable Rights

The largest shift in European political thinking began with John Locke's assertion of inalienable rights in his *Second Treatise on Government*, published in 1690. There, he provides a basis for upholding the English Great Revolution and restoration, which goes well beyond Hobbes's very narrow and exceedingly limited set of rights coinciding with his law of self-preservation.[37] Prior to Locke (and in a very limited sense Hobbes), Western society did not recognize rights as being natural or inalienable. The dominant view was that rights should be granted to people, but that it was up to the sovereign to do so. Similarly, while the idea of the social contract was ancient, as expressed by Plato in *The Crito*, the people had no right to enforce the contract.[38] The rise of the idea of inalienable rights arose directly from contact with the spread of the idea of freedom. It was first expressed by Locke, who read extensively about Indians and met with some of them who came to England. His writing in the *Second Treatise* is filled with references to Indigenous Americans, as shown below.

The change in European thought that came with contact also included a shift in the myth of the Golden Age in Europe. Originally that involved living well in an ordered state, but did not yet include freedom for the people.[39] Based upon his theory of inalienable rights, Locke was also the first modern Western theorist to pose a philosophical basis for democracy, at a time of democratic movements in Europe. At the time of Locke's writing, except for a few scattered city-states (including Rousseau's Geneva, and some Italian city-states), democracy was rare in Europe, so that democratic inspiration came partly from accounts of ancient Greece and Rome that were revived with the Renaissance. The main source of democratic inspiration came from Europeans who went to the Americas, and especially the British and French in North America, who directly experienced extremely democratic societies, with high qualities of political and social life among many Native tribes. They saw small villages and bands functioning effectively on the basis of inclusive consensus-based decision-making, with mutual respect and support for community members. They also witnessed large democratic confederations of thousands of people, such as those of the Iroquois, Huron, and Muscogee. The European visitors and colonists noted that these participatory societies functioned extremely well, balancing respect for the individual's freedom with concern for the whole (family, clan, band, tribe, etc.), as is set out in chapter 1 of this volume.

Section 3: The Impact of American Indian Politics and Society upon John Locke

Stephen M. Sachs

A cursory examination of John Locke's *Second Treatise on Civil Government* shows numerous direct references to American Indians (in Sections #9, #14, #25, #29, #41, #43 #46, #49, #65, #102, #105 #108, #184), as well as many indirect references to them. Many of Locke's ideas are similar to, or seem to echo, practices of peoples in the Americas. On many points, however, there are differences of varying degrees between what Locke proposes, or considers an important principle, and practices in the New World. In the *Second Treatise*, Locke may have been given insights and ideas on some issues from the experiences of Native America. On other points, he may have found Native American experiences good examples in arguing for ideas that he already had, or which may have been strengthened by reports from the Americas or from conversations he had with Indians who came to England.[40] In some cases, his references to Indians are indicative either of a disagreement with some aspect of their ways, or a belief that those ways were not applicable to European life in his era.

Perhaps the most fundamental point in this enquiry is the way in which Locke developed his whole theory of what constituted legitimate government. Having disposed of Filmer's arguments for the divine right of kings in chapter I of the *Second Treatise*, he presents the basis of his theory in chapter II, "Of the State of Nature," by asserting that it is the original state of mankind in its natural, pre-societal condition that is the foundation for all societies and governments. Although there has always been speculation about the pre-societal state of human beings and how societies arose, for instance in Book III of Plato's *Republic* and in Book I of Aristotle's *Politics*, the focus on a "state of nature" as the basis for understanding people in society and the legitimacy of government is a post-contact-with-Indians idea first developed in political philosophy by

Hobbes.[41] There are likely a number of sources for this development, including the rise of natural science, with which Hobbes was
concerned.

However, there appears to be a very direct connection between
the launching of extensive interaction with peoples living close to
nature in the Americas, and the introduction of that concern in
political thought. It was thought that the inhabitants of the New
World would provide a great deal of information about what people were originally like and what the purpose of their society was.
Indeed, as has been shown above, it is known that there was a great
deal of interest in American Indian ways, both in European societies and among Europeans living in America beginning from the
late fifteenth century.[42]

It seems clear Locke believed that "Indians in the woods of
America," as he refers to the Indigenous in his second reference to
them in chapter II, #14, were close to, but not in the state of nature.
In this section, he meets the objection that there were never "any
men in such a state of nature." He argues "that since all princes and
rulers of 'independent' governments all through the world are in a
state of nature [in relation to each other], it is plain that the world
never was, nor will be without numbers of men in that state." He
makes no claim, where he could logically do so, that Indians were
in the state of nature. Yet his discussion shows them to be close
enough to the original state, in comparison with European societies, to provide a good deal of information about it. For example, in
chapter V, "Of Property," in #36 he writes:

> For, supposing a man or family, in the state they were at first,
> peopling of the world by the Children of Adam or Noah, let
> him plant in some inland vacant places of America.

And in #49:

> Thus, in the beginning all of the world was America, and
> more so than it is now.

Indication that this was a widely held view by Europeans is still evident in Native Americans being considered "primitive" people, meaning first people, and being considered "savage" by some, meaning partly, or wholly, prior to society or civilization. It is significant that, to the current time, museums of "natural history" have been engaged in studying Indians and publishing and presenting displays about them. Indeed, until the recent launching of the National Museum of the American Indian at the Smithsonian Institution, the places to go to find out about Indians were the anthropology departments of the Smithsonian's Museum of Natural History and the American Museum of Natural History in New York.[43]

In contrast to Hobbes, Locke describes the state of nature as:

a state of perfect freedom [and] ... A state also of equality, wherein all the power and jurisdiction is reciprocal [in #4] ... But though this be a state of liberty, yet it is not a state of license [in #6].

He tells us (in #15):

I, moreover affirm, that all men are naturally in that state, and remain so till, by their own consents, they make themselves members of some politic society... [and adds], in Ch. 4, "of Slavery," [1n #14], The natural liberty of man is to be free from any superior power on earth, and not to be under the will or legislative authority of man, but to have only the law of Nature for his rule. The liberty of man in society is to be under no other legislative power but that established by consent in the commonwealth, nor under the dominion of any will, or restraint of any law, but what that legislative shall enact according to the trust put in it.

The idea that the establishment of, and continued life in, a society involves a social contract is very old. It can be found, for instance, in Socrates's conversation with the laws of Athens in Plato's *Crito*.

That man is by nature free, possessing inalienable rights, and could only be governed by his consent, however, was a post-contact idea in Europe, not asserted until the "Great Revolution." Although it may have some other roots, it was completely reflective of American Indian society of the time, as indicated above. Thus American Indian experience is likely a most important, if not the primary source for Locke's view that human beings are naturally free and can legitimately be governed only by their consent.

Indeed, the use of consensus decision-making by Native Americans is an active expression of that principle. Locke does not require what he saw as the more developed governments of his day to decide by consensus. He only requires that everyone consent to the decision-making process, which he prefers to be representative on the basis of majority vote (chs. VII–X). But it is essential, in his view, that government do nothing in normal domestic affairs that is not by the consent of the governed, and, furthermore, that government does not violate inalienable rights (ch. XI).

If people living under a government are unhappy with it, Locke tells us that they are free to move to another place, or to unclaimed land, at least until they have explicitly consented to being a member of a commonwealth. That someone might move to another country if they objected to the laws of the nation where they are living is an idea that can be found in Western thought at least as far back as Socrates's discussion with the Laws of Athens in Plato's *Crito*. It was not so strongly asserted, however, until Locke, who would have been quite aware that moving to or forming a new community because of dissatisfaction with where one was living was a common Indian practice, in agreement with the notions of human freedom that Locke shares with Indigenous Americans. At the very least, it would seem that the Native American examples strengthened Locke's views on this issue. Here, as in a number of other matters, however, he does not go so far as Native people. For Locke does say that the right to move can be lost when one explicitly pledges allegiance to a "commonwealth," a regime operating by consent of the governed.

Indians commonly did not assert such a limitation (in what Locke likely considered their less civilized condition).

For Locke:

> the great and chief end, therefore, of men uniting into commonwealths and putting themselves under government, is the preservation of their property, to which in the state of nature there are many things wanting [ch. 9, #124] ... [property of people consisted of] their lives, liberties and estates [#123].

In discussing estate in chapter V, "Of Property," his view holds that in the state of nature everything is owned in common, with the law of nature allowing everyone to take from nature what they need to live:

> The fruit or venison which nourishes the wild Indian, who knows no enclosure, and is still a tenant in common, must be his—*i.e.*, a part of him, that another can no longer have any right to it, before it can do him any good for the support of his life [#25].

The limit is that in the state of nature, nature's law prohibits anyone from taking from nature more of anything than they can use, in order that there be enough for everyone (#30, #31). This was precisely the Native practice in the Americas, to which Locke refers. For while there could be bad winters or other hard times due to environmental factors, Indians generally saw that nature provided plenty for a decent life, if one took only what one needed, and did not waste resources.

But with the invention of money, in itself a convention or contract (#36, #47), for Locke it became possible and desirable to move beyond the subsistence society of pre-Columbian America. On this point he sets a philosophical basis for capitalism and is critical of

Native ways, as he sees laboring for economic development, including widespread tilling of land, as a duty:

> There cannot be a clearer demonstration of anything than several great nations of the Americas are of this, who are rich in land and poor in all the other comforts of life; whom Nature, having furnished as liberally as any other people with materials of plenty—*i.e.*, a fruitful soil, apt to produce abundance what serve for food, raiment, and delight; yet, for want of improving it by labor, have not one hundredth part the conveniences we enjoy, and a king of a large and fruitful territory there feeds, lodges, and is clad worse than a day laborer in England [#41].

In making this critique he understands the subsistence existence of Native peoples, even as he asserts the necessity of humans to evolve to what he believes to be a higher level of economic development:

> And as different degrees of industry were apt to give men possessions in different proportions, so this invention of money gave them the opportunity to continue and enlarge them. For supposing an island, separate from all possible commerce from the rest of the world, wherein there were but a hundred families, but there were sheep horses and cows, with other useful animals, wholesome fruit, and land for corn for a hundred thousand times as many, but nothing in the island, either because of its commonness or perishableness, fit to supply the place of money. What reason could anyone have there to enlarge his possession beyond the use of his family, and a plentiful supply to its consumption, either in what their own industry produced, or they could barter for like perishable, useful commodities with others [#48]?

> Thus in the beginning, all the world was America, and more so than it is now [#49].

On a number of points, Locke uses what he knows of the Americas to develop a theory of human development, for which he also draws upon biblical and other history as sources. In addition to the above example of economic evolution, Locke refers to Indians in illustrating the natural state of the family including the limited extent of "paternal power." For Locke, the parental duty is to nourish and educate children until they have attained reason and can govern themselves:

> So little power does the bare act of begetting give a man over his issue, if all his care ends there, and this be all the title he hath to the name and authority of a father. And what will become of this paternal power in that part of the world where one woman hath more than one husband at a time? Or in those parts of America where, when the husband and wife part, which happens frequently, the children are left to the mother, follow her, and are wholly under her care and provision [#65]?

Thus Indian examples are important to him in showing that there is no natural political authority stemming from fatherhood or parenthood, and that women, in principle, have the same fundamental rights as men — though, within the British legal tradition, not necessarily in practice:

> But the husband and the wife, though they have but one common concern, yet having different understandings, will unavoidably sometimes have different wills too. It therefore being necessary that the last determination (*i.e.*, the rule) should be placed somewhere, it naturally falls to the man's share as the abler and the stronger. But this, reaching to the things of their common interest and property, leaves the wife in the full possession of what by contract is her peculiar right, and at least gives the husband no more power over her than she has over his life; the power of the husband being

so far from that of an absolute monarch that the wife, has in many cases, a liberty to separate from him where natural right or their contract allows it, whether that contract be made by themselves in the state of Nature or by the custom or laws of the country they live in, and the children, upon such separation, fall to the father or mother's lot as such contract does determine [#82].

Drawing upon reports from the Americas, biblical accounts and ancient European histories,[44] Locke asserts that early societies were often formed:

by the uniting together of several men, free and independent one of another, amongst whom there was no natural superiority or subjection. And if Josephus Acosta's word may be taken, he tells us that in many parts of America there was no government at all. "There are great and apparent conjectures," says he, "that these men (speaking of those of the empire of Peru), for a long time had neither kings nor commonwealths, but lived in troops, as they do today in Florida-the Cherquanas [Cherokees], those of Brazil, and many other nations, which have no certain kings, but, as on occasion is offered in peace or war, they choose their captains as they please [#102]."

He continues by asserting that in early times:

where a family was numerous enough to subsist by itself [and it should be noted that in the Americas and elsewhere, tribes generally functioned as extended families], and continued entire together, without mixing with others, as it often happens, where there is much land and few people, the government commonly began in the father.... He was fitted to be trusted: paternal affection secured their property and interest under his care, and the custom of obeying him in their childhood made it easier to submit to him than any other.... .

Or where several families met and consented to continue together, it is not to be doubted that but they used their natural freedom to set up whom they judged the ablest and most likely to rule over them. Conformable hereunto we find the people of America, who—living out of the reach of the conquering swords and spreading domination of the two great empires of Peru and Mexico-enjoyed their own natural freedom, though, *caeteris paribus*, they commonly prefer the heir of their deceased king; yet, if they find him any way weak or incapable, they pass him by, and set up the stoutest and bravest man for their ruler [#105].

Quite correctly, Locke also saw that tribal leaders, or "kings," were quite limited in their power, too:

Thus we see that the kings of the Indians, of America, which is still a pattern of the first ages of Asia and Europe, whilst the inhabitants were too few for the country, and want of people and money gave men no temptation to enlarge their possessions of land or contest for wider extent of ground, are little more than generals of their armies; and though they command absolutely in war, yet at home, and in time of peace, they exercise very little dominion, and have but a moderate sovereignty, the resolutions of peace and war being ordinarily in the people, or in a council, though the war itself, which admits not of pluralities or governors, naturally evolves into the king's sole authority [as Locke goes on to say was also the case in ancient Israel] [#109].

Yet, when ambition and luxury, in future ages, would retain and increase the power, without doing the business for which it was given, and aided by flattery, taught princes to have distinct and separate interests from their people, men found it necessary to examine more carefully the original and rights of government,[45] and to find out ways to restrain the exorbitances and prevent the abuses of that power, which they have entrusted in another's hands, only for their own good, they found was made use of to hurt them [#111].

Locke's entire theory of legitimate government rests upon his view of people in the state of nature, and his analysis of their development from nature into society. It is clear that while American Indians are not the only source of his thinking, they contributed significantly to Locke's ideas about freedom and representative government. Since Locke had an exceedingly strong and direct influence upon the US founders, continues to be the single most influential political thinker upon political ideas in the United States, and remains a seminal thinker in the development of political thought in the West generally, Indigenous American influences upon Locke alone would be sufficient to have a major impact upon Western political thought and practice. Their direct influence, however, has been much wider in its impact, as has already been indicated, and further can be seen by an examination of writings by Charles-Louis de Secondat, Baron de La Brède et de Montesquieu, who developed modern concepts of separations of power and checks and balances applied in the US and other constitutions,[46] and Jean-Jacques Rousseau.

Section 4: Montesquieu vs. the Empire of Prejudice: The Indigenous Spirit of Liberty

Jonathon York

The question of whether or not there exists a connection between the Indigenous experience in the Americas and the political thinking of Montesquieu is not an easy one to answer, in part because

Montesquieu's own method of approaching politics is at first daunting, for Montesquieu's writings, especially his most exhaustive work, the *Spirit of the Laws*, does not easily yield itself to examination. As Thomas Pangle wrote in his treatment of Montesquieu and the political philosophy underpinning liberalism as a worldview, most scholars over the past two centuries maintain that "the work lacks order" and that this disorder reflects "the disorder of his thought—a thought which is unconsciously enmeshed in fundamental contradictions."[47]

Bearing this in mind, it is clear that even after having read the *Spirit of the Laws*, it can be difficult to articulate Montesquieu's actual message. His approach, says Pangle, is "peculiar," but one must keep in mind the observation made by Montesquieu's contemporary, the encyclopedist d'Alembert, who suggested that the apparent disorder which so many have observed in the work is misleading only to those "vulgar readers" who are unable to embark on an "assiduous and meditative reading" of the work as a whole. Only after such careful and thorough contemplation of the *Spirit of the Laws* can one recognize and appreciate the overall plan of the work, and thus make "the merit of this book felt."[48] Indeed, Montesquieu's preface to the *Spirit of the Laws* states that the work is an overall design based on long meditated principles. This indirect style of writing requiring careful thought by the reader was also undertaken by Rousseau, discussed below, and by others including Plato and Aristotle who were part of the classical revival of the period.[49]

That such an underlying order to the *Spirit of the Laws* exists, if we are to take d'Alembert at his word, therefore begs the question: Why would Montesquieu write in this manner? And for our purposes here, could this perplexing approach reveal some insight available only after having considered the realities of political systems previously inaccessible, and even alien, to the eastern shores of the Atlantic? Couched in his firm indictment of one empire, Spain, is the suspicion of religious opinion as an accessory to empire; and in his mixture of guarded praise for with subtle condemnation of another empire, England, the careful and assiduous reader of the *Spirit of the Laws* will conclude that the secret to understanding Montesquieu's perspective on politics rests most surely in his treatment of those he calls the Americans, as well as the Mexicans. In short, it is fair to suggest that without some understanding of the Indigenous polities of the Americas, Montesquieu's doctrine of liberty—so central to his contribution to American political thought through the framers of the Constitution of the United States—would likely not have emerged as it did.

Montesquieu also had a strong focus on liberty, consistent with the broad impact that European contact with Indians had on making liberty an important concern in Europe, particularly in England and France, as just discussed. Usually, according to Montesquieu, most people attach the name of liberty to whatever regime is their own. However, at the outset of his work he asserts that people harbor prejudices generally in favor of what is their own, and so their claims on liberty are likely clouded by those prejudices:

> I would be the happiest of mortals if I could make it so that men were able to cure themselves of their prejudices. Here I call prejudices not what makes one unaware of certain things but what makes one unaware of himself. (*Esprit,* preface)[50]

Further, in a single stroke in the very chapter in which he claims to define liberty itself, Montesquieu rejects the common opinion about liberty with the declaration that it "can consist only in having the power to do what one should want to do and in no way being constrained to do what one should not want to do" (*Esprit,* Bk. 11, ch. 3). By making this assertion he implies no single best and most proper regime, state, or government alone is conducive to liberty. Thus he refutes the claims he attributes to the Muscovites that liberty is found in wearing one's beard long, or that it is the right to be armed and to be able to use violence to protect oneself or to remove a dictator:

Men have given this name (liberty) to one form of government and have excluded others. Those who have tasted
republican government put it in this government. Those
who have enjoyed monarchy placed it in monarchy. In short,
each has given the name of liberty to the government that
was consistent with his customs or his inclinations. (*Esprit*,
Bk. 11, ch. 2)

It is reasonable to assert, therefore, that the Indigenous peoples
of the Americas likely would have believed themselves free, as well.
On the surface, a casual reader may yet reach this inference and
thus conclude that Montesquieu's treatment of Native Americans
invites comparison with Thomas Hobbes's unsalutary treatment of
the same in the *Leviathan*, which asserts that the Natives "in many
places in America, except the government of small families, the
concord of which dependeth on natural lust, have no government
at all; and live today in that brutish manner."[51] Indeed, one will find
language in Montesquieu's portrayal of the Natchez in Louisiana
and the Haudenosaunee in New York that seems at first to reinforce the European prejudice of the day that the Indigenous people
of the Americas were indeed "savage." Yet, in a sharp rejoinder to
Hobbes's very idea of the "state of nature" as a fundamentally law-
less state of total war for empire, Montesquieu asserts that such a
condition as Hobbes describes is peculiar to certain states of society, but not all societies, under specific conditions, and is not a feature of nature.

Rather, Montesquieu's inquiry into the nature of liberty, war,
and society is conspicuously designed to refute claims made by
Hobbes and others about human nature and society itself, thus
offering a glimpse of an Indigenous America unfamiliar to his
readers in Europe. In this sense, first by presenting a common
assumption among his fellow Frenchmen about the Natchez and
Haudenosaunee in blunt terms suggesting one not take this claim
seriously, and then by challenging a central claim of war as a feature of the "state of nature," he exposes the putative arguments of

his European brethren as mere prejudice, as fuel for the hypocrisy of Europeans relative to the peoples of the Americas.

Thanks to the prevailing prejudices of his readers, Montesquieu seems forced to defend his claim using the language of his detractors in referring to Indigenous American polities as the "police des sauvages" (*Esprit*, Bk. 11, ch. 8). What is striking about this phrase is the contradiction inherent in its construction, for "police" suggests a kind of management common to ordered communities, while "sauvages" connotes an untamed quality, a wildness foreign to the notion of said communities. Curiously, Montesquieu's reference to the police merits attention as that alone which holds liberty itself as an object. It is certainly not the police of the Spanish in Mexico who carry the stain of having "destroyed the inhabitants" through genocide and forcible conversion. Nor is it the police of England, so often cited by readers as the standard-bearer for political liberty through commerce in *the Spirit of the Laws*. On the contrary, in England liberty appears as in a mirror (*Esprit*, Bk. 11, ch. 5), ever visible yet forever beyond reach. Having alighted on this distinction, Montesquieu's portrayal of Indigenous Americans deserves closer scrutiny, specifically in contrast to those empires of Europe with whom they interacted.

Exploding Prejudice: Natural Liberty and the "Police des Sauvages"

Montesquieu begins his discussion of liberty in *Esprit* with the remark that "no other word has received more different significations and has struck minds in so many ways" (*Esprit*, Bk. 11, ch. 2). Liberty is a desirable goal for most people and, as stated above, most people attach liberty to whatever is their own. Strong in the conviction that they, and no others but those like themselves, enjoy true freedom, these people ensure the internal security of the government under which they live, and provide opportunity for their government to act both at home and abroad for the sake of that perceived liberty. However, this kind of arrangement for Montesquieu constitutes a prejudice that clouds the judgment both of people and of the government they espouse, defining that liberty in so narrow a framework that no other understanding or expression of freedom is tolerated. On the contrary, for Montesquieu liberty depends neither on such regimes for its existence, preservation, or increase. Rather, liberty as an idea remains distinct from any particular state, yet always requires some kind of government.

It is here where the reader must confront the contradiction between liberty and the notion of "savage peoples," i.e., those without government of any kind. It may be claimed, erroneously in Montesquieu's view, that those without government are free from constraint and free from the orders of other men, whether through royal decrees or the faded words of a written "law," which to he who eschews government constitutes another, albeit trans-generational, decree. How can those without government enjoy liberty? And what becomes of those who attempt such a liberty?

Oddly, one must look not to any specific passage in the *Spirit of the Laws*, but to a parable from Montesquieu's earlier, anonymously published *Persian Letters*. There, in a series of letters from the principal character Usbek to Mirza in the Persian city of Ispahan, we find the cautionary fable of the Troglodytes, who, through their folly, once destroyed their nation and very nearly destroyed their people. In this fable, Usbek foreshadows the wives' revolt in his own seraglio, but also illustrates the character of life among men in the absence of government. Rather than choosing liberty, the Troglodytes of Usbek's tale merely trade the despotism of a foreign king for the despotism of Hobbesian ferocity, after the new magistrates themselves prove intolerable. Slowly the Troglodytes of the fable exterminate each other until only two families remain (*Lettres*, p. 12).[52] The last two among these families, distinguished by their humanity and virtue, formed the foundation of a new society, which would come to be known for the citizens' dedication to the common interest. Each individual's interest was tied directly and inextricably to the common interest of the nation.

What led to this realization in Montesquieu's fable? After the people reject government altogether, preferring instead to pursue their narrow individual interests alone, the false liberty in the absence of government proves crueler than the abuses either of the foreign king or their intolerable replacements (*Lettres*, p. 11). For example, during the sowing month in their country, each decided only to plant what they themselves would need without recognizing the common interest. Because their country's terrain is not at all uniform, some farms were more productive than others, and in the dry months the people in the arid districts suffered famine while the people on the rivers had enough but would not share their harvest. In seasons with an excess of rain, the mountains were more fertile than usual and the people in the lowlands were inundated. Famine struck those who formerly had plenty, and the mountain people would not share with them.

Another story recounts the abduction of women from fellow Troglodytes, and the indifference to this of the former influential men of the failed state with their own fields to plough and own interests to serve. None sat in judgment of disputes, and such disputes were settled only with further injustices. For instance, such as when the weak man who lost his wife in turn abducted the wife of the man he previously sought as judge (*Lettres*, p. 11). Fertile farms were attacked, the owners brutally killed, and the usurpers were killed in turn by new marauders.

Yet even in this seemingly hopeless situation, there remained two among the Troglodytes who escaped the national calamity and went on to found a new order by which their nation would live. Even in the cruel despotism of the Hobbesian mold there remains opportunity for a just society to emerge. Montesquieu asserts that these virtuous men:

> were humane; they understood what justice was; they loved virtue. Attached to each other as much by the integrity of their own hearts as by the corruption of others, they saw the general desolation and felt nothing but pity; which was

another bond between them. They worked with equal solicitude in the common interest; they had no disagreements except those which were due to their tender and affectionate friendship. (*Lettres*, p. 12)

Montesquieu through Usbek remarks that the very earth seemed to bear fruit of its own accord at the hands of these virtuous men. They loved their wives and took care that their children would be raised to develop the same virtuous character as they had, and thus these two men "soon ... had the reward of virtuous parents, which was to have children who resembled themselves" (*Lettres*, p. 12). Using the examples of the self-destruction of their fellow countrymen, they taught these children the need and benefit of recognizing that their individual interests were tied to the common interests of all. In time they grew and prospered, yet remained just as fiercely devoted to each other, for as they grew more numerous, their devotion was also strengthened by more numerous examples of the virtue of their citizens. As the late Anne Cohler suggested, in the "absence of any fixed order or ranks in the population," those with the freedom to act, think, and feel within the limits established by law—in this case, the virtue of the survivors—may "abandon themselves to their own humors," but they are also free *not* to wallow in their narrow passions.[53] This is the hope of natural liberty.

The lesson of the Troglodytes in form bears a strong resemblance to fables characteristic of the Lenape Confederacy, especially the "Story of the Cranberry" and the "Hunter and the Owl," told specifically to instruct in the ways of civil conduct. In the "Story of the Cranberry," when Lenape, who traveled with the wooly mammoths called Yakwawi, reach the eastern shore, the Yakwawi become mad and trample all who are near them, forcing a meeting of all peoples—Man, Animal, and Manitou—to address the problem. Everyone resolves to subdue and destroy the maddened Yakwawi if necessary. When the last of the Yakwawi recognize the united opposition, they head to the far north, never to be seen again. The war scars the land and the people starve. However, within a year the pits the people had dug to stop the Yakwawi eventually produce fruits, which are useful and nourishing, but bitter, serving to remind the people of the war, the famine, and the Yakwawi who once were their friends.

In the "Hunter and the Owl," a Hunter is made to keep a promise to share the heart and fat of his kill with the Owl who helped him find his quarry. After he dresses the deer, the hunter starts to take the whole carcass home instead of leaving the heart and fat of the deer for the Owl as promised. With each step the venison grows heavier, until the hunter cannot proceed; if he takes one more step he would collapse, dead from exhaustion. The Owl stands before the weary hunter and reminds him of his promise, and only when the hunter keeps his word is he able to return to his family.[54]

Each of these three stories carries a similar lesson, albeit in a slightly different context. While no evidence remains to show Montesquieu's specific familiarity with Lenape fables, it is just these sorts of stories one expects the Troglodytes in his own fable to have told their children.

Furthermore, the prosperity of the virtuous survivors in the Troglodyte fable, where the earth seemed to bear fruit of its own accord, finds a parallel in Montesquieu's treatment in the *Spirit of the Laws* regarding the cultivation of crops by the Indigenous Americans (*Esprit*, Bk. 18, ch. 9). For the Troglodytes, the appearance of the earth to bear fruit by itself is seen as a result of the moderation of despotism both by nature and virtue, while in the *Spirit of the Laws* it is seen as an obstacle to the formation of states such as those with which European reader would be more familiar. In the Troglodyte nation of Montesquieu's fable, one traces a transition from despotism to failed republic followed by the genuine savagery akin to Hobbes's state of nature, and ending in the emergence of a new nation founded on a republican virtue previously unknown to the principal characters. In this sense, the fable of the Troglodytes in the *Persian Letters* serves to coax the reader into deeper consideration of the Americans.

By the same token, Montesquieu's approach to the Americans throughout the *Spirit of the Laws* evidently serves a purpose, and assumes his readers are already familiar with the Troglodyte fable from his earlier work. At first glance he appears to draw the European reader into a consideration of the Americans as wholly uncivilized, worse than barbaric, even "savage." Yet, no sooner than he attracts the reader with lurid references to brutality and even cannibalism, he next strikes with an evident contradiction that shakes this prejudice to its core.

For instance, where he claims that an American woman's garden sprouts corn as soon as she cultivates it à *la* the Troglodyte fable from the *Persian Letters*, he nevertheless admits she must still cultivate the land, a telltale sign of civilization (*Esprit*, Bk. 18, ch. 9). In his account of the Iroquois (Haudenosaunee) nations he makes the ghastly claim that they devour their prisoners, but also that they send and receive embassies and recognize the rights of war and peace. Additionally, he recounts a practice among the "savages" of Louisiana of felling a tree to gather its fruit rather than picking the fruit and leaving the tree to stand as a metaphor for despotic government. However, this practice does not imply the absence of government. Rather, this brutal absurdity reminds the reader of the brutal absurdity of French actions against the Natchez themselves.

Moreover, in Book 17, regarding the spirit of laws as related to climate, Montesquieu's references to the peoples of the Americas is for the absence of language referring to them as savage nations. In an effort to explain the degree of moderation or despotism among nations as related to geographic position, anticipating perhaps the geographic determinism of Hegel in his *Philosophy of History*,[55] he notes that the "despotic empires of Mexico and Peru were near the equator, [while] almost all of the small free peoples were and still are toward the poles" (*Esprit*, Bk. 17, ch. 2). If there be any weight at all to the notion implied by the Troglodyte fable in the *Persian Letters* that a nation of savages destroys itself, and that the Americas are seen to be peopled with a variety of nations ranging from despotic to free, then one must conclude that anyone who calls Indigenous Americans "savage" commits a serious error. This notion is reinforced in Book 18 where Montesquieu describes the hunters of the American forests as "enjoy(ing) a great liberty," so great in fact that "it necessarily brings with it the liberty of the citizen" (*Esprit,* Bk. 18, ch. 14). Among such people "equality is forced; thus their leaders are not despotic" (*Esprit,* Bk. 18, ch. 17).

Since the liberty of the citizen is cultivated among the hunters of the American forests, and since the idea of the citizen is generally understood to be the hallmark of civil societies, the reader of Montesquieu's treatment must confront the error of thinking Indigenous Americans to be "savage."

"Noble Savages" and Savage Nobles: The Prejudice of Spanish Empire

Not only does Montesquieu aim to cure men cure themselves of their prejudices about Indigenous Americans, he also must demolish the prejudices European audiences hold about themselves. Only through this means can other ideas, particularly those imported from the New World, find purchase and take root among them. To this end he chooses the two powers of Europe that had the earliest, most frequent, and direct contact with the Native Americans, namely Spain and England. Montesquieu squares the prejudicial claims of both monarchies, both rivals for hegemony in America along with his own homeland of France, with observed experience, especially as they conduct themselves in America.

Beginning with the Spanish Empire, Montesquieu forces the reader to confront an evident hypocrisy in that nation's attachment to the trappings of Catholic Christianity. While the role religious zeal plays in the overt despotism of Spain *vis-a-vis* America appears on its surface inconsistent with his treatment of Christianity itself, as with his treatment of the Americans above, these apparent inconsistencies impeach the prejudices of the European reader. Certain contradictory passages, when placed side by side, reveal the paradox of the teachings of Catholic Christianity common to both Spain and France. Montesquieu asks:

> What good could the Spanish not [have] done the Mexicans? They had a gentle religion to give them; they brought them a raging superstition. They could have set the slaves free, and they made men slaves. They could have made clear to them that human sacrifice was an abuse; instead they exterminated them. (*Esprit*, Bk. 10, ch. 4)

How can Spain, ostensibly devout after the Reconquista of the fifteenth century, subject Mexico to savage cruelty upon meeting its peoples only a generation later? After all, as Montesquieu says in the third chapter of Book 24, Christianity is "opposed to the despotic fury with which a prince would mete out his own justice and exercise his cruelties" (*Esprit*, Bk. 24, ch. 3). Furthermore, the power of religion is supposed to temper the mores of the people who embrace it, so that the cruelties of despotism may be avoided, and serve as a check against the whim of the despot. "Where would Spain…have been after the loss of their laws, without the power that alone checks despotic power?" (*Esprit*, Bk. 2, ch. 4). As one of the great bastions of Catholicism in the world after Ferdinand came to the throne of Castilla and Aragon, Spain had waged a campaign at home to drive the Moors from Iberia. In the eyes of Spanish Christians, Spain had been liberated from despots, yet Montesquieu's account of their actions in Mexico suggest Spain itself had instead become despotic.

As rivers run into the sea, so monarchies are lost in despotism (*Esprit*, Bk. 8, ch. 17). Monarchies run perilously close to the arbitrary rule of one; the role of religion in such regimes is to check that arbitrary power. The Catholic Church in Spain failed to do this; instead, it granted license for the Spaniards to commit their atrocities. Those who use religion to reduce to servitude those whose beliefs differ from their own embrace the spirit of despotism, especially if they deem their own faith more worthy than any other. Such was the mode of religion that moved the Spaniards to destroy the Aztec Triple Alliance in Mexico. The purpose, he holds, of these peoples' efforts to enslave those of different beliefs, is to facilitate the spread of their own beliefs. "On this idea (the Spaniards) founded the right of making so many peoples slaves; for these brigands, who absolutely wanted to be both brigands and Christians, were extremely devout" (*Esprit*, Bk. 15, ch. 4). Given the typical assumptions about Christianity by a reader in France, how then can one reconcile the crimes of the brigand with devotion to Christianity? Given the experience of an Indigenous American in sixteenth-century Mexico, they are one and the same.

One must recall how Montesquieu understands the link between despotism and prejudice. In the seventh chapter of Book 3 he writes that the alleged principle of monarchy is honor. For him the nature of honor is to demand preferences, to seek a distinction from others within a society, and, according to Montesquieu, honor "has good effects in monarchy" (*Esprit*, Bk. 3, ch. 7). The ambition characteristic of a regime oriented around honor, however false that honor may be, "gives life to that government" rather than threatens its principles, for the honor within monarchy is bestowed according to the rule of the king. Thus the relation of king to his subjects is not unlike the relation of the sun to its planets, "where there is a force constantly repelling all bodies from the center and a force of gravitation attracting them to it" (*Esprit*, Bk. 3, ch. 7). In a monarchy, honor makes the entire body politic move in concert, and each person moves for the sake of the common good, which is preservation of the system, despite his opinion to the contrary. Honor allows subject and monarch alike to perform difficult actions "with no other reward than the renown of those actions" (*Esprit*, Bk. 3, ch. 7).

While honor serves as the principle of a monarchy, it cannot be so for despotism. Men in a despotic state "are all equal, one cannot prefer oneself to others" (*Esprit*, Bk. 3, ch. 8). Furthermore, while the monarch may have power over his subjects because of the honor his position and his actions afford him, the despot only has power because he can kill his subjects with impunity. Honor is absent in despotism because all men in such a state, including the despot himself, are enslaved by the despot's arbitrary whim. Honor, on the other hand, "has its laws and rules and is incapable of yielding." Hence one finds honor "only in states whose constitution is fixed and whose laws are certain" (*Esprit*, Bk. 3, ch. 8). The principle of despotism is fear, which Montesquieu makes clear in Book 3 of the *Spirit of the Laws*, and while honor tempers fear among princes and nobles under monarchic regimes, it remains absent in despotisms.

Montesquieu's distinction between monarchy and despotism cautions the reader not to conflate the two; under monarchy, "the prince is enlightened and the ministers are infinitely more skillful and experienced" than under despotism. By contrast, despotism's only education is that which inspires fear into the hearts of those who must live under it. Those under despotism are dull, ignorant people, for "education is, in a way, null there" (*Esprit*, Bk. 4, ch. 4). In fact, education of any kind threatens the security of the despotic state; thus those under despotic governments are utterly enslaved. By contrast, the small, free peoples of North America do not live in a despotic system; they do not submit to fear, and they successfully resist Spain's encroachment, as the Pueblo Revolt of 1680 demonstrates.

For Montesquieu, in the absence of knowledge comes prejudice, which replaces education. "Knowledge makes men gentle, and reason inclines toward humanity; only prejudices cause these to be renounced" (*Esprit*, Bk. 15, ch. 3). Where there is no knowledge, prejudice abounds and in such a state there can be neither education nor virtue. This, for Montesquieu, forms the foundation for the Spanish Empire. Particularly, the empire maintains a prejudice in favor of that which is its own and harbors disdain and revulsion at anything not Spanish. In chapter 15 of Book 3 we find that the Spanish, upon their encounter with Americans' baskets of "produce—crabs, snails, crickets and grasshoppers," consider the Indigenous produce a crime of the Americans. These and other Indigenous American customs, including the use of tobacco and wearing one's beard in an altogether un-Spanish-like fashion, not only were alien to Spain but were declared criminal and established a pretext for the enslavement of Indigenous peoples.

Moreover, the ignorance, fear, and prejudice on which Montesquieu rests his indictment of Spain acquire a religious dimension, augmenting its savagery. As stated before, the Spanish, after having driven the Moors from Spain, asserted themselves as a Christian state. In a truly Christian state, Montesquieu holds that the citizens would be "infinitely enlightened about their duties and [have] a very great zeal to perform them... the more they believed they owed to their religion, the more they would think they owed to their homeland" (*Esprit*, Bk. 25, ch. 6). The Spanish certainly must have attributed at least a part of their success in driving out the Muslims from Spain to the truth of Christianity prevailing over the infidels. This would engender greater loyalty to the Christian religion, and as long as Ferdinand was identified as El Rey Catolico, then to the Spanish state as well. Spain may not have been a Christian state in point of fact, but the Spaniards certainly believed otherwise. The more one attributes to the triumph of Christianity, the more people would think they owed the Spanish state. Therefore, the Spaniards served the throne with great zeal and identified Spanish custom as good Christian behavior.

Consequently, the Spanish Catholicism formed the basis of Spanish prejudice for their own mores, manners, and customs. "When a religion is born and formed in a state, it usually follows the plan of government in which it is established, for the men who accept it and those who make it accepted entertain scarcely any ideas about the police other than those of the state in which they were born" (*Esprit*, Bk. 24, ch. 5). In this view, the character of the Church is nothing more than a reflection of the character of the state, and in the same stroke impeaches the very notion of religion as universal. Rather, religious opinion and practice are tied either to the place in which they originate, or tied to the place where they live. If the religion is imported, it will necessarily be transformed by the community and the place that receives it.

Although moderate government is presumed to be better suited to the opinions of Christianity than despotism, Christianity clearly does not determine whether or not government is moderate. "We owe to Christianity," says Montesquieu, "both a certain political right in government and a certain right of nations in war, for which human nature can never be sufficiently grateful" (*Esprit*, Bk. 24, ch. 3). The right of nations, in a moderate Christian context, ostensibly would leave the lives, liberties, goods, laws and religion of the defeated intact. The Spanish left none of these to the Indigenous people of Mexico. "Let Spain not be cited as an example (of moderate government).... In order to hold America it did what despotism itself does not do; it destroyed the inhabitants" (*Esprit*, Bk. 8, ch. 18). Montesquieu's account of the brutality of Spain's treatment of the Americans stands in the *Spirit of the Laws* as perhaps his sternest indictment of the arrogance of despotic conquerors, thus refuting the notion that Spaniards, and Europeans generally, are civilized while Indigenous Americans are not.

The Prejudice of Religious Opinion:
An Accessory to Empire

It is apparent from several passages in the *Spirit of the Laws* that while one may hold the opinion that Christianity is of a gentle nature and "opposed to the despotic fury" of princes, the religion is nevertheless merely "remote from pure despotism" without being detached from despotism in principle (*Esprit*, Bk. 24, ch. 3). The established religions of the world and the assumptions these established religions make about human nature stand in stark contrast to the small groups of free peoples of North America, and so it should come as no surprise that outside the empires of central Mexico, one cannot adequately describe the practices of Indigenous Americans as "religion" in the sense that religion is understood in Europe.

Montesquieu is clearly aware of the peculiar character of established religion and consequently counts religion itself as among despotic regimes. One can only speculate whether this assessment was heightened by an awareness of the Indigenous religious opinions the Church sought to supplant in the Americas, whereby through the institution of dogma, religion becomes merely another form of despotism, and the absolute rule of dogma dictates the behavior of men and states, granting license for all sorts of abuses. Although he expressly exempts Christianity from this despotic character, his linkage of Christianity with the innumerable evils that the Spanish Empire, under pretext of religious zeal, committed against the Mexicans suggests an altogether contrary position.

For Montesquieu, because religion speaks to the heart rather than to the head (*Esprit*, Bk. 24, ch. 7), the actions that arise from religious zeal are generally bold and in many cases extreme. Making specific reference to the violence characteristic of the early growth of Islam, where "the Mohammadan religion, which speaks only with a sword, continues to act on men with the same destructive spirit that founded it" (*Esprit*, Bk. 24, ch. 4), Montesquieu manages also to remind readers of Spain's religious adventures both in driving out the Moors from Iberia and the razing of Tenochtitlan. The first case appears to give the Western reader a familiar frame of reference from which to understand his stronger point, namely the indictment of Spanish Christianity for its role in the atrocities in Mexico. Yet as we shall soon see, the source of Montesquieu's indictment of religion is not to be found in his experience as a Westerner, but in his advocacy of another means of religious opinion imported from the Americas.

But first, we must consider Montesquieu's critique of Western religion in general. After the Spaniards drove back the Moors who had dominated the Iberian Peninsula for nearly half a millennium, they expanded their reach and within half a century destroyed the Mexica capital so that nothing remained of their temples. "People who have no temples," says Montesquieu, "have little attachment to their religion" (*Esprit*, Bk. 25, ch. 5). If people have their temple destroyed, and in its place the destroyers erect a new temple, in time the people will forget their old religion. It could well be noted that in Mexico today, the people, who are largely descended from those thus enslaved by the Spaniards, overwhelmingly profess the religion of the destroyers.

Nevertheless, there is more to a religion than its houses of worship. It is neither easy to profess a religion in the European mode without dogma, nor is it easy to maintain a religious belief if that belief has no heart. To that end Montesquieu identifies six principal elements that bind men to a religion (*Esprit*, Bk. 25, ch. 2):

First among these is the dogma of a supreme spiritual being, an otherworldly focus. Yet if people are naturally drawn to idolatry, even though they may not be drawn to idolatrous religions, then that dogma would necessarily join the otherworldly focus to more material aspects of worship. This is accomplished through temples, sacred sites, relics, icons, and fetishes. In this way the motivation to acknowledge a supreme spiritual being is "joined to our natural penchant for things that can be felt". (*Esprit*, Bk. 25, ch. 2).

Second, religion "gives the idea of a choice made by the divinity, and a distinction between those who profess it and those who do not" (*Esprit*, Bk. 25, ch. 2). Jewish adherents claim to be God's chosen people, citing a covenant made with Abraham and later the Israelites in their sacred texts. Muslims cite the Koran, which makes a strong distinction between those who profess Islam, i.e., submission to the will of God, and the "infidels," meaning those who do not. In Christianity, John Calvin in his *Institutes* divides even the faithful into the elect and the damned. In this regard religion separates men from each other, and "such separation … is generally linked to the spirit of despotism" (*Esprit*, Bk. 19, ch. 18).

Third, "a religion burdened with many practices attaches people more strongly than another that has fewer" (*Esprit*, Bk. 25, ch. 2). Here he calls attention again to Islam and Judaism, characterized by innumerable religious practices, and the tenacity of believers in these religions invites a contrast with those who do not have such practices, namely "barbarian and savage peoples who, wholly occupied with hunting or warring, scarcely burden themselves with religious practices" (*Esprit*, Bk. 25, ch. 2). Such people are therefore more likely to be free from the despotism of religious opinion than others. One possible exception to this assertion is the example of the Mexica, who maintained elaborate rituals to honor their deities, even to the point of ritual execution. After the arrival of the Spaniards they appeared to abandon their old gods and embrace the Catholic Church *en masse*, as William Prescott would later remark, "in about twenty years from the advent of the missionaries, one...could make the pious vaunt that nine millions of converts...had been admitted within the Christian fold."[56] However, all of the former houses of worship the Mexica had labored to build and maintain had been nearly erased, along with their sacred texts. Even so, a close examination of Christian churches in Mexico will nevertheless show that much of the pre-Hispanic iconography of the Mexica and others has been incorporated into an ostensibly Christian context.

Fourth, a part of the power of religion is to be found in the notions of punishment and reward. Since "men are extremely drawn to hope and fear...a religion that had neither hell nor paradise would scarcely please them" (*Esprit*, Bk. 25, ch. 2). The manner in which the idea of eternal reward or punishment attaches men to religious opinion is twofold in Montesquieu's assessment. First, there is attachment to the notion of reward and punishment— hope for reward and terror of punishment—which together direct the actions of men, and serve to check against wicked thoughts or actions that run counter to the laws of the state. This of course assumes that established religion "follows the plan of government in which it is established," as Montesquieu holds they typically do (*Esprit*, Bk. 24, ch. 5). In such condition crimes of the state are construed by the faithful as sin while rewards of the state are signs of righteousness, for religion is fundamentally a mirror of the state. Reinforcing the notion of reward and punishment, especially in political systems where clever criminals are seen reaping undeserved rewards, is the notion of eternity and an afterlife. In this way the believer may maintain his opinion of righteousness and restrain himself from committing clever wickedness out of fear of eternal punishment.

Nevertheless, this is not often sufficient to deter crime, for under such a system of religious opinion the afterlife is vague and distant. For the same reason the idea of eternal reward is insufficient to maintain hope among the unfortunate. Consequently, it becomes necessary for religion to establish a fifth element to bind the faithful: a pure, general morality that directs whole communities to render judgment and deter wickedness. Crowds, after all, are pleased by "the feelings that morality professes" and offended by "those that it disapproves" (*Esprit*, Bk. 25, ch. 2). Taken individually, religion assumes that men are sure to pursue whatever they think will provide the greatest gain, without regard to God or religion. Once placed in a multitude, however, their opinions will change, if for no other reason than the fear they will be labeled as scoundrels and punished, either by a magistrate or a malignity of opinion. Attention to the opinions of the many restrains people from acting on the desire to sin.

Finally, the established religions familiar to Montesquieu and his audience bind men to them through the "externals of worship": vestments, temples, votive artwork, and all the tangible aspects of religious practice impress people and motivate them to maintain and uphold the religion. This is not because the splendor of any of these externals pleases the deity, but because it pleases the worshipper. "When the externals of worship are magnificent," says he, "we are flattered and we become very attached to the religion. Wealth in the temples and the clergy affects us greatly" (*Esprit*, Bk. 25, ch. 2). Still, one would think that the disenfranchised and the destitute would shun the ostentatious religion. However, this is not so; when a church has the capacity for liberality, and especially when it upholds charity as righteous, then they flock to wealthy churches, for "divinity is the refuge of the unfortunate" (*Esprit*, Bk. 25, hc. 3). Impressed by the great luxury of the temple, even poverty becomes a motive to attach to religion. People, especially the poor who seek the church's aid, see themselves as dependent upon that church, and by maintaining their opinion, they maintain the church (*Esprit*, Bk. 25, ch. 2).

All of these motives are grounded in either prejudice or fear. In the first case, people in such religions assume they have the capacity to honor or glorify a deity; that God would want to be worshipped; that there is a proper way to worship, and that they're doing it. In the second, worshippers are again prejudiced toward themselves, in that they believe God favors some over others, and that their particular clutch of worshippers constitutes the favored lot. In the third case, men are affected by what they see, mystified by the complexity of ritual which either they or the priests perform; attention to these elaborate ceremonies constitutes a cathartic experience for the believers. While involved in the ritual, worshippers separate themselves from the rest of the world; for the believer, all the universe is contained within the ceremony. Surrounding himself with sacred artifacts and filling his mind with the order of the ceremony focuses the worshipper on the ceremony itself and whatever mystery it's supposed to represent. He thereby surrounds himself with his own prejudiced opinion.

The fourth case incorporates a combination of both prejudice and fear. Fear of damnation is evident, but ultimately depends on an overinflated opinion of the believer that he can in whatever way through his own actions offend, injure, or insult the supreme deity, that he is capable of so transgressing God that he may merit eternal punishment. Similarly the believer hoping for the eternal rewards of heaven is equally prejudiced toward himself, in that he is somehow singled out among God's favorites. Calvin in his *Institutes* attempted to relieve people of the fear that their sins would earn them never-ending punishment in the afterlife, yet could not free himself from the notion that some were to be damned while others would be in paradise. Hope of experiencing an afterlife had merely been shifted from one's actions or faith into a hope that one was a member of the elect.

Prejudice of any of these sorts automatically renders judgment on all others, whether they belong to other religions or not. Poor people see scoundrels gain great honors and take comfort in being more righteous than they, believing that in time the scoundrels will earn their just punishments, if not in this life, then in the next. Lastly, the externals of worship appeal to our vanity; our opinions of ourselves and our innumerable arts bring us to favor that which is our own. What Christian has not marveled at the splendor of St. Peter's Basilica in the Vatican, thinking it a fitting tribute to the Almighty, who crafted out of nothing the entirety of the universe? Temples are not for the benefit or the greater glory of God; they are for our own benefit.

Thus the Uey-Tlatoani Motecuzoma, according to Montesquieu, was not at all absurd when he said to Cortez that "the religion of the Spanish was good for their country and that of Mexico good for his own" (*Esprit*, Bk. 24, ch. 24). That Montesquieu includes this reference from Spain's early contact with the Triple Alliance in Mexico indicates he was at least aware of an Indigenous American sense of the peculiarity of certain religious opinions both to people and to place, quite distinct from the universalism claimed by Christianity. From this perspective, religions may be seen as "complexes of attitudes, beliefs and practices fine-tuned to harmonize with the lands on which people live."[57]

Religions in general are shown through their motivations to be particular to certain groups of people, and despite Montesquieu's assertion that Christianity with its claim to universal truth is exempt from these prejudices, he takes pains to show through example that they apply especially to Christianity. In Book 24, chapter 25, he holds that although "there are many drawbacks in transferring a religion from one country to another," Christianity is supposedly excused, for as he pointedly states in the first chapter of the same book, "the Christian religion is the first good" (*Esprit, Bk.* 24, ch. 1). Nevertheless, this same chapter calls attention to the tendency of Christianity to suffer from precisely the same prejudices and fears shared by all other world religions. For although it "wants the best political laws and the best civil laws for each people," it nevertheless "orders men to love one another" (*Esprit*, Bk. 24, ch. 1). Christianity must compel men to love one another. The dogma is absolute, and one may conclude based on all the above prejudices and fears that the faithful are coerced into this arrangement. Is this sense, Montesquieu evokes an Indigenous American sense of the unique bond of spirit and place to refute the universalism of Western religion. That he is particularly sensitive to this bond is evident throughout Book 26, which treats "laws in relation they should have with the order of things upon which they are to enact" (*Esprit*, Bk. 26). In particular, chapter 22, on the "unhappy lot of the Inca Atahualpa," once more indicts the Spanish of violating all of the principles that bind both religion and law to place: "The height of stupidity was that they (the Spaniards) did not condemn him by the political and civil laws of his country, but by the political and civil laws of their own" (*Esprit*, Bk. 26, ch. 22).

The religious belief predominant in Europe, as Montesquieu reveals in the *Spirit of the Laws,* is founded on two basic principles: prejudice towards one's own, and fear both in the next world and this one. This sort of religion therefore ultimately derives its strength from the well of despotism. For this reason dogmatic religion has more influence in despotic states than in any other—it is a fear added to fear. Established through fear, religion in the Western mode serves as a shackle against liberty. This is how Spain reconciled its Catholicism with the Inquisition's burning of Jews and heretics and how it razed Tenochtitlan in the name of its church. As Vine Deloria Jr. noted in his observations of "The Group" in *God Is Red: A Native View of Religion*, "The history of Christianity would seem to indicate that attempts to form a religious community capable of maintaining an arena for religious experiences are doomed to become involved in everything but religious experiences."[58]

Native "Religion" as a Cure for Empire

What alternative to the despotic fury of organized religion does Montesquieu propose? Religion as Europe knew it, rooted in prejudice, passing judgment often as the Spaniards passed judgment on the Mexica or Atahualpa and as the Muslims passed judgment on pagans and Christians alike, offers no solution unless rendered less visible by the power of human passions that hold it in check. "It is much more evident," says he, " ... that a religion should soften the mores of men than that a religion is true" (*Esprit*, Bk. 24, ch. 4). This turn of phrase is peculiar, and indicates an assumption on Montesquieu's part that the reader may not be wholly converted to a consideration of religious opinion counter to the familiar claim to universal truth mandated by Christianity. Here the religion he advocates serves to check the furies of a potentially despotic community, to "soften mores" instead of demanding unswerving fealty. In this sense the alternative religion would serve a worldly rather than an otherworldly aim.

Second, he proposes that "various sects of philosophy ... could be considered as kinds of religion." An especially useful sect for Montesquieu is Stoicism. For while Stoics "considered wealth, human greatness, suffering, sorrows, and pleasures to be vain things, they were occupied only in working for men's happiness" (*Esprit*, Bk. 24, ch. 10) and in exercising their duties as citizens and as men. Stoicism does not concern itself with the propagation of the faith, nor does it hope for a reward beyond this world, nor does it fear the torments of hell. Rather, the Stoics were "born for society; they all believed that their destiny was to work for it; it was the less burdensome as their rewards were all within themselves" (*Esprit*, Bk. 24, ch. 10). Such a religion would bother neither with the externals of worship, nor with a dogmatic morality expressed in public but eschewed in private. In its place one would see a restrained morality, rewarded from within the person who would but accept it, whose expression would ultimately depend both on people and place, rather than on time.

Montesquieu's religion of liberty, if in fact it is a religion at all, is precisely that described in the last century by Deloria in his treatise on American Indian religion, *God Is Red*. According to Deloria, the tribal expression of religion carries "no demand for a personal relationship with a personal savior. Cultural heroes are representative of community experience."[59] Instead, the revelation that defines the community and guides its conduct, bringing with it the sacramentals of the tribe, is "a communal affair in which the community participates but in which no individual claims exclusive franchise."[60] Even so, the free individual still figures prominently in the tribal experience of religion, for the person "fasting and praying must remain open and keenly aware that he might be chosen by the Great Mystery as a holy person ... there is not the emotional dimension of the evangelistic crusades present in this aspect of Indian religious experience.... The individual doggedly and determinedly fasts and sings sacred songs with the hope that he or she will be granted a religious vocation to serve the people."[61] Nor is there the "western preoccupation with history and a chronological description of reality."[62] When religion remains peculiar to a particular people and place, religious controversies such as those that shook Europe during the Protestant Reformation simply cannot arise, for the common historical experience of the people and the place prevent it.[63] In this way, the individual seeker of a vocation need not preoccupy himself or herself with a particular set of religious opinions; he or she need only to wait for that vocation to be revealed privately.

Furthermore, the call of the "religious" in the American tribal context, should it fall upon the person who fasts and prays in the context and for the sake of his tribal community, confers neither privilege nor reward for the Indian holy man. Deloria says:

> The Indian religious leader views his religious powers partly as a blessing and partly as a curse because of the added burdens of social responsibility.... Indian religions consequently do not need the massive buildings, expensive pipe organs, fund-raising drives, publications, and other activities that the Christian denominations need to perpetuate themselves.[64]

If this be so, then a European would hardly recognize Indian religious practice or experience as a religion at all, but instead as a worldview, akin to but not identical with philosophy. In this regard, as George Anastaplo noted in his treatment of non-Western thought, *But Not Philosophy*, "The Indians were more conscientious in living up to their principles than the Europeans were in living up to theirs."[65] Hence, it is a misnomer even to call such localized and individually experienced practices "religion"—certainly not in the sense that it is understood in Europe.

When considering his treatment of the Stoics, and the larger question of finding a link between Montesquieu and Indigenous American thought, we are led to wonder whether when referencing the Stoics, Montesquieu has in mind the likes of Epictetus or Marcus Aurelius, or whether he has fallen victim to an early stereotype of the American Indians of North America, that of the "Noble Savage." Or, conversely, has Montesquieu alighted on an understanding of the proper relationship of religion to community as conceived by Indigenous America? And if so, from what Indigenous stream did he draw this water?

It is peculiar that aside from his passing salutary reference to the Stoics in Book 24, Montesquieu has remarkably little to say about the details of Stoicism, either in theory or in practice. Thomas Pangle asserts that he praises the effects of Stoicism as "a kind of religion" where the source of the Stoics' benevolence was a "belief" that a "sacred spirit" and a sense of "destiny" lay within themselves, but that he offers no praise for the metaphysics of Marcus Aurelius and others who doubtlessly brought about these effects.[66] This conspicuous absence, as well as his stark contrast with Spinoza's view of the contemplative life engendered by the Stoics familiar to European readers,[67] suggests that Montesquieu's source for "Stoic" humanity lies not in an appreciation for the Stoics of the Roman system, but somewhere else entirely, and that in order to maintain the reader's attention by invoking the familiar, he must present this alternative water in a Western vessel.

This brings us to consider the second possibility: that Montesquieu, by invoking the Stoics, has in mind instead the now well-worn stereotype of the "Noble Savage" Rousseau would later adopt in his interpretation of the social contract, where man is born free but is everywhere in chains. This stereotype of Indian people, one of the oldest and most persistent of the past half-millennium, is identified by David Wilkins as:

> seemingly "positive" depictions of indigenous people as "noble savages" or as "enlightened savages," which portray Indians as friendly, courteous, natural environmentalists, hospitable to whites, and capable of full assimilation, though invariably poor and relatively defenseless ... helpless victims because of European and Euro-American policies that devastated tribal nations by taking Indian lands and resources, and due to the natives' apparent cultural and technological deficiencies. These largely benevolent stereotypes tended to emphasize the physical strength, manual dexterity, quiet (stoic) demeanor and modest nature of Indians.[68]

To what extent had the seeds of this stereotype already taken hold in Europe, and to what extent, if at all, did Montesquieu nourish his view of a religion appropriate to liberty in the *Spirit of the Laws* with the waters of the spring that fed it?

According to Ter Ellingson, the stereotype of the "nobility" of "savages," often attributed to Rousseau, has its true origins in the writings of seventeenth-century traveler-ethnographers such as Marc Lescarbot, a Parisian lawyer who, about a century before Montesquieu, spent a year living among the Mi'kmaq people of eastern Canada, which was then claimed by the French.[69] In his *Histoire de la Nouvelle France*, Lescarbot asserts that the people of New France:

> are more humane, and live but with that which God hath given to Man, not devouring their like, Also we must say of them that they are truly noble, not having any action but is generous, whether we consider their hunting, or their employment in the wars, or that one search out their domestical actions, wherein the women do exercise themselves, in

that which is proper unto them, and the men in that which belongeth to arms, and other things befitting them."[70]

As Ellingson observes, the Americans of Lescarbot's ethnography enjoy a means of subsistence and a pattern of conduct which the author identifies with the nobility of Europe, and even notes in passing the religious connection whereby holy men would engage in hunt planning in some American societies. That such activity, a *marque de noblesse*, is carried out "without distinction of persons" among the people of New France legally distinguishes them as equal in stature and privilege to the oligarchies of his homeland.

Moreover, Lescarbot's treatment of the Americans counterposes their perceived virtues and vices generally against those of the people of Europe, averring that:

> there is no more to be reproved in them than in us—yea, I will say less, in that which concerneth the venereal action, whereto they are little addicted....
>
> So have they quarrels very seldom. And if any such thing do chance to happen the Sagamos [*sic*] quieteth all, and doth justice to him that is offended, giving some bastinados to the wrongdoer, or condemning him to make some presents to the other.... Corruption is not among them, which is the fostering mother of physicians and of magistrates, and of the multiplicity of officers and of public extortioners which are created and instituted for to give order unto it and to cut off the abuses. They have no suits at law (the plague of our lives) to the prosecuting whereof we must consume both our years and our means, and very often one cannot obtain justice.[71]

Using reports on Native peoples of the Americas to critique European society was a long tradition begun by Thomas More, just after first contact, as discussed above. Sharpening the critique of French society by using the idea of the "Noble Savage" as a counterpoint was another travel-ethnographer contemporary of Montesquieu, Louis-Armand de Lom d'Arce, Baron de Lahontan, a petit noble himself and thus of equal stature in the French society of the *ancien regime*, but having been exiled from France for publishing his inflammatory anticlerical views. Perhaps this was a reason for Montesquieu and others not to be too direct in criticizing the church, especially in France, and writing in a more circumspect manner. After losing his estate in a series of lawsuits over inheritance and moving to Canada,[72] Lahontan resolved to denounce the political corruption evident in France with an account of Indigenous America that is by turns "sharply observed" and fanciful, to serve as a stern rebuke of French political and legal intrigue. Most notable is an imagined dialogue between the author and a Huron named Adario, where the European view and Lahontan's view of the "Noble Savage" meet head-on. The character Adario seems to be based on Native orators Lahontan had observed in the 1680s, especially Kondiaronk of the Wendat/Huron but also Grangula of the Iroquois. Lahontan presents Adario as admonishing him to:

> turn *Huron*...for I see plainly a vast difference between thy Condition and mine. I am Master of my own Body, I have absolute disposal of myself, I do what I please, I am the first and last of my Nation, and I depend only upon the Great Spirit; Whereas thy Body, as well as thy Soul, are doom'd to a dependence upon thy great Captain [King]; thy Vice-Roy disposes of thee; thou hast not the liberty of doing what that hast a mind to; thou'rt afraid of Robbers, false Witnesses, Assassins, &c. and thou dependest upon an infinity of Persons whose Places have rais'd them above thee.[73]

Thanks to accounts such as those of Lescarbot and Lahontan, the notion of the Americans as equal in stature to the nobility of Europe had entered literate circles and theatre in France for around a century by the time Montesquieu would lift his pen.[74] However, this characterization steeped either in a "vanishing feudalism of the age that inspired it" for Lescarbot[75] or else an exhortation to "go native" rather than accept French hypocrisy[76] would not be widely adopted by the humanism that characterized the Enlightenment in general. Nevertheless, one sees in the *Histoire de la Nouvelle France* and in Lahontan's fictional dialogue an antecedent for the way of life depicted in Montesquieu's Troglodyte fable and Rica's malleable identity in the *Persian Letters*, as well as references to the "small free peoples" in the *Spirit of the Laws*.

Further evidence of Montesquieu's debt to Lahontan and other European commentators on Indians can be seen in his books referring to marriage as "domestic slavery," advocating for the expansion of the acceptable grounds for dissolution of marriage to include repudiation (initiated by wives) as well as divorce (initiated by husbands) (*Esprit*, Bk. 16, chs. 11 and 15). For in his *Dialogues* Lahontan writes that women are:

> very careful in preserving the Liberty and Freedom of their Heart, which they look upon as the most valuable Treasure upon Earth: From whence I conclude that they are not altogether so savage as we are.... A Young Woman, say they is Master of her own body, and by her Natural Right of Liberty is free to do what she pleases.[77]

Yet one must not confuse Lahontan's "Adario" for a genuine Native voice, though its spirit can be used with great effect to indict the state of affairs in Montesquieu's France. Rather, Lahontan's portrayal of the Wendat/Huron leader stands, as Sayre writes, as:

> a synthesis of Indian culture and European radical deism whose speeches denounce prostitution, inequitable taxation, and absolute monarchy as well as praising the Hurons' control of their passions and disdain for the temptations of wealth.[78]

Even so, through his fictional dialogue with Adario, Lahontan shows his debt to Native America in shaping his "deism and primitivism."[79] This is the well from which Montesquieu must have drawn water, especially when confronted with Lahontan's "philosophically constructed savage, with his Greco-Roman head and fig-leaf superimposed on a naked dark body," *niip* and *mataht* held aloft, and with the trappings of the *ancien regime* underfoot.[80] This is also the image that undergirds Montesquieu's substitution of Native religious ideas for those of the Roman Stoics.

Political Liberty and the Constitution: England vs. Indigenous America

With the Book, Crown, and Scepter thus trod upon, we finally arrive at the other monarchy with regular and direct contact with the Americans: England. Montesquieu's treatment of England in the *Spirit of the Laws* is viewed by many as largely salutary, especially in the formation of its constitution, which embodies the powers of government as "legislative power, executive power over the things depending on the laws of nations, and executive power over the things depending on civil right" (*Esprit*, Bk. 11, ch. 6). However, the manner in which Montesquieu opens his discourse on the constitution of England, while it carries a superficial resemblance to the England of Montesquieu's day, does not necessarily paint an accurate portrait of the English government itself.

First of all, Montesquieu emphasizes the necessity of the separation of legislative powers from executive powers, and especially how the power of judging must be distinct from both. "All would be lost if the same man or the same body of principal men, either of nobles, or of the people, exercised these three powers: that of making the laws, that of executing public resolutions, and that of judging the crimes or the disputes of individuals" (*Esprit*, Bk. 11, ch. 6). A casual glance at the government of the United Kingdom in Montesquieu's day suggests that this separation of powers may in fact prevail in eighteenth century England.

However, a closer look reveals that such is not the case. The Crown in the eighteenth century may have been limited by the Parliament in its power to propose resolutions, but the Crown could also issue the "royal negative"—an absolute veto—against acts of Parliament, as well as suspend the Parliament altogether. In this way the Parliament, despite the elective, ostensibly representative character of its House of Commons, served ultimately at the pleasure of the Crown. Additionally, the House of Lords, composed of hereditary English nobility whose titles derived from a Crown decree, would have been inclined to support the position of the Crown, for without it they would not even exist.

Furthermore, the judicial power was generally left either to magistrates pulled originally from Lords under the Justices of the Peace Act of 1361, implying a parliamentary connection, or else from wealthy members of the community serving as Trading Justices if unpaid and charging a fee for their services, or as Court Justices if they were paid.[81] This system, far from ensuring that "one citizen cannot fear another citizen," instead guaranteed a court led by a magistrate who was not "of the same condition as the accused, or his peers," and therefore was in a more or less position of arbitrary power over the accused or the plaintiff (*Esprit*, Bk. 11.6). When compared against the realities of the eighteenth-century British government, Montesquieu's cautions about how mixing powers eliminates liberty indict rather than extols the English constitution. Liberty there indeed appears "as in a [funhouse] mirror": distorted, reversed, and forever beyond reach.

By contrast, Montesquieu's account of a constitution that begets political liberty is reminiscent of Cadwallader Colden's account of the Iroquois in his *History of the Five Indian Nations Depending on the Province of New York in America*, first published in 1727, and presages the separation of powers principle evident in the US Constitution of 1787. Colden's treatment of the Five Nations suggests an admiration of the people of the Gayanashagowa, the Great Binding Law of the Haudenosaunee Confederacy, that Montesquieu would later echo, though he would not make specific reference to the Iroquois in doing so. "Their Great Men," says Colden:

> are generally poorer than the common people for they affect to give away and distribute all the Presents of Plunder they get in their Treaties or War, so as to leave nothing for themselves. If they should be once suspected of selfishness they would grow mean in the opinion of their Countrymen, and would consequently lose their authority.[82]

Montesquieu generalizes such public-mindedness as a fundamental principle important enough for him to emphasize by writing in all caps: "THE WELL-BEING OF THE PEOPLE IS THE SUPREME LAW" (*Esprit*, Bk. 26, ch. 23). Under such a regime, if liberty consists only in "having the power to do what one should want to do and in no way being constrained to do what one should not want to do" (Esprit, Bk. 11, ch. 3), then one should want to ensure the well-being of the people, and not be compelled to do what is contrary to that well-being. This is precisely what Colden's image of the Great Men of the Iroquois shows, and also, through the power of the opinion of their countrymen, what maintains their authority. This principle saturates the Gayanashagowa, from the specific roles of Confederate Lords in keeping the Council, to the power of the Royaneh to remove Lords who do not represent the well-being of their nation or of the Five Nations, to the recognition of Pine-Tree Chiefs and their banishment from the Council Fire if they prove factious, yet retain their title as a potential badge of shame.[83] Under laws which establish a government whose leadership depends on the public opinion regarding the well-being of the community, one finds liberty and the public good braided together in a manner incomprehensible to other systems of government. In such a society one could discover a peace of mind that arises from a feeling of safety.

Montesquieu says political liberty is "tranquility of spirit which comes from the opinion each one has of his security, and in order for him to have this liberty the government must be such that one citizen cannot fear another citizen" (*Esprit*, Bk. 11, ch. 6). The constitution to which he refers as having political liberty as its object is clearly not the actual English constitution of his day, for it provides ample room for subjects to fear other subjects. Rather, the real constitution of liberty could only be found in Native America.

Thus, on careful reading, there is much indication that American Indians had a significant impact on the thinking and writing of Montesquieu, and in turn on the separation of powers and checks and balances in the United States and other constitutions. It must also be recognized that some of the constitutional influence, especially for the United States, was more direct. Discussion in chapter 2 has shown the close relations between numerous European American leaders and Indians, especially with the Haudenosaunee.

Section 5: The Impact of American Indian Politics and Society upon Jean-Jacques Rousseau

Stephen M. Sachs

Perhaps the most influential of the Europeans impacted by contact with American Indians was Jean-Jacques Rousseau.[84] Rousseau writes somewhat differently, according to the context of his concern, both between different writings and in different places within the same work—contributing to the range of interpretations that have been given to his views. The focus here is primarily upon the *Social Contract*, with some reference to *A Discourse on the Origins of Inequality* and to *A Discourse on the Arts and Sciences*.[85] As a developmental thinker, he was concerned with nature both in relation to the original state of mankind and in relation to what it was at least ideally possible for people to achieve, in order to overcome the depredation into which he thought much of society had fallen.[86] Thus he states at the beginning of the Social Contract, "I mean to enquire if, in the civil order, there can be any sure and legitimate rule of administration, men being as they are, and laws as they might be" (3).

To understand the original state and what could be gleaned there of human nature, as well as the whole course of human development, Rousseau enquired extremely widely. The histories of Rome and Greece and of other ancient societies, along with more contemporary developments, were given much consideration. He also delved into what he could find of Native peoples, most particularly accounts from the Americas, which are frequently referred to in the three writings considered here, and very occasionally from Africa.[87] His beginning point for all of this was his experience as a citizen of the free city of Geneva, a participatory democracy small enough for all its citizens to know and care about each other: a naturally good condition that he felt had been lost in most of Europe.[88]

For Rousseau, the problem of establishing legitimate government was to create and maintain a social contract that retained the natural liberty and freedom of men within the civic order. A reading of *the Social Contract* shows Rousseau to be passionate about liberty:

> If we ask what precisely consists the greatest good of all, which should be the end of every system of legislation, we shall find it reduce itself to two main objects, liberty and equality [Bk. II, ch. XI, p. 49].

> To renounce liberty is to renounce being a man, to surrender the rights of humanity and even its duties. For him who renounces everything no indemnity is possible. Such a renunciation is incompatible with man's nature; to remove all liberty from his will is to remove all morality from his acts. Finally, it is an empty and contrary convention that sets up, on one side, absolute authority, and on the other, unlimited obedience [Bk. I, ch. IV, p. 9].

That liberty was natural, Rousseau saw in Indians of the Americas, following what has been described of their societies above:

> The American savages, who go naked, and live entirely on the products of the chase, have always been impossible to subdue. What yoke, indeed, can be imposed on men who need nothing [*A Discourse on the Arts and Sciences*, "The First Part," p. 147, footnote 1]?

> So savage man will not bend his neck to the yoke to which civilized man submits without a murmur, but prefers the most turbulent state of liberty to the most peaceful slavery... when I behold numbers of naked savages, that despise European pleasures, braving hunger, fire, the sword, and death, to preserve nothing but their independence, I feel that it is not for slaves to argue about liberty [*A Discourse on the Origin of Inequality*, "The Second Part," p. 256].

Where for Locke, the way to protect natural liberty within society was through a social contract setting up limited government under which citizens gave up certain rights to representative decision by the government, for Rousseau:

> The problem is to find a form of association which will defend and protect with the whole common force the person and goods of each associate, and in which each, while uniting himself with all, may still obey himself alone, and remain as free as before [Bk. I, ch. VI, pp. 13–14].

This is the fundamental problem, for which the *Social Contract* offers this solution:

> These clauses, properly understood, may be reduced to one—the total alienation of each associate, together with

all his rights, to the whole community; for in the first place, as each gives himself absolutely, the conditions are the same for all; and, this being so, no one has interest in making them burdensome to others [Bk. I, ch. VI, pp. 13–14].

For this to be the case, the people had to be the sovereign, extremely involved in the affairs of the state, and making all legislative decisions directly by their own vote without intervening representatives. This required a good quality decision making process so that the result would be the "general will," and not the subverted "will of all" (Bk. I, ch. VII; Bk. II, chs. I, III, and IV; Bk. III, chs. XII–XV).

Rousseau learned of this very participatory form of politics from his own Geneva, from ancient history and from reports of Indigenous Americans:

I dare not speak of those happy nations who did not even know the name of many vices which we find difficult to suppress; the savages of America, whose simple and natural mode of government Montaigne preferred, without hesitation, not only to the laws of Plato, but to the most perfect vision of government philosophy can suggest [*A Discourse on the Arts and Sciences*, "The First Part," p. 153, footnote 1].

As we have seen in our brief overview of traditional Indian governance in chapter 1, many Native American nations enjoyed what Rousseau required: an extremely active citizenry, concerned about every aspect of community affairs, deciding with the participation of everyone concerned. There were, however, two differences between Indian politics and the functioning "sovereign" of Rousseau. First, in Indian societies decisions were generally made by some sort of consensus, to the point of unanimous consent, where Rousseau called for majority vote, except on important matters where a greater level of agreement might be required (Bk. IV, ch. II, p. 106). Second, Indian nations were organized as tribes, and did not have the strength of sovereignty that constituted Rousseau's state, which would have run counter to Indian sensibility in limiting individual (whether person, family, or other grouping) freedom, except on special occasions, such as the later buffalo hunts of Plains tribes, after the arrival of the horse, where coordinated hunting was enforced to prevent the herd from being stampeded away before the bulk of the hunters could position themselves to descend upon the buffalo in a coordinated manner.[89]

Nevertheless, several fundamental aspects of the way in which Rousseau would have participatory decision making function are in agreement with the way American Indian democracy functioned, as was generally the case with tribal societies, including those discussed in ancient histories to which Rousseau makes frequent reference, including in Bk. III, ch. XII, p. 90, where he says:

> If we went back to the earliest history of nations, we should find that most ancient governments, even those of monarchical form, such as the Macedonian and Frankish, had similar councils [of the whole people regularly deciding public issues].

Some of these practices continued in post-tribal democracies, such as in Rome, which Rousseau discusses at length. In these cases, it is hard to say which of these sources had what degree of influence upon his thinking. It seems likely that they often interacted with each other, with current reports from America often providing depth of insight to points developed from ancient history, as well as reinforcing some of those views.

For example, Rousseau is very concerned about the development and maintenance of democratic culture (Bk. II, chs. III, VII–X and XII; Bk. III, chs. IV, V, XIV, and XV; Bk. IV, chs. I, II, IV, VII, and VIII), and about public opinion as a major force in governance:

> Along with these three kinds of law goes a fourth, most important of all, which is not graven on tablets of marble

or brass, but on the hearts of citizens. This forms the real constitution of the State, takes every day new powers, when other laws decay or die out, restores them or takes their place, keeps a people in the ways it was meant to go, and insensibly replaces authority by the force of habit. I am speaking of morality, of custom, above all of public opinion; a power unknown to political thinkers, on which none the less the success of everything depends. With this the great legislator [founder] concerns himself in secret, though he seems to confine himself to particular regulations; for these are only the arc of the arch; while manners and morals, slower to rise, form in the end its immovable keystone [Bk. II, ch. VI, p. 53].

In a republic the public voice hardly ever rises raises to the highest positions men who are not enlightened and capable, and such as to fill them with honor; ... The people is far less often mistaken in its choice than the prince [Bk. III, ch. VI, p. 72].

The better the constitution of a State is, the more do public affairs encroach on private in the minds of the citizens. Private affairs are even of much less importance, because the aggregate of the common happiness furnishes a greater proportion of that of each individual, so that there is less for him to seek in particular cares. In a well-ordered city every man flies to the assemblies: under a bad government no one cares to stir a step to get to them, because no one is interested in what happens there, because it is foreseen that the general will not prevail, and lastly because domestic cares are all absorbing. Good laws lead to the making of better ones; bad ones bring about worse. As soon as any man says of the affairs of the State, *What does it matter to me?* The State may be given up for lost [Bk. II, ch. XV, pp. 93–94].

As we have seen, in traditional American Indian communities, the people were extremely involved with public affairs, often making great efforts to attend public discussions, where they participated enthusiastically. For leaders, the people chose those with the best qualities for the position, and in honoring them made them strong role models. Indian societies were quite flexible to changing conditions, applying their basic values in new ways according to changes of circumstance. The basic values were maintained, first, through the teachings of respected elders, who provided wisdom in how to apply them to new conditions;[90] and second, by the women of the community, individually as mothers, but especially "grandmothers" (a role played by any elder women in the community who might encounter children, or adults who were their juniors, and were called "Grandmother," and in one sense were considered to be so related, even though they might not be related by blood), and by the collective voice of women, led by their elders.[91]

Rousseau recognizes this role for women in a well-working participatory society, saying of the women of Geneva, they are "the chaste guardians of our morals, and the sweet security for our peace, exerting on every occasion the privileges of the heart and of nature, in the interests of duty and virtue (*A Discourse on the Origin of Inequality*, "Dedication to the Republic of Geneva," p. 187). More important, Rousseau perceived that "The most ancient of all societies, and the only one that is natural, is the family" (Bk. I, ch. II, p. 4). He saw in tribal relations the closeness of an extended family in which everyone was aware of and enjoyed their relationship to everyone else, with its interlocking set of obligations and affinities of the heart.[92] This perception of oneness of the citizenry, which he also speaks of as a virtue of a small community, is an important element for him in a well-working, strong, participatory state that needs to avoid divisive differences of wealth (Bk. II, ch. XI) and religion (Bk. IV, ch. VIII).

As to the role that religion or spirituality played in maintaining and supporting well-working Indian nations, Rousseau had so much evidence from various sources of religion's playing an essential role in the maintenance of the state, that the aboriginal American examples likely only confirmed his already strongly held conclusions. The interesting thing is that in dealing with the problem of the multiplicity of religions of his own time, he, knowingly or unknowingly, followed the same principles that guided traditional Indian people in dealing with diversity, though likely for partially different reasons.

In the final chapter, before concluding *The Social Contract*, on "Civil Religion" (Bk. IV, ch. VIII, p. 140), he says that "tolerance should be given to all religions that tolerate others, so long as their dogmas contain nothing contrary to the duties of citizenship." This is in complete agreement with the principles of respect and of the circle, which though stated differently by different peoples, were widely accepted across pre-Columbian America. First, as all people, all beings, and indeed all things are alive with spirit and are all related, everyone and everything is worthy of respect. Second, each person is born into a different place in the circle of life or being. The places in the circle have no meaning without the context of the whole circle, but there is no circle without each individual place, which has its own quality and way of seeing. Therefore, no decision can be made without hearing from everyone. While no one can completely understand the whole, in order to live well, one needs to come to know something about all the places.

When it came to leadership and administration—which Rousseau called "government"—he approved the fact that Indian communities, along with tribally oriented ancient societies generally, chose their best and most experienced people as leaders, whether formally or by informal consensus:

> The first societies governed themselves aristocratically. The heads of families took counsel together on public affairs. The young bowed without question to the authority of experience. Hence such names as priests, elders, senate, and

gerontes. The savages of North America govern themselves in this way even now, and their government is admirable.

. . . .

There are then three sorts of aristocracy—natural, elective and hereditary. The first is only for simple peoples; the third is the worst of all governments; the second is the best, and is aristocracy properly called [Bk. III, ch. V, p. 67].

Rousseau recognized that direct democracy alone was best suited for small nations. Understanding that the Europe of his age required large countries, he hinted at some possible solutions for adapting his participatory principles for government—the only regime he accepted as legitimate, in principle—to large nations:[93]

if the State cannot be reduced to the right limits, there is still one resource; this is to allow no capital, to make the seat of government move from town to town, and to assemble by turn in each the Provincial Estates of the Country [Bk. III, ch. XIII, p. 91].

This was the way in which the Muscogee (Creek) Nation, of what is now the Southeastern United States, decided federation affairs (and it is essentially representative of the practice of traditional tribal federations). By doing so, they assured a balance of participation over time and maintained the principle of equal respect for people everywhere, as Rousseau appears to have been aware. Thus, this first method is related to the second that he only hints at in Book III, chapter XV, when he says:

I will show later on how the external strength of a great people may be combined with a convenient polity and good order of a small state....

I had intended to do this in a sequel to this work, when in dealing with external relations I came to the subject of confederations. The subject is quite new, and its principles have still to be laid down [pp. 96–97].

Leagues of cities, as alliances and trading networks, had long been used in Europe by Rousseau's time, and city-states had sometimes set up colonies that either had a degree of autonomy or were essentially independent allies who paid tribute to the place (city-state) of origin. But fully democratic federations, such as those of the Muscogee, Huron, and Six Nations, were not known to Europeans prior to their coming to the New World. Benjamin Franklin and others among the US founders acknowledged the merit of federating as Indian nations had, by first proposing the Albany Plan of Union for the British Colonies, and then by putting the idea into practice, initially under the Continental Congress and the Articles of Confederation, and later with the federalism of the Constitution. There is no question that on this point Native Americans had a profound effect upon Western political thought and practice.[94]

There are a number of comments that Rousseau makes in *A Discourse on the Origin of Inequality* about people at the earliest times in the state of nature that do not accurately describe Indians. For example:

Now savage man, being destitute of every species of intelligence, can have no passions save those of the latter kind: his desires never go beyond his physical wants. The only goods he recognizes in the universe are food, a female and sleep, the only evils he fears are pain and hunger [The First Part, p. 210]....

His soul, which nothing disturbs, is wholly wrapped up in the feeling of its present existence, without any idea of the future, however near at hand; while his projects, as limited as his views, hardly extend to the close of the day [The First Part, p. 211].

These statements clearly do not fit Indian people of the fifteenth century who valued wisdom and planned carefully for the future, as far as the seventh generation to come, as Rousseau would agree. These descriptions are Rousseau's view of the earliest times in the state of nature, "before men had so multiplied that the natural produce of the earth was no longer sufficient for their support" (The First Part, p. 212). He clearly sees Indians at a later stage, and not even of the later stages of the state of nature, but somewhat beyond it, for he refers to the "Caribbeans, who have as yet least of all deviated from the state of nature" (The First Part, p. 229).

Most of Rousseau's observations about Indians at the time they first became widely known to Europeans were correct, contributing significantly to his political thought. Rousseau, among many in France in his day interested in the idea of liberty coming from Indigenous Americans, was the most influential thinker for the French Revolution, whose battle cry of "Liberty, Equality, Fraternity" was revived directly by Rousseau, with American Indian inspiration, out of the remnants of European Indigenous democracy and mutual support, as it had expanded in the Middle Ages, before being repressed by the rising hierarchy. Evidence of the long history of this slogan, for example, is that there are ancient statues representing these three values in Notre Dame Cathedral in Paris.[95]

Through leading intellectuals like Rousseau, as well as Locke and Montesquieu, American Indians have had a considerable impact upon European thinking about politics and society. Much of this has come back to impact views and events in the United States, as in Franklin Roosevelt's New Deal Liberalism. Moreover, the rise of the idea of freedom, particularly as it was transmitted by Locke, was so strongly received in the West that it has changed the framework of discussion ever since, causing a great many of those favoring privilege to make their arguments in terms of freedom, by interpreting the concept to mean freedom to use one's money and property as one wishes, to the point that in the case of *Citizens United v. Federal Election Commission*[96] the court majority effectively said that money is speech, and one has the right to spend as much as one wishes in expressing one's opinion. Thus freedom in elections could be seen as upholding the principle of "one dollar, one vote," rather than "one person, one vote."

Section 6: American Indian Impact on the Development of Socialism and Anarchism into the Nineteenth Century and Beyond

Stephen M. Sachs

The Native American roots of socialism and anarchism in the West sprang from the large number of widely circulated reports by Europeans coming to the Americas in the early years of contact, to the effect that Indigenous people held property in common, and that with no government and much mutual support, the Indians lived freely and well. The pictures of Indigenous peoples in these reports as living naturally according to what were later called socialist and anarchist principles were amplified in the "Old World" by numerous European writers, beginning with Thomas More's aforementioned *Utopia*, which had the rise of the socialist and anarchist traditions in Europe. As Friedrich Engels noted much later,[97] such ideas were put forth in the sixteenth, seventeenth, and eighteenth centuries by a range of French writers, including Montaigne, Voltaire, and above all Rousseau, who were greatly influenced by the aborigines of the Americas. This was followed at the end of the eighteenth and beginning of the nineteenth century by the further promotion of such ideas in the writings of the "Utopian Socialists,"[98] including Saint-Simon, Fourier, and Robert Owen.

The influence of American Indians was mostly, if not entirely, indirect for a great many of the socialist and anarchist writers and leaders. In most instances, it comes through Native-influenced chains of thought launched by their distant predecessors, including those discussed above. In contemplating the socialists below, the connection of each of these thinkers to their predecessors is developed as far as possible. It needs to be noted, also, that as ideas and perspectives enter a culture, they spread and evolve more subtly over time, as they interact with other lines of thought. Collectively and individually, the mix of past and current ideas is received by each person and social group through the lenses of their experience, becoming transformed as they are passed on to varying extents in a dynamic process that is difficult, and at times impossible, to delineate. Often the best that can be done to illuminate the possibility of an indirect influence is to show a connection to such thought in the past, and then to find consistencies in the expression or action of the individual being considered with the perspective of the suspected influence. That is part of the undertaking below. In most cases, however, it is impossible to do more than estimate the extent of an influence, as similar thoughts are often independently created or arise from different yet somewhat similar sources of inspiration, or emerge from quite different perspectives, coming to similar conclusions.

The Instance of Robert Owen and Guild Socialism

Robert Owen[99] is particularly interesting to consider, in exploring the question of what the Native American impact may have been on his thinking, as well as upon other founders of the socialist movement. Owen was born in the small Welsh town of Montgomeryshire, Great Britain, in 1771 to a small businessman and a farmer's daughter. There he received all of his formal education by the age of ten. At twenty-one, having worked in several factories, he became manager of the Chorlton Twist Mills in Manchester, England. As a result of his managerial skills, entrepreneurial spirit, and developing progressive moral ideas, he was elected to the Manchester Literary and Philosophical Society, which discussed the work and proposals of Enlightenment philosophers and reformers. He was intellectually and practically active until his death on November 17, 1858.

There is no evidence that Owen read Rousseau in particular, to whom some of his educational and sociopolitical ideas seem similar—in fact he said that his ideas were his own, coming out of his personal experience. But his experience included discussion of the progressive ideas of his time and earlier, which reflected the influence of Indians, among other continuing and newer strands of thought. As G. D. H. Cole points out, Owen read widely to stimulate his own thinking, not to adopt the ideas of others. Even if Owen's ideas were his own, they were developed from his reading and in dialogue with others.[100]

Indeed, while it may be more true of Owen than of most people, most individuals, however influenced by others, make their own choices, and express their unique creativity within the context of their circumstances. Consistent with Owen's own view that one's character and thinking are shaped by one's environment, it appears that his thinking was impacted by the stream of ideas with Native American roots that were common in Britain in the late eighteenth and early to mid-nineteenth century.[101] Even if Owen's ideas were entirely his own, without the slightest indirect impact of American Indian thinking, it is unlikely they would have had much impact had they not been relevant to the thinking and events of his time and place, which included developments arising from American Indigenous influences among many interacting and developing sources of ideas. Thus, Owen's case is helpful for indicating the complexity of the issue of determining the sources of influence on someone, for these can range from the very direct and obvious to the quite indirect and subtle.[102]

Robert Owen's reformist ideas and efforts involved important initiatives in several fields. The first concerned education, which he believed critical for any society, as it was the means for forming character, as well as the basis of happiness. To Owen, sufficient proper education was the basis of good living, good fellowship, and good work, which were directly interrelated.[103] Consistent with American Indian views about young people's needing to learn early to be respectful of each other and of all beings—including oneself—in order to become collaborative members of society, Owen understood that proper education was the foundation for developing a harmonious society and friendly international relations.[104] He believed, as did Indigenous Americans, that to be a proper participant in a collaborative democratic community, one had to combine a strong sense of self with a respectful attitude and collaborative values. Indeed, he believed the proper way for humanity to proceed, via education for, and experience of, collaboration, was to achieve a single worldwide "Co-operative Commonwealth" united by the bonds of reason and affection. An important source of Owen's persuasiveness and influence was the feeling he gave all with whom he interacted that he cared about them. His assertion of equalitarianism appears to have been based in a genuine love of all people.[105]

Also, Owen followed the American Indian view of the uniqueness of every individual, which needed to be taken into account in their upbringing. He asserted that teachers should study the mind of each child, treating each as a unique reasoning creature, to help the child understand things in their own terms and in light of their own experiences. Referring to children's minds, which he saw as quite "plastic," Owen wrote: "These original compounds, like other works of the Great Directing Power, possess endless variation," so that each needs to be worked with according to its own way of learning, in order to create thoughtful, collaborative individuals, capable of working, dialoguing, and living together harmoniously.[106]

In line with Indigenous American thinking, Owen agreed with Rousseau that children were naturally good, and that their upbringing ought to empower the development of their qualities. Owen insisted that proper learning needed to be enjoyable, stimulating all the senses, not forcing or overworking the student. Emphasizing forced memorization, common in much of the education of Owen's day, was doubly bad, as it made learning a hard chore—rather than encouraging natural curiosity and joy in learning. The rote learning approach discouraged thoughtfulness and appreciation of difference of perspective. Thus, "boys and girls are to be taught in the school to read, and to understand what they read."[107]

Owen also promoted a well-rounded education. While directly learning reading, writing, and mathematics, children should also enjoy music and dancing, learn through time in nature and in play, as well as in the classroom. Moreover, learning ought to use varied media, including pictures, charts, materials such as colored blocks, and natural objects such as flowers and stones, and diverse activities, as well as reading, lecture, and discussion. For Owen moral education needed to begin at birth, but in order not to overstrain the child, formal schooling ought not begin too early. At the factory Owen managed at New Lanark, this formal education did not begin until young people were at least five. For Owen, schooling was not just for the elite, it was essential for all. Consequently, it was a critical element in his cooperative factory, and in the collaborative communities he initiated and inspired.[108]

What Owen aimed for was an equalitarian cooperative world, composed of collaborative associations and societies. This is fully consistent with Indigenous values. He attempted to put this into practice first, so far as limited conditions would allow, by taking over the management of the cotton mill at New Lanark in 1800.[109] There, he moved to improve the working conditions and lives of the workers. This eventually included rearrangement and improvement of the machinery, shortening of the hours of work (which was accompanied by an increase in production), elimination of labor of children under ten years of age, and the provision of decent housing for all workers, schooling and playgrounds for all employees' children (in a day school for those under ten, and for working children after work), lecture halls for adult education, free medical care for employees and families, along with a sick club. A savings bank, an employee-run system of moral education and regulation at work, and sanitary education and inspection in the houses were also provided.

When an embargo on cotton sales to Britain by the United States forced a factory shutdown in 1806, Owen prevailed on his fellow investors to continue to pay full wages through the production stoppage. With the formation of a new partnership of ownership of the New Lanark mill in 1813, Owen included in the contract that "all profits made in the concern beyond five percent, per annum on the capital invested shall be laid aside for the religious, educational and moral improvement of the workers, and the community at large."[110]

The same equalitarian cooperative principles, paralleling the reciprocal relationships of American Native societies and of writers influenced by them from More through Rousseau, were central to the cooperative communities and enterprises that Owen founded and inspired.[111] At New Harmony, in Indiana, for instance, a committee drew up an initial constitution founded on the equality of all settlers. The village was segmented into six departments: agriculture; manufacturing; literature, science, and education; domestic economy; general economy; and commerce. Each department elected an intendant, who appointed four superintendents, with all of these officers constituting the governing council of New Harmony.

Later, following a philosophical disagreement and some practical problems between Owen and one of the principal investors, William Maclure, the community divided into two distinct groups who lived on outlying portions of the property, each governed directly by its adult members. This governing arrangement was more in keeping with Owen's dislike of the divisive potential of representative democracy, and was more closely aligned with the participatory principles and agreeable separation of irreconcilable factions of Indigenous societies, which was also central to Rousseau. Owen, however, was foremost a proponent of equalitarian cooperation, and less so of participatory democracy per se, particularly as a leader attempting to promote and establish a new way of associating, in which he could at times be fairly inflexible, despite his otherwise strong aversion to dogmatism.[112]

Earlier in his reformist career, Owen had attempted to have his social, political, and economic ideas accepted in society, and enacted by the British Parliament on the basis of logical argument. Despite his success at New Lanark and despite attracting many supporters,

Owen found his powers of persuasion limited. Upon returning to England from the United States in 1829, and particularly after a major political change in England in 1832, Owen shifted to working with the rising working-class movement, of which he became a major leader for a number of years, until conditions again shifted, and his ideas became less relevant in the immediate working-class struggle.[113] In his role as a leader of labor, Owen also developed a new way of evaluating the price of commodities, based primarily on the value of the labor put into producing them, which when used in practice would eliminate factors not related to their actual cost, such as speculation, thus tending to prevent wealth and the power related to it from concentrating.[114] This was entirely consistent with Indigenous socioeconomic values that stressed essential equality, honored contributing to the community (in this case by paying only for labor), and abhorred hoarding. This system was used by a series of labor exchanges, which set prices by adding the cost of the materials, together with the current wages for the time spent in doing the work (which for many items could be averaged and standardized), plus a penny per shilling for the expenses of the exchange. In addition, labor unions began creating worker cooperatives, especially for unemployed workers, which fit the Indigenous values of mutual support and collaboration.

While Owen's immediate reformist efforts had rather limited impact, they produced important long-term legacies. One was the development of the cooperative movement, of worker and consumer cooperatives, which are widespread around the world today. The most developed existing cooperative form is the highly successful federation of worker and supporting cooperatives centered at Mondragon, in Spain (discussed in the politics and economics chapters of part II of this book). The second legacy is the system of guild socialism, featuring worker cooperatives (often supported by consumer and other cooperatives) run by labor unions. Such a system flourished under a Labor government in Great Britain in the early 1900s. It inspired a similar syndicalism in France (and was proposed elsewhere), and likely contributed significantly to

Yugoslavia's development of an economy based on worker and social self-management as an alternative to Soviet-style communism, following Yugoslav President Tito's split with Stalin in 1950.[115]

Marx, Engels, and Scientific Socialism

Karl Marx, born in 1818 in Trier, Prussia, developed his basic theory of "scientific socialism," in which he was later joined by Friedrich Engels (whom he first met in 1842), long before he is known to have read directly of American Indians or other Indigenous peoples. But a clear chain of awareness of Indian ways for Marx is evident through Locke, Rousseau, and other prior writers, whom Marx began to read at least as early as 1836, as a philosophy student.[116] Indeed, Marx refers to and quotes Locke and Rousseau a number of times. For Locke, this includes: in *Capital*, part 1 ("Commodities and Money"), chapter 1, "Commodities," quoting, "The natural worth of anything consists in its fitness to supply the necessities, or serve the conveniences of life;"[117] and discussing Locke's rhetorical importance in "the bourgeois transformation of English society" in *The Eighteenth Brumaire of Louis Bonaparte*."[118] Engels also mentions Locke, including in discussing the shift of looking at objects in isolation from the sciences to philosophy, which "begot the narrow, metaphysical mode of thought of the last [eighteenth] century" in *Socialism: Utopian and Scientific*.[119] In the letter to Joseph Bloch, September 21–22, 1890, on historical materialism, Engels wrote, "and when the fight of absolute monarch against the people was beginning in England. Locke, both in religion and politics, was the child of the class compromise of 1688."[120]

Rousseau, whom we have shown above to be closer to Indigenous thinking than Locke, and whose philosophy is closer to that of Marx and Engels than his English predecessor, is discussed by both scientific socialists. In *On the Jewish Question*, a young Marx, in 1843, in building on a quote from Rousseau, begins to indicate the need for humanity to evolve to the point of returning, in an expanded form, to the original freedom of Indigenous societies, a major part of his and Engels's historical theory, as we show below.

As Marx states in considering how, consistent with Indigenous principles, people need to be transformed from alienated competing individuals into fully human collaborating members of a mutually supporting society:

> The abstract notion of political man is well formulated by Rousseau:
>
> "Whoever dares undertake to establish a people's institutions must feel himself capable of changing, as it were, human nature itself, of transforming each individual who, in isolation, is a complete but solitary whole, into a part of something greater than himself, from which in a sense, he derives his life and his being; [of changing man's nature in order to strengthen it;] of substituting a limited and moral existence for the physical and independent life [with which all of us are endowed by nature]. His task, in short, is to take from a man his own powers, and to give him in exchange alien powers which he can only employ with the help of other men."
>
> Every emancipation is a restoration of the human world and of human relationships to man himself.
>
> Political emancipation is a reduction of man, on the one hand to a member of civil society, an independent and egoistic individual, and on the other hand, to a citizen, a moral person.
>
> Human emancipation will only be complete when the real, individual man has absorbed into himself the abstract citizen; when as an individual man, in his everyday life, in his work, and in his relationships, he has become a species-being; and when he has recognized and organized his own powers (forces propres) as social powers so that he no longer separates this social power from himself as political power.[121]

Later, in the introduction of the *Grundrisse*, Marx mentions Rousseau's approach in the Frenchman's *The Social Contract*, "which brings naturally independent, autonomous subjects into relation and connection by contract," in partial contrast to the "naturalism" of most eighteenth-century discussion of natural man as being abstracted from the social and historical contexts of human existence.[122] Engels later takes this further in *Socialism: Utopian and Scientific*, in discussing Rousseau and other eighteenth-century thinkers as being limited to the historical level of development of their own era, so that Rousseau's social contract "came into being, and could only come into being, as a democratic bourgeois republic."[123]

Engels speaks more of the development of ideas, especially by leading philosophers, in relation to the unfolding of history in speaking of Rousseau in two additional places in *Socialism: Utopian and Scientific*:

We saw how the French Philosophers of the Eighteenth Century, the forerunners of the Revolution, appealed to reason as the sole judge of all that is. A rational government, a rational society were to be founded; everything that ran counter to eternal reason was in reality nothing but the idealized understanding of the Eighteenth Century citizen, just then evolving into the bourgeois. The French Revolution had realized this rational society and government.

But the new order of things, rational enough as compared with earlier conditions, turned out to be by no means absolutely rational. The state based upon reason completely collapsed. Rousseau's *Contract Social* had found its realization in the Reign of Terror, from which the bourgeois, who had lost their confidence in their own political capacity, had taken refuge first in the corruption of the Directorate, and, finally, under the wing of Napoleonic Despotism. The promised eternal peace was turned into an eternal war of conquest. The society based upon reason had fared no better. The antagonism between rich and poor, instead of dissolving into general prosperity, had become intensified by the removal of the guild and other privileges, which had to some extent bridged it over, and by the removal of the charitable institutions of the Church. The "freedom of property" from feudal fetters, now virtually accomplished, turned out to be, for the small capitalists and landlords, to be the right to sell their property, crushed under by the overmastering competition of the large capitalists and landlords, to these great lords, and thus, as far as small capitalists and peasant proprietors were concerned, became "freedom from property."[124]

For Marx and Engels, the reasoning of Rousseau and other French thinkers was compatible with the values that ultimately ought to be achieved by advanced human societies. These values that were seen in primitive (meaning first) tribal social relations, but until socioeconomic relations advanced to the necessary historical stage, it was premature to attain them. The same was true of the "Utopian Socialists" going back to Thomas More, who in his *Utopia* was regarded as being well ahead of his time. Engels notes, in speaking of early uprisings by a not-yet-developed bourgeois class:

> There were theoretical enunciations corresponding with these revolutionary uprisings of a class not yet developed; in the sixteenth and seventeenth century, Utopian pictures of ideal social conditions, in the Eighteenth, actual communistic theories (Morelly and Mably). The demand for equality was no longer limited to political rights [as in Locke]; it was extended also to social conditions and individuals. It was not simply class privileges that were to be abolished, but class distinctions themselves.[125]

Engels was quite familiar with Robert Owen's work, having gone to Manchester, England, in 1842–44 to complete his business training, and there studying English life and literature as well as reading the British political economists. There, he joined the Chartist movement and published in the Owenite paper, the *New Moral World*. It was in this period, after having attended lectures at the University of Berlin, that he joined the Young Hegelian radical circle. He stopped in Paris to meet Marx, while en route to England. It was then that Engels penned his "Outlines of a Critique of Political Economy," before again meeting Marx and beginning their collaboration in 1844.[126] Thus, continuing in *Socialism: Utopian and Scientific*, Engels wrote,

> Then came the three great Utopians: Saint-Simon, Fourier and Owen, who in the country where capitalist production was most developed, and under the influence of the antagonisms begotten of this, worked out his proposals for the removal of class distinction systematically and in direct relation to French materialism.
>
> One thing is common to all three. Not one of them appears as a representative of the interests of the proletariat which historical development had, in the mean time, produced. Like the French philosophers, they do not claim to emancipate a particular class to begin with, but all humanity at once. Like them, they wish to bring in the kingdom of reason and eternal justice, but this kingdom, as they see it, is as far as heaven from earth, from that of the French philosophers.[127]

What Marx and Engels thought necessary to achieving human advancement and ultimate liberation was thought and action based upon a dialectical approach to historical unfoldment, which had begun to develop with the French thinkers, and arose more fully with the German historical school of philosophy that followed. They believed that for human beings to return to living as whole people in societies returning to functioning according to the original Indigenous principles, those working for social transformation needed a sound scientific method on which to base their actions. As Engels states later in *Socialism: Utopian and Scientific*:

> To make a science of socialism, it had first to be placed upon a real basis.
>
> In the meantime, along with and after the French philosophy of the Eighteenth Century had arisen, the new German philosophy, culminating in Hegel. Its greatest merit was the taking up again of dialectics as the highest form of reasoning.... Outside philosophy in the restricted sense, the French nevertheless produced masterpieces of dialectics. We need only call to mind Diderot's *Le Neveu de Rameau* and Rousseau's *Discours sur l'ongine et les fondements de l'inegualite parmi les homes.*[128]

This New German philosophy culminated in the Hegelian System. In this system—and herein is its greatest merit—for the first time the whole world, natural, historical, intellectual, is represented as a process, i.e. as in constant motion, change, transformation, development; and the attempt is made to trace out the internal connection that makes a continuous whole of all this movement and development. From this point of view the history of mankind no longer appeared as a wild whirl of senseless deeds and violence, all equally condemnable at the judgment-seat of mature philosophic reason and which are best forgotten as quickly as possible, but as the process of evolution of man himself. It was now the task of the intellect to follow the gradual march of this process through all its devious ways, and to trace out the inner law running through all its apparently accidental phenomena.

That the Hegelian system did not solve the problem it propounded is immaterial. Its epoch-making merit was that it propounded the problem.... To these limits a third must be added. Hegel was an idealist. To him the thoughts within the brain were not the more or less abstract pictures of actual things and processes, but, conversely, things and their evolution were only the realized picture of the "idea," existing somewhere from eternity before the world was. This way of thinking turned everything upside down, and completely reversed the actual connection of things in the world....

The perception of the fundamental contradiction in German idealism led necessarily back to materialism, but not, nota bene, not to the simply metaphysical, exclusively mechanical materialism of the Eighteenth Century.... Modern materialism embraces the more recent discoveries of natural science, according to which Nature also has its history in time, the celestial bodies, like the organic species that, under favorable conditions, people them, being born and perishing. And even if Nature, as a whole, must still be said to move in recurrent cycles, these cycles assume infinitely larger dimensions....

The new facts made imperative a new examination of all past history. Then it was seen that all past history, with the exception of its primitive stages, was the history of class struggle; that these warring classes of society are always the products of modes of production and of exchange—in a word, of the economic conditions of their time; that the economic structure of society always furnishes the real basis, starting from which we can alone work out the ultimate explanation of the whole superstructure of juridical and political institutions as well as of the religious, philosophical and other ideas of a given historical period.[129]

For Marx and Engels, the dialectics of history arose following early tribal times, before the increasing population required production beyond simple hunting and gathering, and greater production led to the surplus necessary for discrete struggling classes to arise. In that pre-historical time, individuals and their extended families generally lived good whole (well-rounded) lives in collaboration with each other. Property, beyond a small amount of personal property, was held in common, as had been set out in the numerous early reports coming from the "New World" to Europe. This had given rise to the idea that human rights were natural, or "inalienable," first set forth by Locke. As the young Marx understood from previous writers, people in tribal societies were free from exploitation by others, and did not begin to suffer under the "superstructure" of repressive governments until their economies developed beyond subsistence and the rudimentary division of labor transformed into a clear segmentation as he set forth in *The German Ideology*:

> The first form of ownership is tribal [*Stammeigentum*] ownership. It corresponds to the underdeveloped stage of production, at which a people lives by hunting and fishing, by the rearing of beasts, or in the highest stage, agriculture. In the latter case it presupposes a great mass of uncultivated stretches of land. The division of labor is at this stage still very elementary and is confined to a further extension of the natural division of labor existing in the family. The social structure is, therefore, limited to an extension of the family; patriarchal family chieftains, below them the members of the tribe, finally slaves. The slavery latent in the family only develops gradually with the increase in population, the growth of wants, and with the extension of external relations, both of war and barter.[130]
>
> The family, which to begin with is the only social relationship, becomes later, when increased needs create new social relations and the increased population new needs, a subordinate one.[131]
>
> Further, the division of labor implies the contradiction between the interest of the separate individual or the individual family and the communal interest of all individuals who have intercourse with one another. And indeed, the communal interest does not exist merely in

the imagination, as the "general interest," but first of all in reality, as the mutual interdependence of the individuals among whom the labor is divided. And finally, the division of labor offers us the first example of how, as long as man remains in natural society, that is as long as a cleavage exists between the particular and the common interest, as long therefore as activity is not voluntary, but naturally, divided, man's own deed becomes an alien power opposed to him, which enslaves him instead of being controlled by him. For as soon as the distribution of labor comes into being, each man has a particular, exclusive sphere of activity, which is forced upon him and from which he cannot escape. He is a hunter, a fisherman, a shepherd or a critical critic, and must remain so if he does not want to lose his livelihood; while in a communist society, where nobody has one exclusive sphere of activity but each may become accomplished in any branch he wishes, society relegates the general production and thus makes it possible for me to do one thing today and another tomorrow, to hunt in the morning, fish in the afternoon, rear cattle in the evening, criticize after dinner, just as I have a mind, without ever becoming hunter, fisherman, shepherd or critic. This fixation of social activity, this consolidation of what we ourselves produce into an objective power above us, growing out of our control, thwarting our expectations, bringing to naught our calculations, is one of the chief factors in historical development up until now.[132]

Thus for Marx, even before having much direct knowledge of tribal societies, the way of living in those first societies was natural and good, allowing people to live as well-rounded human beings, as social animals relating to one another in a harmonious and egalitarian community where their own interests were to a large extent the common interest. The realities of economic development, and thus of social and political development as well, removed human beings from that desirable state of living. History then passed through a series of class struggles founded upon the internal contradictions in evolving economic social relations. The fundamental problem for human beings, then, is to find a way to combine technologically advanced and efficient production with a social order that distributes benefits equitably and eliminates class antagonisms, which would return society to the basic "communist" principles and values of tribal society. For Marx and Engels this does not mean returning to the simple technology and small scale of organization in tribal society, but to living as whole human beings in a more advanced and complex society, according to the fundamental values that are natural to human beings and governed early societies.[133]

Some time later, taking into account some direct reports of remnants of ancient society, Marx writes of common property:

It is the primitive form that we can show existed among Romans, Teutons, Celts, and even to this day we find numerous examples, ruins though they be, in India.[134]

Speaking further of the examples in India, in 1867, he writes in *Capital*:

Those small and extremely ancient Indian communities, some of which have continued down to this day, are based on common ownership of the land, on the association of agriculture and handicrafts, and upon an unalterable division of labor, which serves, whenever a new community is started, as a plan and scheme already cut and dried. Occupying areas from 100 to up to several thousand acres, each forms a self-sufficient productive entity. The greater part of the products is destined for direct use by the community itself, and does not take the form of commodities. Hence, production here is independent of that division of labor brought about, in Indian society as a whole, by means of the exchange of commodities. It is only the surplus products which become commodities, to a large extent through the State, into whose hands from time immemorial a certain quantity of these products has found its way in the shape of rent in kind. The constitution of these communities varies in different parts of India. In those of the simplest form, the land is tilled in common, and the produce divided among the members. At the same time, spinning and weaving are carried out by each family as subsidiary industries. Side by side with the masses thus occupied in the same kind of work, we find the "chief inhabitant," who is judge, police-man and tax gatherer in one;... [along with a few other officials. Professionals, and craftsmen.] This dozen or so of individuals is maintained at the expense of the whole community. If the population expands, a new community is founded, on the pattern of the old one, on unoccupied land. The whole mechanism discloses a systematic division of labor; but a division like that in manufacturing is impos-sible, since the smith and carpenter, etc., find an unchang-ing market, and at most there may be, according to the size of the villages, two or three instead of one. The law that regulates the division of labor in the community acts here with the irresistible authority of a law of Nature, while each individual artisan, the smith, the carpenter, and so on, con-ducts in his workshop all the operations of his handicraft in the traditional way, but independently, and without recog-nizing any authority over him. The simplicity of the orga-nization for production of these self-sufficing communities that constantly reproduce themselves in the same form, and if destroyed, by chance spring up again on the same spot and with the same name—this simplicity supplies the key to the secret of the unchangeableness of Asiatic societies, and unchangeableness in such striking contrast with the constant dissolution and refounding of Asiatic states, and the never ceasing changes of dynasty. The structure of the economic elements of society remains untouched by the storm-clouds of the political sky.[135]

Stephen M. Sachs

The Direct Indigenous American Influence on Marx and Engels in Later Years

The anthropologist Lewis Henry Morgan published in 1877 *Ancient Society or Researches in the Lines of Human Progress from Savagery through Barbarism to Civilization.* Morgan had undertaken considerable field research with the Haudenosaunee (reported in *League of the Iroquois,* referred to and quoted in chapter 1, above), which informed a good deal of the discussion of tribal society in *Ancient Society,* including analyses of the ways of a number of other American Indian tribes. A copy was brought to Marx, who from 1880 to 1882 undertook an extensive study of it, along with the anthropological writings of John Budd Phaer, Henry Sumner Maine, and John Lubbock, as well as a number of other works of ethnography including those of George M. Maurer and Maxim M. Kovalevsky. Marx and Engels found that Morgan and these other authors confirmed and expanded their view of tribal society. Marx was preparing to include this new information in his own writing, but his ethnographic-based work was cut short by his death in 1883. His extensive notes were later published as *The Ethnological Notebooks of Karl Marx.*

Engels worked with these notebooks, as well as with Morgan's *Ancient Society,* and in the preface to *Manifesto of the Communist Party,* German Edition of 1883, he comments:

> In 1847, the pre-history of society, the social organization existing previous to recorded history, was all but unknown. Since then, Haxthausen discovered common ownership in Russia, Maurer proved it to be the social foundation from which all Teutonic races started in history, and by and by village communes were found to be, or to have been the primitive form of society everywhere from India to Ireland. The inner organization of the primitive Communistic society was laid bare, in its typical form by Morgan's crowning discovery of the true nature the gens and its relation to the

tribe. With the dissolution of these primeval communities society begins to differentiate into separate and finally antagonistic classes.[136]

Marx's Notebooks and Morgan's volume were major sources in Engels's writing *The Origin of the Family, Private Property and the State*, where he discusses the ways of a number of Indian nations, and some of their evolution away from their original socioeconomic relations.[137] It is significant that Engels concludes this work by quoting Morgan's own conclusion to *Ancient Societies*, although their theories of social evolution are different:

Since the advent of civilization, the outgrowth of property has been so immense, its forms so diversified, its uses so expanding and its management so intelligent in the interest of its owners that it has become, on the part of the people, an unmanageable power. The human mind stands bewildered in the presence of its own creation. The time will come, nevertheless, when human intelligence will rise to the mastery over property, and define the relations of the state to the property it protects, as well as the obligations and limits of the rights of its owners. The interests of society are paramount to individual interest, and the two must be brought into just and harmonious relation. A mere property career is not the final destiny of mankind, if progress is to be the law of the future as it has been of the past. The time which has passed away is but a fragment of the ages yet to come. The dissolution of society bids fair to become the termination of a career of which property is the end and aim, because such a career contains the elements of self-destruction. Democracy in government, brotherhood in society, equality in rights and privileges, and universal education foreshadow the next higher plane of society to which experience, intelligence and knowledge are steadily tending. It will be a revival in a higher form of the liberty equality and fraternity of the ancient gentes. (Morgan, *Ancient Society*, 552)[138]

The influence of American Indians and other Indigenous peoples upon the ongoing traditions of socialism that came through Marx, Engels, and others, including the "Utopian Socialists" (discussed in part, above) and the anarchists (discussed in part below), continues in various ways and to various degrees in the different branches of socialism which have developed. For instance, Marx believed, and many socialists continued to believe, that the political repression found in the capitalist state would force the working class into a revolution (and some socialists believed that the leaders of the working class would foment a revolution), to bring a socialist society into being and begin the return to natural human relations at a higher level. Edward Bernstein, in *Evolutionary Socialism*,[139] in 1899, expounded and furthered the view of likeminded others, that since Marx had written, conditions had changed, and new developments had occurred, including the rise of strong labor unions, that made possible the gradual development of socialism in society, by peaceful and democratic means. This development has carried the Indigenous influences on socialism into the social-democracies and social-democratic movements of Europe and other places around the world.

Peter Kropotkin and the Anarchist Tradition

Anarchism in Europe—and later beyond—has the same American Indian roots as socialism, and there is much overlap and interaction between the two traditions. Often anarchists are called libertarian socialists. Of those called or calling themselves socialists, anarchists are generally among the most participatory democrats, favoring extensive decentralization of government and other institutions. At the least democratic and most authoritarian extreme of those calling themselves socialists are the Stalinists of the Soviet Union, its satellite states and related movements, which many critics consider to be socialist in name only. They saw the Soviet Union as a system based on an economy of state capitalism, rather than socialism, and violating the human rights and democratic participation required for true socialism.[140]

The term "anarchist," meaning without government, was coined in the seventeenth century and derived from the mistaken belief that American Indian nations had no government.[141] In many instances, those calling themselves anarchists have agreed with much of Marx's and Engels's critique of capitalism. They generally have believed that once the capitalist state and economy were properly replaced, return to a natural human governance and society would be rather quick, and would not require the longer, step-by-step transition, that Marx, Engels, and many other socialists believed necessary. In the late nineteenth century in Russia (and to some extent elsewhere), some of the more violence-prone anarchists believed that if the state apparatus were smashed, a socialist libertarian society would quickly arise. Consequently, some of these anarchists focused on assassinating police chiefs and other officials.

To date, the best-known examples of anarchist self-governing communities that have been formed are the short-lived anarchist collectives that arose during the Spanish Civil War of the late 1930s. These fell with the victory of General Franco's forces, so that it is difficult to analyze how successful they might have been if they had not been forcibly repressed.[142] The numerous socialist Kibbutzim in Israel, organized as equalitarian participatory communities, were directly influenced by anarchist, as well as socialist ideas.[143] Among the many intentional communal communities in the United States, a fair number were organized on anarchist and socialist principles, while others were formed directly reflecting American Indian ideas, including "hippy" communes.[144] It can be argued that at its most liberal point under Tito, Yugoslavia had begun to move in the direction of an anarchist or decentralist participatory democratic socialism, through its system of social and worker self-management in a decentralized federalist system. However, Yugoslavia only suggested that model, for its political system became increasingly oligarchic, as it moved from the local to the national level. The varied set of cultures in the multiethnic country were to different degrees hierarchical, undercutting both political and workplace democracy. Moreover, a lack of equalizing legislation led to a laissez-faire market socialism, allowing mergers that tended to build oligopoly, while salaries plus bonuses were based on "the results of work," which without a sufficiently progressive income tax system, led to fairly wide income differentials, even for the same work (though not to the point of producing a wealthy upper class and quite poor lower class).[145]

The Work of Peter Kropotkin

The best known of the early anarchists, in terms of the question of Native American influence upon the rise of the tradition, is Peter Kropotkin. He was a young man when Marx was a mature writer and thinker.[146] Though the son of a Russian prince, at age thirteen, Kropotkin became disillusioned with Russian politics and society and began exploring alternative social thought, including becoming familiar with the American Indian–impacted strands of Western thought (encompassing Rousseau and others). When he became a vocal dissident in Russia, Kropotkin was jailed in 1874. In 1876 he was moved to a Russian military hospital, from which he escaped and fled to western Europe, where he worked and wrote as a professional geographer.

He read the works of the Social Darwinists, whose extremely competitive view of nature he knew to be wrong from his observations about wildlife as a young man in Siberia, where he had instead found natural life to be strongly cooperative, though containing competitive aspects. Thus, in writing *Mutual Aid: A Factor in Evolution*, first published in 1902, he opens the introduction with:

Two aspects of animal life impressed me most during the journeys which I made in my youth in Eastern Siberia and Northern Manchuria. One of them was the extreme severity of the struggle for existence which most species of animals have to carry on against an inclement nature;...And the other was, that even in those few spots where animal life teamed in abundance, I failed to find—although I was eagerly looking for it—that bitter struggle for the means of existence, among animals belonging to the same species, which was considered by most Darwinists (though not always by Darwin himself) as the dominant characteristic of struggle for life, and the main factor in evolution.[147]

On the other hand, whenever I saw animal life in abundance, as, for instance, on the lakes where scores of species and millions of individuals came together to rear their progeny;...in all these scenes of animal life which passed before my eyes, I saw Mutual Aid and Mutual Support carried on to an extent which made me suspect in it a feature of the greatest importance for the maintenance of life, the preservation of each species, and its further evolution.

Kropotkin's view that nature is largely cooperative is entirely consistent with the Native American view of nonhuman species, often called nations, whom North American tribal people greatly respected and learned a great deal from relating to their own behavior. This is illustrated in a very considerable number of Native stories.

Kropotkin adds that in 1880, at the Congress of Russian Naturalists, he heard the Dean of St. Petersburg University, zoologist Professor Kessler state:

besides the law of mutual struggle, there is in nature the law of mutual aid, which, for the success of the struggle for life, and especially for the progressive evolution of the species, is far more important than the law of mutual contest.[148]

Kropotkin saw this idea as "nothing but a further development of the ideas expressed by Darwin himself in The Descent of Man," and goes on to point out:

The importance of the Mutual Aid factor—"if its generality could only be demonstrated"—did not escape the naturalist's genius so manifest in Goethe [in an observation in 1827].

Concerning human evolution and history, he writes:

It is not love to my neighbor—whom I often do not know at all—which induces me to seize a pail of water and rush towards his house when I see it on fire; it is a far wider, even though more vague feeling or instinct of human solidarity and sociability which moves me. So it is also with animals. It is not love, and not even sympathy (understood in its proper sense).... It is a feeling infinitely wider than love or personal sympathy—an instinct that has been slowly developed among animals and men in the course of an extremely long evolution, and which has taught animals and men alike the force they can borrow from the process of mutual aid and support, and the joys they can find in social life....

But it is not love and not even sympathy upon which Society is based in mankind. It is the conscience—be it only at the stage of instinct—of human solidarity. It is the unconscious recognition of the force that is borrowed by each man from the practice of mutual aid; of the close dependency of everyone's happiness upon the happiness of all; and of the sense of justice, or equity, which brings the individual to consider the rights of every individual as equal to his own. Upon this broad and necessary foundation the still higher moral feelings are developed....

The number and importance of mutual-aid institutions which were developed by the creative genius of the savage and half-savage masses, during the earliest clan-period of mankind and still more during the next village-community period, and the immense influence which these institutions have exerted upon the subsequent development of mankind, down to the present times, induced me to extend my researches to the later historical periods as well....

I should certainly be the last to underestimate the part which self-assertion of the individual has played in the evolution of mankind. However, this subject requires, I believe, a much deeper treatment than the one it has hitherto received. In the history of mankind, individual self-assertion has often been, and continually is, something quite different from, and far larger and deeper than, the petty, unintelligent, narrow-mindedness, which, with a large class of writers, goes for "individualism" and "self-assertion." Nor have history-making individuals been limited to those whom historians have represented as heroes.... When the Mutual Aid institutions—the tribe, the village community, the guilds, the mediaeval city—began, in the course of history, to lose their primitive character, to be invaded by parasitic growths, and thus to become hindrances to progress, the revolt of individuals against these institutions took always two different aspects. Part of those who rose up strove to purify the old institutions, or to work to a higher form of commonwealth, based upon the same Mutual Aid principles; they tried, for instance, to introduce the principles of "compensation," instead of the lex talionis, and later on, the pardon of offences, or a still higher ideal of equality before the human conscience, in lieu of compensation, according to class-value. But at the very same time, another portion of the same individual rebels endeavored to break down the protective institutions of mutual support, with no other intention but to increase their own wealth and their own powers. In this three-cornered contest, between the two classes of revolted individuals and the supporters of what existed, lies the real tragedy of history.[149]

These views of the anarchist writer are quite in keeping with those of traditional American Indians, as set out in chapter 1.

Indigenous North Americans considered all life to be naturally relational, involving a high degree of cooperation, respect for individual rights and differences, with individuals' egos and power needing to be kept in balance with community needs. Numerous traditional Indians have criticized what they saw as the excessive individualism of Europeans, leading to a poor distribution of goods and selfish values in unbalanced communities.

Kropotkin, therefore, begins his study of mutual aid as a factor in evolution, in chapters I and II, with a consideration of mutual aid among animals (supported by several appendices) along the lines laid out in the introduction. He then proceeds in chapter III to make a broad examination of what was known in the late nineteenth century of band and tribal societies worldwide, including some examples from North America, drawing on the anthropological work up to his day. It is clear from his references (including the appendixes) that he was widely read, including of Morgan. In so doing, Kropotkin showed the cooperative nature of Indigenous societies, along the general lines described among traditional American Indian societies in chapter 1 of this book. Going further, he indicates the parallels in animal species and Indigenous societies operating largely in terms of providing mutual aid. He notes:

> It is not possible to study primitive mankind without being deeply impressed by the sociability it has displayed since its very first steps in life.[150]

In the following chapters, Kropotkin traces the continuing, though uneven persistence of human relations based upon mutual aid, sometimes remnants of Indigenous ways in modified forms, including in Europe. He also illuminates recreations and re-emergences of collaborative ways in the face of or following the breakdown of hierarchical control, because human cooperation is natural, and indeed necessary, for human survival and well-being. As Kropotkin has already been quoted as saying, competition also has a compatible place in a well-working human system, though it creates major harms and problems when it extends out of bounds. When, for example, the ascension of the narrowly personal and the competitive aspect of human nature goes too far, it causes very serious damages and imbalances in human life. Kropotkin shows that, with ups and downs, social vehicles and institutions of mutual aid in Europe remained particularly strong through the Mediaeval period and that there has been more of a struggle for them since the rise of the modern state.

In the history of humanity through its many stages and tribulations, in terms of mutual aid, Kropotkin finds:

[In earlier stages of society,] notwithstanding all tyranny, oppression, robberies and raids, tribal wars, glutton kings, deceiving witches and priests, slave-hunters, the ivory robbers, and the like, these populations have not gone astray in the woods; ... they have maintained a certain civilization, and have remained men, instead of dropping to the level of straggling families of decaying orangutans. The fact is, the slave-hunters, the ivory robbers, the fighting kings, the Matabele and the Madagascar "heroes" pass away, leaving their traces marked with blood and fire; but the nucleus of mutual-aid institutions, habits and customs, grown up in the tribe and village community, remains; and it keeps men united in societies, open to the progress of civilization, and ready to receive it when the day comes that they shall receive civilization instead of bullets.

The same applies to our civilized world. The natural and social calamities pass away. Whole populations are periodically reduced to misery or starvation; the very strings of life are crushed out of millions of men, reduced to city pauperism; the understanding and the feelings of millions are vitiated by teachings worked out in the interest of the few. All this is certainly part of our existence. But the nucleus of mutual-support institutions, habits and customs remains alive with millions; It keeps them together; and they prefer to cling to their customs, beliefs and traditions rather than to accept the teachings of a war of each against all, which are offered to them under the title of science, but are no science at all.[151]

[I]t is especially in the domain of ethics that the dominating importance of the mutual-aid principle appears in full. That mutual-aid is the real foundation of our ethical conceptions seems evident enough. But ... as far back as the lowest stages of the animal world; and from these stages we can follow its [mutual aid's] uninterrupted evolution, in opposition to a number of contrary agencies, through all degrees of human development, up to the present times. Even the new religions which were born from time to time—always at epochs when the mutual-aid principle was falling into decay in the theocracies and despotic states of the East, or at the decline of the Roman Empire—even the new religions have only reaffirmed that same principle. They found their first supporters among the humble, in the lowest downtrodden layers of society, where the mutual-aid principle is the foundation of every-day life; and the new forms of union which were introduced in the earliest Buddhist and Christian communities, in the Moravian brotherhoods and so on, took the character of a return to the best aspects of mutual-aid in early tribal life.[152]

Finally, Kropotkin concludes that in all of the religions and widely accepted ethical systems:

Man is appealed to be guided in his acts, not merely by love, which is always personal, or at best tribal, but by the perception of his oneness with each human being. In the practice of mutual-aid, which we can retrace to the earliest beginnings of evolution, we thus find the positive and undoubted origin of our ethical conceptions; and we can affirm that in the ethical progress of man, mutual support—not mutual struggle—has had the leading part. In its wide extension, even at the present time, we also see the best guarantee of a still loftier evolution of our race.[153]

It is interesting to note that his views on the importance of cooperation within a species for its survival and evolutionary advancement is very much in keeping with the mainstream of early twenty-first century evolutionary biology. E. O. Wilson, one of the leading early twenty-first century evolutionary biologists, sounds much like Kropotkin in commenting:

Group selection is clearly the process responsible for advanced social behavior. It also possesses the two elements necessary for evolution. First group-level traits, including cooperativeness, empathy and patterns of networking, have been found to be heritable in humans—that is, they vary genetically in some degree from one person to the next. And second, cooperation and unity manifestly affect the survival of groups that are competing.[154]

The Overall Impact of American Indian Ways in Europe

It is clear that from first contact to the present moment, European contact with Indigenous peoples of the Americas has had profound and continuing effects on social, political, and economic thinking in Europe. Every major tradition of thought across the political spectrum has been greatly changed, from Hobbesian law-and-order conservatism, through Lockean and Rousseauian perspectives to the varieties of socialist and anarchist thinking. The Indians' impact on Europeans and European Americans in North America in the first three centuries following contact also continued from the nineteenth century to the current day, and is the topic of the next chapter.

Notes to Chapter 3

1. See William Brandon, *New Worlds for Old: Reports from the New World and Their Effect on the Development of Social Thought in Europe, 1500–1800* (Athens: Ohio University Press, 1986).

2. In terms of writers reacting to the reports reflecting national developments, see Brandon, *New Worlds for Old*. For the background in England, see John M. Barry, *Roger Williams and the Creation of the American Soul* (New York: Viking Adult, 2012). On Indigenous (traditional) remnants in European society, which had been politically and socially important in the Middle Ages, see Peter Kropotkin, *Mutual Aid: A Factor of Evolution* (Lawrence, KS: Digireads, 2010); the background is in chaps. 3–6, and the direct discussion in chaps. 7 and 8, while the Reformation included some democratizing movements, as for example the Anabaptists, 120n251.

3. Brandon, *New Worlds for Old*, chap. 2, and 36–44, 155–65.

4. Sharon O'Brien, *American Indian Tribal Government* (Norman: University of Oklahoma Press, 1989), 37. See Angie Debo, *A History of the Indians of the United States* (Norman: University of Oklahoma Press, 1970), 19 (First Voyage, "A gentle people"). The text of Christopher Columbus's first voyage to America in the year 1492 is available online at Fordham's "Medieval Sourcebook: Christopher Columbus; Extracts from Journal," http://www.fordham.edu/halsall/source/columbus1.html, with selected passages from the journal of Columbus's voyage of 1492. From the Sourcebook:

Thursday, 11 October

At two o'clock in the morning the land was discovered, at two leagues' distance; they took in sail and remained under the square-sail lying to till day, which was Friday, when they found themselves near a small island, one of the Lucayos, called in the Indian language Guanahani. Presently they descried people, naked, and the Admiral landed in the boat, which was armed, along with Martin Alonzo Pinzon, and Vincent Yanez his brother, captain of the Nina. The Admiral bore the royal standard, and the two captains each a banner of the Green Cross, which all the ships had carried; this contained the initials of the names of the King and Queen each side of the cross, and a crown over each letter Arrived on shore, they saw trees very green many streams of water, and diverse sorts of fruits. The Admiral called upon the two Captains, and the rest of the crew who landed, as also to Rodrigo de Escovedo notary of the fleet, and Rodrigo Sanchez, of Segovia, to bear witness that he before all others took possession (as in fact he did) of that island for the King and Queen his sovereigns, making the requisite declarations, which are more at large set down here in writing. Numbers of the people of the island straightway collected together. Here follow the precise words of the Admiral: "As I saw that they were very friendly to us, and perceived that they could be much more easily converted to our holy faith by gentle means than by force, I presented them with some red caps, and strings of beads to wear upon the neck, and many other trifles of small value, wherewith they were much delighted, and became wonderfully attached to us. Afterwards they came swimming to the boats, bringing parrots, balls of cotton thread, javelins, and many other things which they exchanged for articles we gave them, such as glass beads, and hawk's bells; which trade was carried on with the utmost good will. But they seemed on the whole to me, to be a very poor people. They all go completely naked, even the women, though I saw but one girl. All whom I saw were young, not above thirty years of age, well made, with fine shapes and faces; their hair short, and coarse like that of a horse's tail, combed toward the forehead, except a small portion which they suffer to hang down behind, and never cut. Some paint themselves with black, which makes them appear like those of the Canaries, neither black nor white; others with white, others with red, and others with such colors as they can find. Some paint the face, and some the whole body; others only the eyes, and others the nose. Weapons they have none, nor are acquainted with them, for I showed them swords which they grasped by the blades, and cut themselves through ignorance. They have no iron, their javelins being without it, and nothing more than sticks, though some have fish-bones or other things at the ends. They are all of a good size and stature, and handsomely formed. I saw some with scars of wounds upon their bodies, and demanded by signs the of them; they answered me in the same way, that there came people from the other islands in the neighborhood who endeavored to make prisoners of them, and they defended themselves. I thought then, and still believe, that these were from the continent. It appears to me, that the people are ingenious, and would be good servants and I am of opinion that they would very readily become Christians, as they appear to have no religion. They very quickly learn such words as are spoken to them. If it please our Lord, I intend at my return to carry home six of them to your Highnesses, that they may learn our language. I saw no beasts in the island, nor any sort of animals except parrots." These are the words of the Admiral.

Saturday, 13 October

At daybreak great multitudes of men came to the shore, all young and of fine shapes, very handsome; their hair not curled but straight and coarse like horse-hair, and all with foreheads and heads much broader than any people I had hitherto seen; their eyes were large and very beautiful; they were not black, but the color of the inhabitants of the Canaries, which is a very natural circumstance, they being in the same latitude with the island of Ferro in the Canaries. They were straight-limbed without exception, and not with prominent bellies but handsomely shaped. They came to the ship in canoes, made of a single trunk of a tree, wrought in a wonderful manner considering the country; some of them large enough to contain forty or forty-five men, others of different sizes down to those fitted to hold but a single person. They rowed with an oar like a baker's peel, and wonderfully swift. If they happen to upset, they all jump into the sea, and swim till they have righted their canoe and emptied it with the calabashes they carry with them. They came loaded with balls of cotton, parrots, javelins, and other things too numerous to mention; these they exchanged for whatever we chose to give them. I was very attentive to them, and strove to learn if they had any gold. Seeing some of them with little bits of this metal hanging at their noses, I gathered from them by signs that by going southward or steering round the island in that direction, there would be found a king who possessed large vessels of gold, and in great quantities. I endeavored to procure them to lead the way thither, but found they were unacquainted with the route. I determined to stay here till the evening of the next day, and then sail for the southwest; for according to what I could learn from them, there was land at the south as well as at the southwest and northwest and those from the northwest came many times and fought with them and proceeded on to the southwest in search of gold and precious stones.... The natives are an inoffensive people, and so desirous to possess any thing they saw with us, that they kept swimming off to the ships with whatever they could find, and readily bartered for any article we saw fit to give them in return, even such as broken platters and fragments of glass. I saw in this manner sixteen balls of cotton thread which weighed above twenty-five pounds, given for three Portuguese ceutis...

Sunday, 14 October

In the morning, I ordered the boats to be got ready, and coasted along the island toward the north-northeast to examine that part of it, we having landed first at the eastern part. Presently we discovered two or three villages, and the people all came down to the shore, calling out to us, and giving thanks to God. Some brought us water, and others victuals: others seeing that I was not disposed to land, plunged into the sea and swam out to us, and we perceived that they interrogated us if we had come from heaven. An old man came on board my boat; the others, both men and women cried with loud voices—"Come and see the men who have come from heavens. Bring them victuals and drink." There came many of both sexes, every one bringing something, giving thanks to God, prostrating themselves on the earth, and lifting up their hands to heaven. They called out to us loudly to come to land, but I was apprehensive on account of a reef of rocks.... It was to view these parts that I set out in the morning, for I wished to give a complete relation to your Highnesses, as also to find where a fort might be built. I discovered a tongue of land which appeared like an island though it was not, but might be cut through and made so in two days; it contained six houses. I do not, however, see the necessity of fortifying the place, as the people here are simple in war-like matters, as your Highnesses will see by those seven which I have ordered to be taken and carried to Spain in order to learn our language and return, unless your Highnesses should choose to have them all transported to Castile, or held captive in the island. I could conquer the whole of them with fifty men, and govern them as I pleased.... I determined to steer for the largest [island].... They are all very level, without mountains, exceedingly fertile and populous, the inhabitants living at war with one another, although a simple race, and with delicate bodies.

15 October

... From this island espying a still larger one to the west, I set sail in that direction and kept on till night without reaching the western extremity of the island, where I gave it the name of Santa Maria de la Concepcion. About sunset we anchored near the cape which terminates the island towards the west to enquire for gold, for the natives we had taken from San Salvador told me that the people here wore golden bracelets upon their arms and legs. I believed pretty confidently that they had invented this story in order to find means to escape from us, still I determined to pass none of these islands without taking possession, because being once taken, it would answer for all times. We anchored and remained till Tuesday, when at daybreak I went ashore with the boats armed. The people we found naked like those of San Salvador, and of the same disposition. They suffered us to traverse the island, and gave us what we asked of them. As the wind blew southeast upon the shore where the vessels lay, I determined not to remain, and set out for the ship. A large canoe being near the caravel Nina, one of the San Salvador natives leaped overboard and swam to her; (another had made his escape the night before,) the canoe being reached by the fugitive, the natives rowed for the land too swiftly to be overtaken; having landed, some of my men went ashore in pursuit of them, when they abandoned the canoe and fled with precipitation; the canoe which they had left was brought on board the Nina, where from another quarter had arrived a small canoe with a single man, who came to barter some cotton; some of the sailors finding him unwilling to go on board the vessel, jumped into the sea and took him. I was upon the quarter deck of my ship, and seeing the whole, sent for him, and gave him a red cap, put some glass beads upon his arms, and two hawk's bells upon his ears. I then ordered his canoe to be returned to him, and dispatched him back to land.

Tuesday, 16 October
Set sail from Santa Maria about noon, for Fernandina which appeared very large in the west;...Beat up and down all night, and in the morning arrived at a village and anchored. This was the place to which the man whom we had picked up at sea had gone, when we set him on shore. He had given such a favorable account of us, that all night there were great numbers of canoes coming off to us, who brought us water and other things. I ordered each man to be presented with something, as strings of ten or a dozen glass beads apiece, and thongs of leather, all which they estimated highly; those which came on board I directed should be fed with molasses. At three o'clock, I sent the boat on shore for water; the natives with great good will directed the men where to find it, assisted them in carrying the casks full of it to the boat, and seemed to take great pleasure in serving us.... Now, writing this, I set sail with a southerly wind to circumnavigate the island, and search till we can find Samoet, which is the island or city where the gold is, according to the account of those who come on board the ship, to which the relation of those of San Salvador and Santa Maria corresponds. These people are similar to those of the islands just mentioned, and have the same language and

customs; with the exception that they appear somewhat more civilized, showing themselves more subtle in their dealings with us, bartering their cotton and other articles with more profit than the others had experienced. Here we saw cotton cloth, and perceived the people more decent, the women wearing a slight covering of cotton over the nudities.... They have no religion, and I believe that they would very readily become Christians, as they have a good understanding...

Wednesday, 17 October
...The natives we found like those already described, as to personal appearance and manners, and naked like the rest. Whatever they possessed, they bartered for what we chose to give them. I saw a boy of the crew purchasing javelins of them with bits of platters and broken glass. Those who went for water informed me that they had entered their houses and found them very clean and neat, with beds and coverings of cotton nets. Their houses are all built in the shape of tents, with very high chimneys. None of the villages which I saw contained more than twelve or fifteen of them. Here it was remarked that the married women wore cotton breeches, but the younger females were without them, except a few who were as old as eighteen years. Dogs were seen of a large and small size, and one of the men had hanging at his nose a piece of gold half as big as a castellailo, with letters upon it. I endeavored to purchase it of them in order to ascertain what sort of money it was but they refused to part with it...

Sunday, 21 October
...While we were in search of some good water, we came upon a village of the natives about half a league from the place where the ships lay; the inhabitants on discovering us abandoned their houses, and took to flight, carrying of their goods to the mountain. I ordered that nothing which they had left should be taken, not even the value of a pin. Presently we saw several of the natives advancing towards our party, and one of them came up to us, to

whom we gave some hawk's bells and glass beads, with which he was delighted. We asked him in return, for water, and after I had gone on board the ship, the natives came down to the shore with their calabashes full, and showed great pleasure in presenting us with it. I ordered more glass beads to be given them, and they promised to return the next day.... .

5. Ibid., excerpts from Columbus diary.

6. Brandon, *New Worlds for Old*, 13. That liberty was the most important theme spreading in and from these reports is shown throughout *New Worlds for Old*, but can be seen especially from 32–44.

7. Sir Thomas Moore (or More), *Utopia* (Sioux Falls, SD: NuVision, 2007). Page references to *Utopia* in this chapter are in this edition.

8. Information on *Utopia*'s relationship to Amerigo Vespucci's two accounts of his four voyages are in Thomas More, *Utopia*, ed. George M. Logan (New York: W. W. Norton, 2011), which contains sections about the background of the writing of *Utopia*, including a section "Amerigo Vespucci," 117–21, including related quotes from the accounts of Vespucci's journeys. Logan says that there is today some controversy over the authenticity of those accounts, but that there was no such controversy when More wrote.

9. Ibid. Note that this is plain from More's text, he also gained incites from Plato and other European sources as is discussed in Logan's edition of *Utopia*.

10. Logan, *Utopia*, 119–20 (section, "Amerigo Vespucci").

11. *Utopia* (NuVision), 29–30. Note the passage continues critiquing the European handling of property, including its uncertainty leading to lawsuits, leading Hythloday to say, "I grow more favorable to Plato [in the *Republic*], and do not wonder that he resolved not to make any laws for such as would not submit to a community of all things."

12. Ibid., 36–37.

13. Ibid., 37–44.

14. "Karl Koutsky from *The Roots of More's Socialism*," in Logan, *Utopia*, 162–66. For more on Marx on freedom as man's "generic character," see Guy Besse, *Rapport*, vol. 3, no. 18. Note that More's name was written in Red Square in Moscow as a hero of the Russian Revolution (Brandon, *New Worlds for Old*, 9).

   For more on Marx and Engels's works being influenced by Indigenous American ways, see: T. B. Bottomore, ed. and trans.,

Karl Marx: Selected Writings in Sociology and Social Philosophy (New York: McGraw-Hill, 1964), 39, "introduction." Marx and Engels had read Lewis Henry Morgan, *Ancient Society or Researches in the Lines of Human Progress from Savagery through Barbarism to Civilization* (New York: H. Holt, 1877). For a discussion of the limitations of Morgan's understanding, see Joy Bilharz, "First among Equals? The Changing Status of Seneca Women," in *Women and Power in Native North America*, eds. Laura E. Klein and Lillian A. Ackerman (Norman: University of Oklahoma Press, 1995), 107.

In the German edition of 1883 of the *Manifesto of the Communist Party*, Engels refers to Morgan in a footnote to the opening sentence of part I, "The history of all hitherto existing society is the history of class struggles." In footnote 6 Engels states, "That is all written history," then states that since 1847 much has become known of "common ownership" and "village socialism" in Russia and "all Teutonic races," and "the primitive form of society everywhere from India to Ireland." He then states, "The inner organization of this primitive Communistic society was laid bare, in its typical form, by Morgan's crowning discovery of the true nature of the gens and its relation to the tribe. With the dissolution of these primeval communities society begins to be differentiated into separate and finally antagonistic classes. I have attempted to retrace this process of dissolution in *The Origin of the Family, Private Property and the State*." (This selection is available in Robert C. Tucker, *The Marx-Engels Reader*, 2nd ed. (New York: W. W. Norton, 1978), 473. See also the introductory note to the selection from Friedrich Engels, *The Origin of the Family, Private Property, and the State*, in *The Marx-Engels Reader* (New York: W. W. Norton, 1972), 734.

At the end of *The Origin of the Family*, Engels discuses Morgan's critique of civilization that arose out of the primeval state of human existence on the basis of the development of private property. Engels (writing from Marx's notes on Morgan) agrees with Morgan that

Since the advent of civilization, the outgrowth of property has been so immense, its forms so diversified, its uses so expanding and its management so intelligent in the interests of its owners that it has become, on the part of the people, an unmanageable power. The human mind stands bewildered in the presence of its own creation [that brings about a war between the rich and the poor]. The time will come, never the less, when human intelligence will rise to the mastery over property, and define the relations of the state to the property it protects, as well as the obligations and the limits of the rights of its owners.... Democracy in government, brotherhood in society, equality in rights and privileges, and universal education, foreshadow the next higher plane of society to which experience, intelligence and knowledge are steadily tending. It will be a revival, in a higher form, of the liberty, equality and fraternity of the ancient gentes. (ibid., 758–59)

Thus it is that Marx and Engels saw the full nature of human beings and human relations in Morgan's reports of the Seneca, before pressure of population growth created a need for dehumanizing institutions to increase production, setting in motion the dialectic of class conflict. For Marx and Engels, it is through the solution of the problem of production that human relations can return to their original condition, at a higher level, in late socialism, or communism.

15. Jack Weatherford, *Indian Givers: How the Indians of America Transformed the World* (New York: Fawcett Columbine, 1988), 122–24; and Brandon, *New Worlds for Old*, 87–112.

16. Brandon, *New Worlds for Old*, chap. 1, on European writers.

17. Michel de Montaigne, *Essays*, trans. J. M. Cohen (New York: Penguin, 1993). As this is an abridged edition of the *Essays*, references to the *Essays* in this writing are from this edition, unless otherwise noted. See also Karen Ordahl Kupperman, ed., *America in European Consciousness, 1493–1750*, Institute of Early American History and Culture (Chapel Hill: University of North Carolina Press, 1995), 166–91, on Montaigne, showing Indian influence—at least partly via More—which in turn Montaigne passed on to others, including Shakespeare in *The Tempest*.

Some critics of Montaigne say that he often overstates the virtues of American Indians. That may well be just their own view. Barbara Alice Mann, who discusses this issue in *Iroquoian Women: The Gantowisas* (New York: Lang, 2000), 206, wrote to Stephen Sachs in an email, April 2, 2018:

As for Montaigne, he could be pretty accurate, especially in a commentary in "Des cannibals," one of his *Essais* (1580), where he shows a clear grasp of the twinned nature of the cosmic halves of Indigenous worldview, here, as played out in social organization. Montaigne: "… qu'ils nomment les hommes moitié les uns des autres" ("[so] that they call men the halves of each other") (Michel de Montaigne, Reinhold Deziemeris, and Henri Auguste Barckhausen, "Des cannibales," in *Essais de Michel de Montaigne avec les variantes des* éditions *de 1582 et 1587 publié, Publications de la Société des bibliophiles de Guyenne*, vol. 1 [1580; Bordeaux: *Féret et fils*, 1870–1873], 181). His visiting Indians saw the extremes of poverty on the one hand juxtaposed with the extreme of wealth, on the other hand, and said that they just did not understand why the rich did not aid "their other half," or why the poor did not rise up, seize their unsharing brethren by the throat, set their fine homes on fire, and force them to share the wealth. This is right on the button of Indigenous thought. Maybe Europeans would see that as socialism or anarchy, but Indians see it as righting the cosmic balance.

18. Jean Jacques Rousseau, "A Discourse on the Arts and Sciences," in *The Social Contract and Discourses* (New York: E. P. Dutton, 1950), 153n1, "The First Part.'"
19. From the first English translation of *The Essayes: or, Morall, Politike, and Militarie Discourses of Lord Michael de Montaigne*, 3rd ed., translated by John Florio (London: M. Flesher, 1632), as quoted by Brandon, *New Worlds for Old*, 28.
20. Montaigne, "On Cannibals," in *The Essayes*, 105.
21. Ibid., 108–9.
22. Montaigne, "On Vehicles," in *The Essayes*, 279.
23. Montaigne, "On Cannibals," in *The Essayes*, 114.
24. Montaigne, "On Vehicles," in *The Essayes*, 283.
25. Ibid., 284.
26. Ibid., 277.
27. Montaigne, "On Cannibals," in *The Essayes*, 109–10 (the quote is from Seneca, *Letters* XC, as it appears in a footnote on p. 110). It may be this last statement quoted from Montaigne that Rousseau was referring to in his statement about Montaigne, above (and in the discussion of Rousseau, below).

28. The page numbers given for this book are from M. de Voltaire, *L'ingenu; or, the Sincere Huron: A True History* (London: S. Bladon, 1768; repr., Farmington Hills, MI: Gale ECCO, 2018).

29. Ruben G. Thwaites, ed., *The Jesuit Relations and Allied Documents*, 73 vols. (Cleveland, OH: Burrows, 1896–1901); J. H. Kennedy, *Jesuit and Savage in New France* (New Haven, CT: Yale University Press, 1950); and Brandon, *New Worlds for Old*, 67–70, 83, 91, 100, 100–8, 162.

30. Don Grinde reported to author Stephen Sachs that it is well known that many of the letters Jesuits sent back to France with requests for money accompanied by reports about Indians were read in church, but he could not remember the citation for it. While Sachs could not locate a direct location, he found in Kennedy, *Jesuit and Savage in New France*, numerous references to regular Jesuit missionary requests for donations, and lists of donations given for the New France missionary work, including on pp. 12, 64–68, 70, 77–79, and in chap. 12.

31. For example, see ibid., chap. 2, and 36–41, 155–65.

32. Thomas Hobbes, *Leviathan*, parts I and II (Indianapolis, IN: Liberal Arts, 1958).

33. Naeem Inayatullah and David L. Blaney, *International Relations and the Problem of Difference* (New York and London: Routledge, 2004), pt. I, especially chap. 2. See also Evan Haefeli, *New Netherland and the Dutch Origins of American Religious Liberty* (Philadelphia: University of Pennsylvania Press, 2016).

34. Hamilton Vreeland, *Hugo Grotius: The Father of the Modern Science of International Law* (New York: Oxford University Press, 1917), appendix.

35. Regarding Grotius on international law, see ibid.

36. See Laurence Berns, "Thomas Hobbes," in *History of Political Philosophy*, ed. Leo Strauss and Joseph Cropsey (Chicago: Rand McNally, 1963), 354–78.

37. John Locke, *The Second Treatise on Government* (Buffalo, NY: Prometheus, 1986).

38. Brandon, *New Worlds for Old*, 19–28, 150–53; Jason Caro, "Pre-Revolutionary Liberty: How Freedom was Before the Great Revolution," unpublished paper; Jason Caro, *The Origins of Free Peoples* (New York and London: Continuum, 2011), chaps. 1–3; and personal correspondence with Jason Caro.

39. Brandon, *New Worlds for Old*, 19–24, 150–53.

40. Robert W. Venables, "American Indian Influences on the Founding Fathers," in *Exiled in the Land of the Free,* Lyons et al. (Santa Fe, NM: Clear Light, 1992), 111; and David Armatage, "John Locke: Theorist of Empire?" in *Empire and Modern Political Thought,* ed. Sankar Muthu (New York: Cambridge University Press, 2012), 84–111.

41. Hobbes, *Leviathan,* part I.

42. To which additional support is provided by Venables, "American Indian Influences on the Founding Fathers," in *Exiled in the Land of the Free,* Lyons et al., throughout the article, but European interest is summarized on p. 111. Note that throughout the volume, the various authors give extensive references to European interest in American Indian society from the seventeenth century onward.

43. There is discussion of the role of the American Museum of Natural History, and anthropologist Clark Wissler of that institution, in the study of American Indians in James R. Walker, Raymond J. DeMallie, and Elaine A. Jahner, eds., *Lakota Belief and Ritual* (Lincoln: University of Nebraska Press, 1991), in the preface, acknowledgments, and pt. I, "James R. Walker: His Life and Works."

44. Conceivably also sub-Saharan African accounts, but there is no reference to them in *The Second Treatise,* and far less information was directly available from Africa, as extensive inland European colonization did not take place there until much later.

45. Though in reality, Native people were quite cautious to avoid such problems, as indicated in the Cherokee case reported above and in the Lakota story of the "Festival of the Little People," presented in Charles A. Eastman (Ohiyesa) and Elain Goodale Eastman, *Wigwam Evenings: Sioux Tales Retold* (Lincoln: University of Nebraska Press, 1990), 99–105.

46. See, for example, Biancamaria Fontana, ed., *The Invention of the Modern Republic* (Lausanne, Switzerland: Université de Lausanne, 2007); M. J. C. Vile, *Constitutionalism and the Separation of Powers* (Indianapolis, IN: Liberty Fund, 1998); and "Separation of Powers," Wikipedia, the free encyclopedia, https://en.wikipedia.org/wiki/Separation_of_powers#Montesquieu.27s_tripartite_system.

47. Thomas Pangle, *Montesquieu's Philosophy of Liberalism: A Commentary on* The Spirit of the Laws (Chicago: University of Chicago Press, 1973), 11.

48. Ibid. Supporting the point that *The Spirit of the Laws* has a consistent overall plan and by intention needs to be read carefully, see David

Lowenthal, "Montesquieu," in Straus and Cropsey, eds., *History of Political Philosophy*.

49. Leo Straus, "Plato," in Straus and Cropsey, eds., *History of Political Philosophy*; and Harry V. Jaffa, "Aristotle," in ibid.

50. Charles de Secondat Baron de Montesquieu, *De L'Esprit des Lois* (Paris: Éditions Garnier Frères, 1956). References are indicated in the text as *Esprit*, with the location.

51. Hobbes, *Leviathan*, pt. I, chap. 13.

52. Charles de Secondat Baron de Montesquieu, *Lettres Persanes* (Paris: Booking International, 1993). References are indicated in the text as *Lettres*, with the location.

53. Anne Cohler, *Montesquieu's Comparative Politics and the Spirit of American Constitutionalism* (Lawrence: University of Kansas Press, 1988), 117.

54. Richard C. Adams, *Legends of the Delaware Indians and Picture Writing*, ed. Deborah Nichols (Syracuse, NY: University of Syracuse Press, 1997), 48–49.

55. Georg W. F. Hegel, *The Philosophy of History* (Overland Park, KS: Digireads, 2010).

56. William H. Prescott, *The Conquest of Mexico and the Conquest of Peru* (New York: Random House, 1955). Bk. 7, chap. 2.

57. Vine Deloria Jr., *God Is Red: A Native View of Religion* (Golden, CO: Fulcrum, 2003), 69.

58. Ibid., 309.

59. Ibid., 195.

60. Ibid.

61. Ibid., 196.

62. Ibid., 97.

63. Ibid., 99.

64. Ibid., 213.

65. George Anastaplo, *But Not Philosophy: Seven Introductions to Non-Western Thought* (Lanham, MD: Lexington, 2002), 243.

66. Pangle, *Montesquieu's Philosophy of Liberalism*, 234.

67. Ibid., 324.

68. David E. Wilkins, *American Indian Politics and the American Political System* (Lanham, MD: Rowman & Littlefield, 2002), 227–28.

69. Ter Ellingson, *The Myth of the Noble Savage* (Berkeley: University of California Press, 2001), 13.

70. Ibid., 21–22.

71. Lescarbot, quoted in ibid., 29–30.

72. On Lahontan losing his estate in France and moving to Canada, see Gordon M. Sayre, *Les Sauvages Americains: Representations of Native Americans in French and English Colonial Literature* (Chapel Hill: University of North Carolina Press, 1997), 35.

As to his approach to writing a fictitious account of Indigenous America, Lahontan admits that he decided to present the Native perspective in a European style, after writing a letter with a rather literal translation of a speech by Grangula at treaty talks with the French, getting critical feedback from "an honest Gentleman" about the Iroquois orator's "Metaphorical harangue," and being entreated "not to make a literal Translation of a language that was so stuff'd with Fictions and Savage Hyperboles." Even if there is no evidence that famous native orators like Grangula or Kondiaronk had experienced the fictional Adario's visit to France, Lahontan had met Indians who had been kidnapped and taken there. Moreover, the Huron leader Kondiaronk had often dined and conversed with New France's Governor Frontenac and his officers (Ellingson, pp. 72–73), providing a most plausible source of inspiration for the dialogues with the fictional Adario.

Much of the information about the character, experience, and views of Adario is consistent with other observers' reports on the kinds of Natives Lahontan encountered. Recognition of Lahontan's value for understanding Natives' thinking, as expressed in their rhetoric and ceremonies, is evident in his citation by the foremost published authority on Iroquoian traditions, the pioneering anthropologist Lewis Henry Morgan (Ellingson, pp. 72–73, 123). The latter's thorough ethnographic work in the mid-nineteenth century was enhanced by close consultation with Ely Parker, who became a leader of the Seneca Nation of the Haudenosaunee (Iroquois) League. (Parker later had an illustrious career that included service as an engineer at the Erie Canal, military secretary to General Ulysses Grant, and Commissioner of Indian Affairs during the latter's presidency).

Parts of Lahontan's travelogue, especially regarding the territory and inhabitants west of the Great Lakes, are not credible, as they contain geographic and ethnographic details (about cities, game parks, beards, metallurgy, domesticated buffalo, etc.) that do not match any other accounts. Lahontan's reporting here may be based on faulty secondhand information or an insertion of elements from ancient Eurasian tales to enhance the sensational reputation and marketability of his writings (Gilbert Chinard, *Dialogues Curieux*, Baltimore: Johns Hopkins Press, 1931, pp. 11, 58; Ellingson, *Myth of the Noble*

Savage, pp. 67–68). Some critics have suggested that an editor (especially the defrocked French monk named Nicolas Gueudeville, in exile in Holland) may have made significant modifications of the text, but despite the sharpening of the critique of the French polity and church evident in later editions, the specific observations and general themes remain rather consistent throughout the many versions of Lahontan's work (Chinard, pp. 20, 26, 43). Summarizing the crucial insight of Lahontan's work, despite some of its questionable details, Ellingson (pp. 70–71) writes: "Lahontan may be fictionalizing the historical truth of individual identities and the particular instances of their words and interactions, but the result is a clear and direct representation of one of the profoundest and most unsettling experiential truths confronted by both colonists and Indians[,] ... that their identity, their ethnicity, their freedom were actually subject to their own choice." This is illustrated by the "common and widely known" cases of defectors of European origin or heritage who "went native" and joined Indian societies, despite the risk of colonial governments' drastic punishments for such apostasy.

The originality of the argument for freedom of conscience and of the critique of European social order that Lahontan presents through the dialogues with Adario have been questioned. Similar ideas were "in the air" among nonconformists and libertines in lands (such as Holland and England) where Lahontan found refuge and publishers, after getting into trouble with the authorities in his homeland of France. Yet there is no question that Lahontan helped spread such ideas through his immensely popular writings. He even made his intellectual predecessors (including the English philosophers discussed above) more understandable and influential for his readers, in the light of the published information and reflections on his experiences among North America's Natives (Chinard, pp. 3, 18, 70).

Côté, Tardivel, and Vaugeois (*L'Indien généreux*, 1992, pp. 153–54) raise the interesting question of whether authors like Lahontan were predisposed by their own beliefs to find in Native societies that which fit their expectations and purposes. The fact that similar details and themes were reported by observers who were not rebelling against the established order in their European homelands (Chinard, pp. 28, 48, 69; Ellingson, p. 72) suggests that such selective perception was not a major factor. Moreover, both types of observers expressed surprise at much of what they encountered, which indicates that their expectations did not unduly color their reports. Finally, in Lahontan's case at least, his early writings (letters to relatives in France) are replete with ethnographic details, while the later publications contain more philosophical musings and systematic comparisons, consistent with an evolution in his thinking after he left North America and came into contact with other French exiles in Europe.

73. Baron de Lahontan, *Dialogues de Monsieur le Baron de Lahontan et D'un Sauvage, dans l'Amerique: Contenant une Description Exacte des Mœurs & des Coutumes de ces Peuples Sauvages* (Amsterdam: Chez la Veuve de Boeteman, 1704), quoted in Ellingson, *Myth of the Noble Savage,* 70; Sayre, *Les Sauvages Americains,* 37. For more on Lahontan, see Brandon, *New Worlds for Old,* 87–108, and on the impact of reports coming back to Europe from the Americas, see the entire work.

74. On the idea of "natural liberty" exemplified by images of Indians in numerous French plays, including Delisle de la Drevetier's *Arlequin Sauvage,* performed in Paris in June 1721, see Brandon, *New Worlds for Old,* 100–105.

75. In Ellingson, *Myth of the Noble Savage,* 34.

76. Ibid., 72.

77. Lahontan, quoted in Sayre, *Les Sauvages Americains,* 39.

78. Ibid., 38.

79. Ibid., 31.

80. From the frontispiece of Lahontan's *Dialogues,* reprinted in Ellingson, *Myth of the Noble Savage,* 64.

81. "Justices of the Peace and the Pre-Trial Process." London Lives, 1690–1800: Crime, Poverty, and Social Policy in the Metropolis, http://www.londonlives.org/static/Pretrial.jsp.

82. Cadwallader Colden, *History of the Five Indian Nations Depending on the Province of New York in America* (Ithaca, NY: Cornell University Press, 1958) also available as "The History of the Five Indian Nations of Canada, Which Are Dependent on the Province of New-York in America, and Are the Barrier between the English and French in that Part of the World. With Accounts of their Religion, Manners, Customs, Laws, and Forms of Government; their several Battles and Treaties with the European Nations; particular Relations of their several Wars with the Other Indians; and a True Account of the Present State of Our Trade with Them. In Which Are Shewn the Great Advantage of Their Trade and Alliance to the British Nation, and the Intrigues and Attempts of the French to Engage Them from Us; a Subject Nearly Concerning All Our American Plantations, and Highly Meriting the Consideration of the British

Nation at this Juncture," Project Gutenberg EBook, chap. XV, http://www.gutenberg.org/files/35719/35719-h/35719-h.htm; and quoted in Bruce E. Johansen, *Forgotten Founders: Benjamin Franklin, the Iroquois, and the Rationale for the American Revolution* (Ipswich, MA: Gambit, 1982), 39.

83. "Constitution of the Iroquois Nations, The Great Binding Law Gayanashagowa," http://www.constitution.org/cons/iroquois.htm.

84. Brandon, *New Worlds for Old*, 109.

85. All three writings are available in Jean-Jacques Rousseau, *The Social Contract and Discourses* (New York: E. P. Dutton, 1950). See Brandon, *New Worlds for Old*, 103–4, on Rousseau being influenced by writings and plays in France concerning American Indians, and as a young man in 1742, well prior to writing the discourses and the *Social Contract*, he wrote an operetta about the discovery of the New World. In that operetta, an Indian priest sings of the Spaniards' putting them under an "odious Yoke," causing them to lose "the dearest gifts of heaven ... their liberty, their innocence."

86. In the course of some of his criticism of existing society, it seems that Rousseau is more concerned with man in the original state, as for example, "The more we reflect on it, the more we shall find that this state was the least subject to revolutions, and altogether the very best man could experience; so that he can have departed from it only through some fatal accident, which for the public good should never have happened" ("A Discourse on the Origin of Inequality," *The Social Contract and Discourses*, 2nd pt., 243). Yet, at the opening of the same discourse he quotes Aristotle (who sees the nature of a thing in its telos), *Politics*, Bk. 1, chap. 2, 175, "We should consider what is natural not in things which are depraved, but in those which are rightly ordered by nature."

87. For example he mentions the reports of travelers concerning the "Hottentots of the Cape of Good Hope," in "A Discourse on the Origin of Inequality," *The Social Contract and Discourses*, 1st pt., 207.

88. Rousseau makes this quite clear in the introduction to *The Social Contract*, 3, "As I was born a citizen of a free State, and a member of the sovereign, I feel that however feeble the influence my voice can have on public affairs, the right of voting makes it my duty to study them: and I am happy, when I reflect upon governments, to find my enquiries always furnish me with new reasons for loving that of my own country." He develops this theme further in "A Discourse on the Origin of Inequality," in the lengthy "Dedication to the Republic of

Geneva," in considering "the inequality which nature has ordained between men, and the inequality they have introduced" (*The Social Contract and Discourses*, 176).

89. Hoebel, "Comanche, Kiowa, and Cheyenne: Plains Indian Law in Development," chap. 7 of *The Law of Primitive Man*, 150–53.

90. For a particularly good example of this role of elders, enduring even to the present time, see Loretta Fowler, *Arapahoe Politics, 1851–1978* (Lincoln: University of Nebraska Press, 1982).

91. See Charles A. Eastman (Ohiyesa), *The Soul of the Indian: An Interpretation* (Lincoln: University of Nebraska Press, 1980), chap. 2; LaDonna Harris, Stephen M. Sachs, and Barbara Morris, *Re-Creating the Circle: The Renewal of American Indian Self-Determination* (Albuquerque: University of New Mexico Press, 2011), pt. I, chap. 1.

92. For examples of this from America, among the Cherokee, see Michael Garrett, "To Walk in Beauty: The Way of Right Relationship," in *Medicine of the Cherokee: The Way of Right Relationship*, ed. J. T. Garrett and Michael Garrett (Santa Fe, NM: Bear, 1996), 165. For an excellent discussion of tribal relationships from a Dakota perspective, see Ella Deloria, *Speaking of Indians*, part II, "A Scheme of Life That Worked" (Lincoln: University of Nebraska Press, 1998), 24–25.

93. The contradiction between the practical requirement for participatory democracy, without the use of representatives, to be undertaken in only small states, and the necessity for large states is one of the sources of controversy in how to interpret Rousseau. Some say that Rousseau's democratic ideal is impossible to achieve in modern states. At the extreme, this leads to the idea of mass democracy, where a wise and trustworthy ruler or elite knows the general will better than the large mass of the people can know it, and rules in their best interest. This becomes democracy for, but not of or by, the people. Others argue that since the ideal is impossible, representative democracy has to be used as a distant, second best. Others argue that by using Rousseau's hinted at alternatives, the ideal can be approached. Another interpretation (that is my personal choice) is that, while in practice the ideal of full participation cannot be achieved, it should be approached as closely as possible according to the circumstances, with the kinds of devices that Rousseau only briefly mentions, depending upon the circumstances. This means that, in practice, some representation may be necessary, but to the minimum extent possible, with every effort being made to arrange the use of representatives to come as close as possible to direct democracy. In this view, Rousseau does not want to detract

from the ideal by discussing the ways it can be achieved in some circumstances, especially as just what arrangements are best will vary according to the specifics of the case, as he makes clear throughout Books II and III.

94. See Lyons et al., *Exiled in the Land of the Free*, 239–45, 248, 250, 256, 269–70, 274.

95. Peter Kropotkin, *Mutual Aid: A Factor in Evolution* (Lawrence, KS: Digireads, 2010), 114–15.

96. *Citizens United v. Federal Election Commission*, 558 US 310 (2010).

97. Friedrich Engels, *Socialism: Utopian and Scientific*, in *The Marx-Engels Reader*, 2nd ed., ed. Robert C. Tucker (New York: W. W. Norton, 1972), 681–84.

98. Ibid., 685–94. See also Marx's references to Owen in particular, including in *The Grundrisse* and *Capital*, both published in part in Tucker, ed., *The Marx-Engels Reader*, the former 289 and the latter 412, as well as in the section on "Critical-Utopian Socialism and Communism," in *The Communist Manifesto*, in *Marxism: Essential Writings*, ed. David McLellan (Oxford: Oxford University Press, 1988), 44–46.

99. On Owen, see G. D. H Cole, *The Life of Robert Owen* (London: Ernest Benn, 1925); Robert Owen, *The Life of Robert Owen Written by Himself; With Selections from His Writings and Correspondence*, vol. 1, pt. 1 (Fairfield, NJ: A. M. Kelley, 1977); A. L. Morton, *The Life and Ideas of Robert Owen* (London: Lawrence and Wishart, 1962); John F. C. Harrison, *Robert Owen and the Owenites in Britain and America: Quest for the New Moral World* (New York: Charles Scribner's, 1969); and Frank Podmore, *Robert Owen: A Biography*, vols. 1–2 (London: Hutchinson, 1906).

100. Cole, *The Life of Robert Owen*, chap. 18.

101. There are, of course, other sources of the kinds of ideas that Owen expressed, including a few remnants of European Indigenous ways that Kropotkin discusses, which are considered below.

102. This also raises the question of what, if any, role intuition may play in the development of one's thinking, and whether people may receive information other than through the five senses. This is a large and controversial topic beyond the scope of the current discussion. It is discussed in small part by some of the works cited in the introduction to part II, including Gebser, *The Ever Present Origin*, and Taegel, *The Mother Tongue*.

103. Cole, *The Life of Robert Owen*, 126–27. Chapter VIII focuses on Owen's "Ideas on Education."

104. Ibid., 133–37. On American Indian views of education, see chaps. 1 and 8 of this volume, and Margaret Connel Szasz, *Education and the American Indian: The Road to Self-Determination since 1928*, 3rd ed. (Albuquerque: University of New Mexico Press, 1999); Gregory A. Cajete, *Look to the Mountain: An Ecology of Indigenous Education* (Skyland, NC: Kivaki, 1994); and Harris, Sachs, and Morris, *Re-Creating the Circle*, chap. 5, sec. 3.

105. Cole, *The Life of Robert Owen*, 317–22.

106. Ibid., 136.

107. Ibid., for the quote. The rest of the discussion of Owen's method of education is discussed on 129–37.

108. Ibid., chap. 8.

109. Ibid., chaps 6, 12.

110. Ibid., 206.

111. Ibid., chaps. 10, 11, 13, 14.

112. Ibid., 315–17.

113. Ibid., chaps. 1, 15, 16.

114. Ibid., chap. 15.

115. For a brief history of the rise of the Cooperative Movement, see "The Cooperative Movement," North American Students of Cooperation [University of Michigan], http://www.umich.edu/~nasco/OrgHand/movement.html; and "Robert Owen and the Co-Operative Movement," A Web of English History: The Peel Web, http://www.historyhome.co.uk/peel/economic/owencoop.htm. On Guild Socialism, see G. D. H. Cole, *Guild Socialism Restated* (London: Leonard Parsons, 1920), https://archive.org/details/guildsocialismre00coleuoft; and S. G. Hobson, *National Guilds and the State* (London: G. Bell, 1920), https://archive.org/details/nationalguildsst00hobsuoft. On the likely impact on Yugoslavia's development of social and workers' self-management, see "Thoughts on Syndicalism: Part Three; Parallels with Syndicalism/Guild Socialism in Yugoslavia and Broken Hill," George's Political Blog, http://georgespolblog.blogspot.com/2014_01_01_archive.html.

116. Robert C. Tucker, ed., *Marx-Engels Reader*, "Chronology: The Lives of Marx and Engels" and "Introduction."

117. Ibid., 303n3, quoting Locke's "Some Considerations on the Consequences of the Lowering of Interest."

118. Ibid., 596.

119. Ibid., 695.

120. Ibid., 765.

121. Ibid., 46. The quote from Rousseau is from *Du Contract Social*, Book II, ch. VII, "The Legislator," which Marx quoted in French and added the emphases.

122. Ibid., 222.

123. Ibid., 684.

124. Ibid., 685–86.

125. Ibid., 685.

126. Ibid., xv–xvi, "Chronology: The Lives of Marx and Engels."

127. Ibid., 685.

128. Ibid., 694.

129. Ibid., 697–99.

130. Ibid., 151.

131. Ibid., 156.

132. Ibid., 160.

133. For more on the ends of the history of class struggle for Marx and Engels, see Karl Marx and Friedrich Engels, *The Communist Manifesto*, part II, available in ibid., 483–91, as well as published separately and in other collections such as David McClellan, ed., *Marxism: Essential Writings* (Oxford: Oxford University Press, 1988), 31–38; Friedrich Engels, *Socialism: Utopian and Scientific*; an extract made by Engels from his work, *Anti-Dühring*, among other printings in Tucker, *Marx-Engels Reader*, 683–71; and in part in McClellan, *Marxism: Essential Writings*, 69–75. On 112, Marx is quoted as writing in 1859 of common property.

134. Karl Marx, *Selected Writings in Philosophy and Sociology*, trans. T. B. Bottomore (New York: McGraw-Hill, 1964), 112.

135. Ibid., 110–12.

136. Tucker, *Marx-Engels Reader*, 473n6.

137. On Marx and Engels's reading of Morgan and others on ethnology, see Karl Marx, *The Ethnological Notebooks of Karl Marx*, trans. and ed. Lawrence Kraeder (Assen, Netherlands: Van Gorcum, 1974); Engels, *Origin of the Family*, 734–59.

138. Tucker, *Marx-Engels Reader*, 758–59.

139. Edward Bernstein, *Evolutionary Socialism* (New York: Random House, 1961), excerpts of which are published in McClellan, *Marxism: Essential Writings*, 76–86.

140. Ladislov Rusmich and Stephen M. Sachs, *Lessons from the Failure of the Communist Economic System* (Lanham, MD: Lexington, 2003), pt. I.

141. Jack Weatherford, *Indian Givers: How the Indians of America Transformed the World* (New York: Fawcett Columbine, 1988), 123. For more, see Brandon, *New Worlds for Old*, 87–95, especially 90.

142. Sam Dolgoff, ed., *The Anarchist Collectives: Workers' Self-Management in the Spanish Revolution, 1936–1939* (New York: Free Life, 1974).

143. James Horrox, *A Living Revolution: Anarchism in the Kibbutz Movement* (Oakland, CA: AK Press 2009), chap. 3; Daniel Gavron, *The Kibbutz: Awakening from Utopia* (Lanham, MD: Rowman & Littlefield, 2000); and "Kibbutz," Wikipedia, https://en.wikipedia.org/wiki/Kibbutz.

144. For example, see: "Hippyland," http://www.hippy.com; "Hippy Havens," http://www.hippy.com/havens.htm, lists hippie communities in the US. Fellowship for Intentional Community (FIC).

145. Stephen M. Sachs, "Some Reflections upon Workers' Self-Management in Yugoslavia," *Journal of the Hellenic Diaspora: Critical Thought on Greek and World Issues* 4, no. 1 (1977), reprinted as *Workplace Democracy Paper #4* (Washington, DC: Association for Workplace Democracy, 1981); David Riddell, "Social Self-Government in Yugoslav Socialism," in *Where It's At: Radical Perspectives on Sociology*, eds. John Howard and Stephen Deutsch (New York: Harper and Row, 1970); and Stephen M. Sachs and Nahoma Sachs, "Political Participation in a Macedonian Village," paper presented at Midwest Political Science Association Meeting, Chicago, 1974.

146. Peter Kropotkin, *Mutual Aid: A Factor in Evolution* (Lawrence, KS: Digireads), back cover. On his being familiar with Rousseau, see 47.

147. Ibid., 5.

148. Ibid., 6, which is also the source of the following reported discussion by Kropotkin, including the quotes referring to Darwin and Goethe.

149. Ibid., 7–9.

150. Ibid., 66, in the opening sentence of chap. 4.

151. Ibid., 138.

152. Ibid., 156, near the end of the conclusion.

153. Ibid., 157, at the end of the conclusion. Concerning Kropotkin's comment that mutual aid is the foundation of the teachings of all religions (including Islam), which he mentions in the midst of the discussion in his conclusion, from which the last two quotes in this discussion of his work come, it is interesting to note that the Baha'is ("Bahá'ís of the United States," National Spiritual Assembly of the Bahá'ís of the United States, http://www.bahai.us) and the universalist Sufi teacher, Hazrat Inayat Khan, in *The Unity of Religious Ideals* (New Lebanon, NY: Sufi Order, 1979) say the same thing, while it is

quite clear in the second Sura of the Koran, the holy book of Islam (which means peace, and whose invocation is "we begin in the Name of God, who is most Merciful-Magnanimous and Compassionate"), that all religions are okay, while elsewhere in the Koran it says that God sent many prophets to humanity, and none of them have arguments with each other. Indeed, the Unitarian Universalists have essentially the same teaching (Unitarian Universalist Association, http://www.uua.org), and it is found too in John Locke, *The Second Treatise on Government* (Buffalo, NY: Prometheus, 1986), chap. 2.

154. E. O. Wilson, *The Social Conquest of Earth* (New York: Liveright, 2012), 289–90.

INDEX TO VOLUME 1

CPSIA information can be obtained
at www.ICGtesting.com
Printed in the USA
LVHW032342011221
704984LV00007B/992